The
Insurance
Fact Book

**INSURANCE
INFORMATION**
INSTITUTE

D1088527

TO THE READER

Since its inception more than 50 years ago, the Insurance Information Institute (I.I.I.) Fact Book has provided information to help reporters, businesses, regulators, legislators and researchers understand the trends and statistics shaping the insurance industry.

As always, the book provides valuable information on:

- World and U.S. catastrophes
- Property/casualty and life/health insurance results and investments
- Personal expenditures on auto and homeowners insurance
- Major types of insurance losses, including vehicle accidents, homeowners claims, crime and workplace accidents
- State auto insurance laws

The I.I.I. Insurance Fact Book is meant to be used along with the Institute's website, www.iii.org, which features information for consumers, researchers, public policymakers and businesses alike. The I.I.I. remains a vital source for the media, which rely on the I.I.I.'s spokespersons, Fact Book, Insurance Handbook, videos and other materials for creditable, timely information. Social networks are another way to stay in touch with the I.I.I. We welcome you to like our Facebook page and follow us on Twitter at @iiiorg and @III_Research.

As always, we would like to thank the many associations, consultants and others who collect industry statistics and who have generously given permission to use their data.

This past year for the first time, we began to accept academic and government members. As such we would like to extend a thank you and a warm welcome to those who join us from those ranks, and to all our other new members as well.

Robert P. Hartwig, Ph.D., CPCU
President, Insurance Information Institute
@Bob_Hartwig

Contents

- The U.S. insurance industry's net premiums written totaled $1.1 trillion in 2014, with premiums recorded by life/health (L/H) insurers accounting for 56 percent and premiums by property/casualty (P/C) insurers accounting for 44 percent, according to SNL Financial.

- P/C insurance consists primarily of auto, home and commercial insurance. Net premiums written for the sector totaled $502.6 billion in 2014.

- The L/H insurance sector consists primarily of annuities and life insurance. Net premiums written for the sector totaled $644.5 billion in 2014.

- Health insurance is generally considered separate. The sector includes private health insurance companies as well as government programs. P/C and L/H insurers also write some health insurance.

- There were 6,118 insurance companies in 2014 in the United States (including territories), including P/C (2,583), life/annuities (895), health (857), fraternal (85), title (56), risk retention groups (252) and other companies (1,390), according to the National Association of Insurance Commissioners.

- Insurance carriers and related activities contributed $421.4 billion, or 2.5 percent, of U.S. gross domestic product in 2013, according to the U.S. Bureau of Economic Analysis.

U.S. P/C AND L/H INSURANCE PREMIUMS, 2014
($ billions)

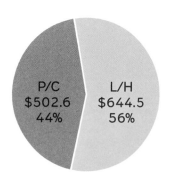

Source: SNL Financial LC.

- The U.S. insurance industry employed 2.5 million people in 2014, according to the U.S. Department of Labor. Of those, 1.5 million worked for insurance companies, including life, health and medical insurers (838,200 workers), P/C insurers (596,000 workers) and reinsurers (25,200 workers). The remaining 1 million people worked for insurance agencies, brokers and other insurance-related enterprises.

- Total P/C cash and invested assets were $1.5 trillion in 2014, according to SNL Financial. L/H cash and invested assets totaled $3.6 trillion in 2014. The majority of these assets were in bonds (61 percent of P/C assets and 74 percent of L/H assets).

- P/C and L/H insurance companies paid $18.1 billion in premium taxes in 2014, or $57 for every person living in the United States, according to the U.S. Department of Commerce.

- P/C insurers paid out $15.5 billion in property losses related to catastrophes in 2014, compared with $12.9 billion in 2013, according to the Property Claims Services division of Verisk Analytics. There were 31 catastrophes in 2014, compared with 28 in 2013.

World Life and Nonlife Insurance in 2014

Outside the United States, the insurance industry is divided into life and nonlife, or general insurance, rather than life/health and property/casualty. World insurance premiums rose 3.7 percent in 2014, adjusted for inflation, after stagnating in 2013, according to Swiss Re's latest study of world insurance. Nonlife premiums rose 2.9 percent in 2014, adjusted for inflation, following 2.7 percent growth in 2013. Life insurance premiums grew by 4.3 percent after inflation in 2014, after having fallen 1.8 percent in 2013, adjusted for inflation.

In 2014 life and nonlife insurance premiums (excluding cross-border business) accounted for 6.2 percent of world gross domestic product (GDP). Premiums accounted for 18.9 percent of GDP in Taiwan, the highest share in the Swiss Re study, followed by 14.2 percent in Hong Kong, 14.0 percent in South Africa, 11.3 percent in South Korea and 11.0 percent in the Netherlands. Premiums represented 7.3 percent of GDP in the United States, the 16th highest share in the study.

TOP 10 COUNTRIES BY LIFE AND NONLIFE DIRECT PREMIUMS WRITTEN, 2014[1]
(U.S. $ millions)

Rank	Country	Life premiums	Nonlife premiums[2]	Total premiums Amount	Total premiums Percent change from prior year	Total premiums Percent of total world premiums
1	United States[3,4]	$528,221	$752,222	$1,280,443	2.1%	26.80%
2	Japan[5,6]	371,588	108,174	479,762	-3.7	10.04
3	United Kingdom[5]	235,321	115,945	351,266	7.9	7.35
4	P.R. China[7]	176,950	151,490	328,439	17.3	6.90
5	France[8]	172,761	97,759	270,520	5.1	5.66
6	Germany[7]	118,475	136,170	254,644	2.8	5.33
7	Italy[9]	145,292	49,443	194,735	15.3	4.08
8	South Korea[6]	101,572	57,943	159,515	9.4	3.34
9	Canada[10,11]	52,138	73,235	125,373	-2.0	2.62
10	Netherlands[5]	21,855	74,100	95,956	-3.5	2.01

[1]Before reinsurance transactions.
[2]Includes accident and health insurance.
[3]Nonlife premiums include state funds; life premiums include an estimate of group pension business.
[4]Life premiums are estimated.
[5]Estimated.
[6]April 1, 2014, to March 31, 2015.
[7]Provisional.
[8]Life premiums are provisional; nonlife premiums are estimated.
[9]Nonlife premiums are estimated.
[10]Life premiums are net premiums.
[11]Life premiums are estimated; nonlife premiums are provisional.

Source: Swiss Re, *sigma*, No. 4/2015.

World Premiums Per Capita

Swiss Re's latest world insurance study is based on direct premium data from 147 countries, with detailed information on the largest 88 markets. In 2014 an average of $662 per capita was spent on insurance, with an average of $136 in emerging markets and $3,666 in advanced markets. Among the 10 largest insurance markets, premiums per capita ranged from a high of $5,689 in the Netherlands to a low of $235 in China. In the United States, the world's largest insurance market, premiums per capita totaled $4,017, including $1,657 for life insurance and $2,360 for nonlife insurance. By region, total premiums per capita were $3,969 in North America; $2,600 in Oceania (Australia and New Zealand); $1,902 in Europe; $307 in Asia; and $61 in Africa.

WORLD LIFE AND NONLIFE INSURANCE DIRECT PREMIUMS WRITTEN, 2014

($ billions)

Nonlife
44%
$2,124

Life
56%
$2,655

Total: $4,778 billion

Source: Swiss Re, *sigma*, No. 4/2015.

WORLD LIFE AND NONLIFE INSURANCE DIRECT PREMIUMS WRITTEN, 2012-2014[1]

(U.S. $ millions)

Year	Life	Nonlife[2]	Total
2012	$2,624,993	$1,976,336	$4,601,329
2013	2,545,045	2,048,587	4,593,632
2014	2,654,549	2,123,699	4,778,248

[1]Before reinsurance transactions.
[2]Includes accident and health insurance.

Source: Swiss Re, *sigma*, No. 4/2015.

Reinsurance

Each year the Reinsurance Association of America (RAA) provides an overview of the countries from which U.S. insurance companies obtain reinsurance, i.e., the countries to which they have ceded, or transferred, some of their risk. The analysis includes premiums that a U.S. insurance company cedes to "offshore" i.e., foreign, reinsurance companies that are not part of the insurer's own corporate group ("unaffiliated offshore insurers" in the chart below), as well as business ceded to overseas reinsurers that are part of the insurer's corporate family ("affiliated offshore reinsurers" in the chart below).

The RAA report compares U.S. insurance premiums ceded to U.S. professional reinsurance companies to the U.S. premiums ceded to offshore, i.e., foreign, companies. U.S. professional reinsurance companies accounted for 38.2 percent of the U.S. premium written that was ceded in 2013, while offshore companies accounted for 61.8 percent. However, a number of U.S.-based reinsurers are owned by foreign companies. Taking this into consideration, foreign reinsurers accounted for 91.9 percent while U.S. professional reinsurers accounted for 8.1 percent.

U.S. REINSURANCE PREMIUMS CEDED TO UNAFFILIATED AND AFFILIATED OFFSHORE REINSURERS BY COUNTRY, 2011-2013[1]

($ millions)

Rank	Country	Unaffiliated offshore reinsurers			Affiliated offshore reinsurers			
		2011	2012	2013	2011	2012	2013	2013 total
1	Bermuda	$9,798	$9,387	$9,676	$21,802	$23,918	$22,597	$32,273
2	Switzerland	1,316	1,151	1,388	7,496	9,013	10,434	11,822
3	United Kingdom	4,680	4,719	4,781	792	544	1,654	6,435
4	Germany	2,697	2,883	3,655	972	1,318	1,579	5,234
5	Cayman Islands	2,548	2,963	3,308	377	591	1,321	4,629
6	Turks and Caicos	733	873	1,047	79	234	270	1,317
7	Channel Islands	1,518	2,883	1,261	NA	NA	NA	1,261
8	Ireland	485	454	490	323	194	174	664
9	Barbados	607	652	659	NA	NA	NA	659
10	France	NA	NA	NA	436	256	630	630
11	British Virgin Islands	355	434	464	NA	NA	NA	464
12	Spain	NA	NA	NA	164	278	266	266
13	Canada	NA	NA	NA	92	96	100	100
	Total, countries shown	$24,737	$26,399	$26,729	$32,533	$36,442	$39,025	$65,754
	Total, all countries	$26,374	$26,790	$28,386	$33,051	$36,929	$37,357[2]	$65,743[2]

[1]Ranked by 2013 total reinsurance premiums. [2]Includes ($1.91) billion in affiliated premiums ceded to Japan.
NA=Data not available.

Source: Reinsurance Association of America.

TOP 10 GLOBAL INSURANCE COMPANIES BY REVENUES, 2014[1]
($ millions)

Rank	Company	Revenues	Country	Industry
1	Berkshire Hathaway	$194,673	U.S.	Property/casualty
2	AXA	161,173	France	Life/health
3	Allianz	136,846	Germany	Property/casualty
4	Japan Post Holdings	129,686[2]	Japan	Life/health
5	Assicurazioni Generali	118,871	Italy	Life/health
6	Prudential plc	98,976	U.K.	Life/health
7	China Life Insurance	87,249	China	Life/health
8	Ping An Insurance	86,021	China	Life/health
9	Legal & General Group	84,805	U.K.	Life/health
10	Munich Re	81,685	Germany	Property/casualty

[1]Based on an analysis of companies in the Global Fortune 500. Includes stock and mutual companies.
[2]Fiscal year ending March 31, 2015.

Source: Fortune.

TOP 10 GLOBAL PROPERTY/CASUALTY REINSURERS BY NET REINSURANCE PREMIUMS WRITTEN, 2013
($ millions)

Rank	Company	Net reinsurance premiums written	Country
1	Munich Reinsurance Co.	$22,545.9	Germany
2	Swiss Re Ltd.	14,542.0	Switzerland
3	Hannover Re S.E.	12,905.8	Germany
4	Berkshire Hathaway Reinsurance Group	11,440.0	U.S.
5	Lloyd's of London	11,363.7	U.K.
6	Scor S.E.	5,931.9	France
7	Everest Re Group Ltd.	5,004.8	Bermuda
8	PartnerRe Ltd.	4,479.1	Bermuda
9	Korean Reinsurance Co.	3,499.0[1]	South Korea
10	Transatlantic Holdings Inc.	3,248.0	U.S.

[1]Fiscal year ending March 31.

Source: Business Insurance, September 1, 2014.

TOP 10 GLOBAL INSURANCE BROKERS BY REVENUES, 2014[1]
($ millions)

Rank	Company	Brokerage revenues	Country
1	Marsh & McLennan Cos. Inc.	$12,966	U.S.
2	Aon P.L.C.	12,019	U.K.
3	Willis Group Holdings P.L.C.	3,767	U.K.
4	Arthur J. Gallagher & Co.	3,530	U.S.
5	Jardine Lloyd Thompson Group P.L.C.	1,714	U.K.
6	BB&T Insurance Holdings Inc.	1,714	U.S.
7	Brown & Brown Inc.	1,567	U.S.
8	Wells Fargo Insurance Services USA Inc.	1,299	U.S.
9	Hub International Ltd.	1,296	U.S.
10	Lockton Cos. L.L.C.[2]	1,231	U.S.

- Revenue generated by the world's 10 largest brokers increased to $41.1 billion in 2014 from $24.8 billion in 2005.

[1]Revenue generated by insurance brokerage and related services.
[2]Fiscal year ending April 30.
Source: Business Insurance, July 20, 2015.

TOP 10 GLOBAL REINSURANCE BROKERS BY GROSS REINSURANCE REVENUES, 2013[1]
($000)

Rank	Company	Gross reinsurance revenues	Country
1	Aon Benfield	$1,505,000	U.K.
2	Guy Carpenter & Co. L.L.C.[2]	1,131,267	U.S.
3	Willis Re	860,000	U.K.
4	JLT Reinsurance Brokers Ltd.	375,869	U.K.
5	Cooper Gay Swett & Crawford Ltd.	158,466	U.K.
6	Miller Insurance Services L.L.P.[3]	93,528	U.K.
7	UIB Holdings Ltd.[2]	67,463	U.K.
8	THB Group Ltd.	58,094	U.K.
9	BMS Group Ltd.	54,300	U.K.
10	Lockton Re[3]	46,029	U.K.

[1]Includes all reinsurance revenue reported through holding and/or subsidiary companies.
[2]Includes aviation reinsurance business placed by Marsh L.L.C.
[3]Fiscal year ending April 30.
Source: Business Insurance, October 27, 2014.

International Sales

The U.S. Department of Commerce provides estimates on two methods of international delivery of insurance services: cross-border trade, in which a domestic company transacts directly with a foreign company (for example, a European firm purchasing insurance from a U.S. firm through a broker), and sales by subsidiaries of multinational corporations (for example, sales to the European market through a European-based subsidiary of a U.S. insurer). The combination of these methods of delivery creates a broad measure of insurance services provided and received from abroad.

U.S. INSURANCE SALES ABROAD, 2007-2013
($ millions)

Year	Sold directly[1]	Sold through majority-owned foreign affiliates of U.S. multinational corporations[2]
2007	$10,841	$55,290
2008	13,403	61,794
2009	14,586	61,609
2010	14,397	58,379
2011	15,114	59,942
2012	16,534	65,829
2013	16,096	NA

[1]Largely based on premiums. Includes adjustments for "normal" i.e., expected losses and premium supplements (income due to policy holders). BEA refers to this category as "cross border sales." Includes property/casualty, life insurance and reinsurance.
[2]Based on sales by primary industry of the affiliate; there could be other services, such as financial services, included in the data. NA=Data not available.

Source: U.S. Department of Commerce, Bureau of Economic Analysis (BEA), International Division.

INSURANCE BUSINESS IN THE U.S. WRITTEN BY SUBSIDIARIES OF FOREIGN CONTROLLED COMPANIES, 2013
($ billions)

Life 66% $143.4
Nonlife 34% $74.2

Total: $217.6 billion

Source: Organization for Economic Cooperation and Development.

INSURANCE BUSINESS IN THE U.S. WRITTEN BY SUBSIDIARIES OF FOREIGN CONTROLLED COMPANIES, 2009-2013
($ millions)

	Gross premiums written				
	2009	2010	2011	2012	2013
Life	$172,464	$132,870	$139,311	$141,524	$143,429
Nonlife	103,296	78,504	82,199	69,668	74,219
Total[1]	**$275,760**	**$211,374**	**$221,511**	**$211,192**	**$217,648**

[1]Calculated from unrounded data.

Source: Organization for Economic Cooperation and Development.

Captives and Other Risk-Financing Options

Over the years, a number of alternatives to traditional commercial insurance have emerged to respond to fluctuations in the marketplace. Captives—a special type of insurance company set up by a parent company, trade association or group of companies to insure the risks of its owner or owners—emerged during the 1980s, when businesses had trouble obtaining some types of commercial insurance coverage. Alternative risk transfer (ART) arrangements include self insurance, risk retention groups and risk purchasing groups and more recent innovations such as catastrophe bonds and microinsurance.

LEADING CAPTIVE DOMICILES, 2013-2014

Rank	Domicile	Number of captives	
		2013	2014
1	Bermuda	831	800
2	Cayman Islands	759	759
3	Vermont	588	587
4	Utah	342[1]	422
5	Anguilla	295	379
6	Delaware	298	333
7	Guernsey	318[1]	321
8	Nevis	276	281
9	Barbados	264	271
10	Luxembourg	226[1]	224
11	Hawaii	184	194
12	District of Columbia	170[1]	191
13	Montana	150	177
14	Nevada	148	160
15	South Carolina	145	158
16	Puerto Rico	107[1]	152
17	British Virgin Islands	147	146
18	Isle of Man	123[1]	122
18	Kentucky	128	122
20	Arizona	106	114
	Total, top 20	**5,605**	**5,913**
	Total, all captives	**6,412**	**6,876**

[1]Restated.

Source: Business Insurance, March 16, 2015.

The Securitization of Insurance Risk: Catastrophe Bonds

Catastrophe (cat) bonds are one of a number of innovative risk transfer products that have emerged as an alternative to traditional insurance and reinsurance products. Insurers and reinsurers typically issue cat bonds through a special purpose vehicle, a company set up specifically for this purpose. Cat bonds pay high interest rates and diversify an investor's portfolio because natural disasters occur randomly and are not associated with economic factors. Depending on how the cat bond is structured, if losses reach the threshold specified in the bond offering, the investor may lose all or part of the principal or interest.

Catastrophe bond issuance reached a record high of $8.0 billion in 2014, up from $7.1 billion in 2013, according to the GC Securities division of MMC Securities Corp. Included in the 2014 number was the largest catastrophe bond in history, a $1.5 billion issue sponsored by Florida's Citizens Property Insurance Corp. Catastrophe bond risk capital outstanding rose to $22.9 billion during the same period, also a record high. The first quarter, which historically is particularly active in terms of issuance for the property/casualty market, was especially so for 2015, with $1.49 billion of risk capital issued—the highest first-quarter volume in history, according to GC Securities.

TOP 10 CATASTROPHE BOND TRANSACTIONS, 2014
($ millions)

Rank	Special purpose vehicle	Sponsor name	Risk amount	Peril	Risk location
1	Everglades Re 2014-1	Citizens (Florida)	$1,500	Hurricane	Florida
2	Sanders Re Ltd. 2014-1	Allstate	750	Hurricane and earthquake	U.S.
3	Kilimanjaro Re 2014-2	Everest Re	500	Earthquake	U.S. and Canada
4	Tradewynd Re Ltd. 2014-1	AIG/National Union/Chartis	500	Hurricane and earthquake	U.S. and Canada
5	Kilimanjaro Re 2014-1	Everest Re	450	Hurricane and earthquake	U.S.
6	Alamo Re Ltd. Series 2014-2	TWIA	400	Hurricane	Texas
7	Ursa Re Ltd.	California Earthquake Authority	400	Earthquake	California
8	Nakama Re Ltd. 2014-2	Zenkyoren	375	Earthquake	Japan
9	Merna Re V 2014-1	State Farm	300	Earthquake	New Madrid
10	Nakama Re Ltd. 2014-1	Zenkyoren	300	Earthquake	Japan

Source: GC Securities, a division of MMC Securities Corp., a U.S. registered broker-dealer, member FINRA/SIPC, and Guy Carpenter.

CATASTROPHE BONDS, ANNUAL RISK CAPITAL ISSUED, 2005-2014

($ billions)

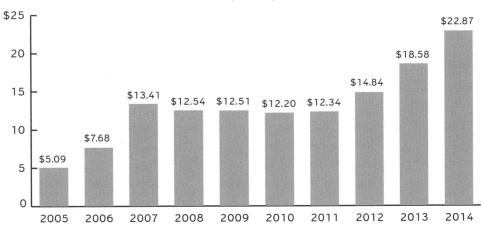

Source: GC Securities, a division of MMC Securities Corp., a U.S. registered broker-dealer, member FINRA/SIPC, and Guy Carpenter.

CATASTROPHE BONDS, RISK CAPITAL OUTSTANDING, 2005-2014

($ billions)

Source: GC Securities, a division of MMC Securities Corp., a U.S. registered broker-dealer, member FINRA/SIPC, and Guy Carpenter.

Microinsurance and Emerging Markets

A growing number of insurers are tapping into markets in developing countries through microinsurance projects, which provide low-cost insurance to individuals generally not covered by traditional insurance or government programs. Microinsurance products tend to be much less costly than traditional products and thus extend protection to a much wider market. Microinsurance products vary in type and structure but are generally distinguished by high volumes, low cost and efficient administration. Microinsurance policies may be offered along with a small loan, with premiums a small percentage of the loan amount. The approach is an outgrowth of the microfinancing projects developed by Bangladeshi Nobel Prize-winning banker and economist Muhammad Yunus, which helped millions of low-income individuals in Asia and Africa to set up businesses and buy houses. Today a number of innovative microinsurance products have been developed to protect the working poor against the financial impact of losses.

A 2014 A.M. Best report states that about 500 million people globally have microinsurance and that there is increasing evidence from numerous academic studies that its impact has been beneficial for the poor in many ways. The report also cites a 2011 survey by the Microinsurance Network that found that 33 of the world's largest insurance companies were involved in microinsurance projects, up from seven in 2005. The report sums up 95 microinsurance projects that cover more than 1 million people in Asia or Latin America or at least 500,000 in Africa. Findings include: About 50 percent of microinsurance projects provide different types of life insurance such as term life, credit life and funeral. Also about 50 percent of the projects receive subsidies that mainly target agricultural and health insurance. The report also notes a 2014 Economist Intelligence Unit survey of insurers that found that 45 percent of respondents believe that the work of international organizations to inform policymakers in the developing world of the value of insurance is a top priority.

The 10th International Microinsurance Conference in 2014 brought together some 400 participants from 54 countries. The Latin America and the Caribbean 2014 study, presented at the conference by the Munich Re Foundation and the Microinsurance Network, showed that coverage in the region has grown from 7.6 percent to 7.9 percent between 2011 and 2013, and that premiums now total $830 million. In addition, 18.3 million clients in Mexico have some kind of coverage. With 15 percent of the population covered, Mexico is a leader. The potential number of clients in the region is estimated to be between 250 million and 300 million, of whom 48.6 million already have some sort of microinsurance. In relation to the total population, this is a much stronger outreach than in Africa and Asia. Another interesting finding of the study was the shift in distribution channels. Microfinance organizations have played a key role in past years, but alternative channels such as utility companies have substantially gained in market share and continue to grow.

The Microinsurance Consortium, which formed the Blue Marble Microinsurance group in early 2015, is committed to launching 10 microinsurance ventures over the next 10 years and will deliver solutions to address the risk management needs of the underserved. Blue Marble Microinsurance has identified several potential strategic partners and is in advanced discussions to establish these relationships. Those partners will include companies with expertise in distribution, technology and social impact issues, as well as donor organizations and government and quasi-government entities. The venture will provide innovative technology-enabled platforms, achieve sustainability through adequate levels of profitability and advance the role of insurance in society. The group aims to develop the business services necessary to achieve scale and profitability in the market including unique distribution methods, local partnerships, product development and impact services such as measuring and monitoring social impact. It is currently evaluating opportunities in Latin America, Africa and emerging Asia, with the initial venture scheduled to launch in 2015. The consortium behind Blue Marble consists of American International Group Inc., Aspen Insurance Holdings Ltd. and Guy Carpenter & Co. LLC, together with Marsh & McLennan Cos. Inc., Hamilton Insurance Group Ltd., Old Mutual PLC, Transatlantic Reinsurance Co., XL Catlin and Zurich Insurance Group.

Insurance in Emerging Markets

With limited growth prospects in the insurance markets of developed countries, insurers see emerging economies as presenting significant potential for growth and profitability. Premium growth in developing countries has been outpacing growth in industrialized countries. Swiss Re's 2015 *sigma* report on world insurance markets found that premiums in emerging countries rose 7.4 percent in 2014, after adjusting for inflation, following a 5.9 percent rise in 2013. Growth in developing markets outpaced growth in advanced markets, which increased by 2.9 percent in 2014 after falling 1.0 percent in 2013. Emerging markets accounted for almost 18 percent of total global premium volume in 2014, up from 17 percent in 2013.

Swiss Re identifies emerging markets as countries in South and East Asia, Latin America and the Caribbean, Central and Eastern Europe, Africa, the Middle East (excluding Israel), Central Asia, and Turkey. Emerging market premiums rose from $778 billion in 2013 to $839 billion in 2014, driven by strong growth in both the nonlife and life sectors. Each year since 2006, emerging market nonlife premiums have risen 1.5 times the annual average economic growth rate, according to Swiss Re. Life sector premiums had 6.9 percent growth in 2014, adjusted for inflation, compared with 3.6 percent in 2013.

Microinsurance and Emerging Markets

INSURANCE IN EMERGING MARKETS, 2014
($ millions)

	Direct premiums written, 2014	Percent change from 2013[1]	Share of world market	Premiums as a percent of GDP[2]	Premiums per capita
Total industry					
Advanced markets	$3,939,311	2.9%	82.4%	8.2%	$3,666
Emerging markets	838,936	7.4	17.6	2.7	136
World	**$4,778,248**	**3.7%**	**100.0%**	**6.2%**	**$662**
Life					
Advanced markets	2,232,524	3.8	84.1	4.7	2,090
Emerging markets	422,025	6.9	15.9	1.4	68
World	**$2,654,549**	**4.3%**	**100.0%**	**3.4%**	**$368**
Nonlife					
Advanced markets	1,706,787	1.8	80.4	3.5	1,576
Emerging markets	416,912	8.0	19.6	1.4	67
World	**$2,123,699**	**2.9%**	**100.0%**	**2.7%**	**$294**

[1]Inflation-adjusted. [2]Gross Domestic Product.
Source: Swiss Re, *sigma*, No. 4/2015.

According to Swiss Re, China is the largest emerging market country based on insurance premiums written (including life and nonlife business) with $328 billion in premiums written in 2014, followed by Brazil with $85 billion and India with $70 billion. However when measured by insurance density, Macao ranked first, with $1,915 in premiums per capita (including life and nonlife business).

TOP 10 EMERGING MARKETS BY INSURANCE DENSITY, 2014[1]

Rank	Country	Total premiums[2]	
		Per capita (U.S. dollars)	As a percent of GDP[3]
1	Macao	$1,915	1.9%
2	Bahamas	1,894	8.4
3	Slovenia	1,246	5.0
4	Qatar	979	1.0
5	United Arab Emirates	974	2.2
6	South Africa	925	14.0
7	Trinidad and Tobago	809	4.4
8	Venezuela	735	3.6
9	Czech Republic	721	3.5
10	Mauritius	613	6.0

[1]Based on insurance premiums per capita. Excludes cross-border business. [2]Life and nonlife premiums. Data are estimated except for Slovenia and Czech Republic, which are provisional. [3]Gross Domestic Product.

Source: Swiss Re, *sigma*, No. 4/2015.

Net Premiums Written, Property/Casualty and Life/Health

There are three main insurance sectors. Property/casualty (P/C) consists mainly of auto, home and commercial insurance. Life/health (L/H) consists mainly of life insurance and annuity products. Most private health insurance is written by insurers whose main business is health insurance. However, L/H and P/C insurers also write this coverage. P/C net premiums written rose by 4.4 percent, and L/H net premiums written rose by 15.1 percent in 2014.

PROPERTY/CASUALTY AND LIFE/HEALTH INSURANCE NET PREMIUMS WRITTEN, 2005-2014
($000)

Year	Property/casualty[1]	Life/health[2]	Total
2005	$422,448,786	$520,220,499	$942,669,285
2006	447,803,479	564,983,111	1,012,786,590
2007	446,179,922	596,148,902	1,042,328,824
2008	440,318,983	607,250,216	1,047,569,199
2009	423,528,077	491,637,251	915,165,328
2010	425,878,773	560,608,885	986,487,658
2011	441,562,154	602,296,889	1,043,859,043
2012	460,486,285	623,258,729	1,083,745,014
2013	481,265,997	559,949,077	1,041,215,074
2014	502,584,384	644,503,730	1,147,088,114
Percent change, 2005-2014	**19.0%**	**23.9%**	**21.7%**

[1]Net premiums written after reinsurance transactions, excludes state funds.
[2]Premiums, annuity considerations (fees for annuity contracts) and deposit-type funds for life/health insurance companies.

Source: SNL Financial LC.

U.S. PROPERTY/CASUALTY AND LIFE/HEALTH INSURANCE PREMIUMS, 2014[1]

$502.6 billion — Property/casualty 44%

Life/health 56% — $644.5 billion

Total: $1,147.1 billion

[1]Property/casualty: net premiums written after reinsurance transactions, excludes state funds; life/health: premiums, annuity considerations (fees for annuity contracts) and deposit-type funds.

Source: SNL Financial LC.

GROWTH IN U.S. PREMIUMS, PROPERTY/CASUALTY AND LIFE/HEALTH INSURANCE, 2005-2014
(Percent change from prior year)

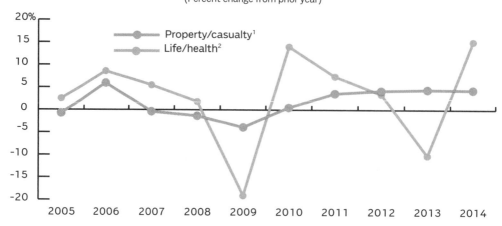

[1]Net premiums written after reinsurance transactions, excludes state funds.
[2]Premiums and annuity considerations (fees for annuity contracts) for life/health insurance companies.

Source: SNL Financial LC.

Direct Premiums Written, Property/Casualty and Life/Health

PROPERTY/CASUALTY AND LIFE/HEALTH INSURANCE DIRECT PREMIUMS WRITTEN, 2005-2014
($000)

Year	Property/casualty[1]	Life/health[2]	Total
2005	$494,700,641	$559,584,322	$1,054,284,963
2006	508,324,604	600,580,462	1,108,905,066
2007	510,979,916	645,651,813	1,156,631,729
2008	498,690,753	661,930,391	1,160,621,144
2009	483,081,379	608,285,532	1,091,366,911
2010	484,404,467	613,073,913	1,097,478,381
2011	502,005,179	656,968,773	1,158,973,951
2012	523,881,547	684,868,448	1,208,749,995
2013	546,136,268	646,652,656	1,192,788,924
2014	570,731,653	662,304,443	1,233,036,096
Percent change, 2005-2014	**15.4%**	**18.4%**	**17.0%**

[1]Direct premiums written before reinsurance transactions, excludes state funds. Includes all business written by U.S. filing companies including business in U.S. territories, Canada and other alien areas.
[2]Premiums, annuity considerations (fees for annuity contracts) and deposit-type funds for life/health insurance companies.

Source: SNL Financial LC.

Leading Companies

TOP 10 WRITERS OF PROPERTY/CASUALTY INSURANCE
BY DIRECT PREMIUMS WRITTEN, 2014
($000)

Rank	Group/company	Direct premiums written[1]	Market share[2]
1	State Farm Mutual Automobile Insurance	$58,508,587	10.3%
2	Liberty Mutual	29,364,559	5.1
3	Allstate Corp.	28,892,088	5.1
4	Berkshire Hathaway Inc.	26,555,515	4.7
5	Travelers Companies Inc.	22,790,776	4.0
6	Progressive Corp.	20,056,860	3.5
7	Nationwide Mutual Group	18,935,862	3.3
8	American International Group (AIG)	18,653,981	3.3
9	Farmers Insurance Group of Companies[3]	18,611,695	3.3
10	USAA Insurance Group	15,678,176	2.8

[1]Before reinsurance transactions, includes state funds.
[2]Based on U.S. total, includes territories.
[3]Data for Farmers Insurance Group of Companies and Zurich Financial Group (which owns Farmers' management company) are reported separately by SNL Financial.

Source: SNL Financial LC.

TOP 10 WRITERS OF LIFE INSURANCE/ANNUITIES BY DIRECT PREMIUMS WRITTEN, 2014
($000)

Rank	Group/company	Direct premiums written[1]	Market share[2]
1	MetLife Inc.	$95,331,132	16.1%
2	Prudential Financial Inc.	44,720,129	7.6
3	New York Life Insurance Group	28,393,849	4.8
4	Jackson National Life Group	26,708,218	4.5
5	AEGON	25,339,180	4.3
6	Lincoln National Corp.	24,329,107	4.1
7	American International Group (AIG)	23,279,901	3.9
8	Principal Financial Group Inc.	18,894,839	3.2
9	Manulife Financial Corp.	18,513,758	3.1
10	Massachusetts Mutual Life Insurance Co.	16,818,431	2.8

[1]Before reinsurance transactions. Includes life insurance, annuity considerations, deposit-type contract funds and other considerations; excludes accident and health insurance.
[2]Based on U.S. total, includes territories.

Source: SNL Financial LC.

Healthcare Expenditures

Nearly half of the nation's healthcare costs are covered under Medicaid, Medicare and other public programs.

THE NATION'S HEALTHCARE DOLLAR: WHERE IT CAME FROM, 2013[1]

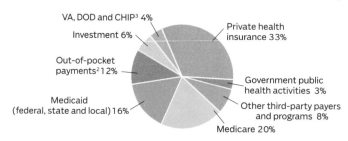

[1]Sum of components does not add to 100 percent due to rounding.
[2]Includes co-payments, deductibles and any amounts not covered by health insurance.
[3]Department of Veterans Affairs, Department of Defense and Children's Health Insurance Program.

Source: Centers for Medicare and Medicaid Services, Office of the Actuary, National Health Statistics Group.

National healthcare expenditures rose 3.6 percent to $2.9 trillion in 2013, the fifth consecutive year of slow growth, according to the U.S. Department of Health and Human Services' Centers for Medicare and Medicaid Services (CMS). Between 1970 and 1993, the beginning of the shift to managed care, healthcare expenditures rose 11.5 percent on an average annual basis. In 2013 the health spending share of the U.S. gross domestic product remained at 17.4 percent. This level has been stable since 2009. Healthcare spending rose to $9,255 per capita in 2013 from $8,996 in 2012, a 2.9 percent increase. CMS projected that annual health expenditures grew 5.5 percent in 2014 and will average 5.8 percent a year through 2024 as coverage expands under the Affordable Care Act and prescription drug spending grows.

NATIONAL HEALTH EXPENDITURES, AVERAGE ANNUAL PERCENT GROWTH FROM PRIOR YEAR, 1993-2018

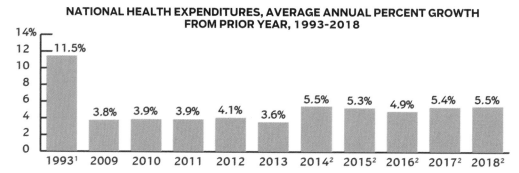

[1]Average annual growth from 1970 through 1993; marks the beginning of the shift to managed care.
[2]Projected.

Source: Centers for Medicare and Medicaid Services, Office of the Actuary.

Employment and Other Economic Contributions

Property/casualty and life/health insurance companies contribute to our economy far beyond their core function of helping to manage risk. Insurers contributed $421.4 billion, or 2.5 percent, to the nation's gross domestic product in 2013. The taxes they pay include special levies on insurance premiums, which amounted to $18.1 billion in 2014, or 2.0 percent of all taxes collected by the states. Insurance companies invested $756.4 billion in state and local municipal bonds and loans in 2014, helping to fund the building of roads, schools and other public projects. They provide businesses with capital for research, expansions and other ventures through their holdings in stocks and bonds, a figure which totaled $4.1 trillion in 2014. The industry is also a major contributor to charitable causes. The Insurance Industry Charitable Foundation, established by the property/casualty insurance industry in 1994, had contributed more than $23.5 million in local community grants and nearly 200,000 volunteer hours to hundreds of community nonprofit organizations by mid-2015. The sector is also a large employer, providing some 2.5 million jobs, or 2.1 percent of U.S. employment in 2014.

EMPLOYMENT IN INSURANCE, 2005-2014
(Annual averages, 000)

| | Insurance carriers | | | | Insurance agencies, brokerages and related services | | | |
| | Direct insurers[1] | | | | | | | |
Year	Life, health and medical	Property/ casualty	Reinsurers	Total	Insurance agencies and brokers	Other insurance-related activities[2]	Total	Total industry
2005	764.9	652.1	28.8	1,445.7	652.5	240.7	893.2	2,338.9
2006	790.6	649.1	28.0	1,467.7	662.4	249.0	911.4	2,379.1
2007	787.1	647.0	27.0	1,461.1	677.8	252.7	930.5	2,391.6
2008	800.8	646.7	27.9	1,475.4	671.6	258.1	929.6	2,405.1
2009	802.8	632.9	27.5	1,463.2	653.3	254.2	907.4	2,370.6
2010	804.1	614.3	26.8	1,445.2	642.3	253.1	895.5	2,340.6
2011	788.9	611.6	25.6	1,426.1	649.2	261.1	910.3	2,336.4
2012	811.3	599.5	25.7	1,436.4	659.6	272.3	931.8	2,368.3
2013	813.2	593.7	26.2	1,433.1	672.3	283.5	955.8	2,388.9
2014	838.2	596.0	25.2	1,459.3	711.7	295.9	1,007.6	2,467.0

[1]Establishments primarily engaged in initially underwriting insurance policies.
[2]Includes claims adjusters, third-party administrators of insurance funds and other service personnel such as advisory and insurance ratemaking services.
Source: U.S. Department of Labor, Bureau of Labor Statistics.

INSURANCE CARRIERS AND RELATED ACTIVITIES EMPLOYMENT BY STATE, 2014[1]

State	Number of employees	State	Number of employees
Alabama	37,319	Montana	8,758
Alaska	2,661	Nebraska	33,791
Arizona	59,953	Nevada	18,333
Arkansas	21,349	New Hampshire	17,476
California	297,159	New Jersey	98,774
Colorado	54,231	New Mexico	12,085
Connecticut	67,623	New York	196,781
Delaware	8,877	North Carolina	77,615
D.C.	4,569	North Dakota	11,000
Florida	203,275	Ohio	133,618
Georgia	101,796	Oklahoma	31,030
Hawaii	10,326	Oregon	33,319
Idaho	12,832	Pennsylvania	157,051
Illinois	144,723	Rhode Island	11,860
Indiana	61,502	South Carolina	41,501
Iowa	55,423	South Dakota	12,273
Kansas	39,578	Tennessee	61,674
Kentucky	41,789	Texas	259,251
Louisiana	35,470	Utah	25,554
Maine	13,571	Vermont	5,090
Maryland	48,009	Virginia	66,237
Massachusetts	80,564	Washington	54,985
Michigan	79,301	West Virginia	11,425
Minnesota	79,851	Wisconsin	79,188
Mississippi	18,656	Wyoming	3,483
Missouri	66,641	**United States**	**3,109,200**

[1]Total full-time and part-time employment.

Note: Does not match data shown shown elsewhere due to the use of different surveys. Data as of September 2015.

Source: U.S. Department of Commerce, Bureau of Economic Analysis, Regional Economic Information System.

Gross Domestic Product

INSURANCE SECTOR'S SHARE OF GROSS DOMESTIC PRODUCT (GDP), 2009-2013
($ billions)

Year	Total GDP	Insurance carriers and related activities	
		GDP	Percent of total GDP
2009	$14,418.7	$357.6	2.5%
2010	14,964.4	365.2	2.4
2011	15,517.9	379.5	2.4
2012	16,163.2	398.9	2.5
2013	16,768.1	421.4	2.5

Source: U.S. Department of Commerce, Bureau of Economic Analysis.

- Gross domestic product (GDP) is the total value of all final goods and services produced in the economy. The GDP growth rate is the primary indicator of the state of the economy.

- The insurance industry contributed $421.4 billion to the $16.8 trillion GDP in 2013.

Ownership of Municipal Bonds

Insurance companies help fund the construction of schools, roads and healthcare facilities as well as a variety of other public sector projects through their investments in municipal bonds. The property/casualty insurance industry invested $322 billion in such bonds in 2014, and the life insurance industry invested $148 billion, according to the Federal Reserve. (See page 33 and page 50 for further information on insurance industry investments.)

INSURANCE COMPANY HOLDINGS OF U.S. MUNICIPAL SECURITIES AND LOANS, 2010-2014
($ billions, end of year)

	2010	2011	2012	2013	2014
Property/casualty insurance companies	$348.4	$331.0	$328.1	$326.4	$321.7
Life insurance companies	112.3	121.8	131.5	141.2	147.8
Total	**$460.7**	**$452.8**	**$459.6**	**$467.6**	**$469.5**

Source: Board of Governors of the Federal Reserve System, June 11, 2015.

Mergers and Acquisitions

The number of global insurance-related mergers and acquisitions (M&A) rose to 722 transactions in 2014 from 695 in 2013, propelled by rising insurer valuations, softening property/casualty rates and runoff transactions in the life sector in the United States, according to an analysis by Conning Research. Outside the United States, several life transactions were driven by regulatory and market pressures. The value of M&A transactions rose to $67.0 billion from $42.6 billion in 2013.

In 2014 the number of insurance-related deals in which a U.S. firm was either a buyer or a target rose 13.0 percent, and the value of properties acquired in such deals almost doubled, according to Conning data. There were 504 U.S. insurance M&A transactions in 2014, up from 446 in 2013. The overall value of U.S. deals increased significantly to $37.5 billion from $19.3 billion in 2013. The number of non-U.S. insurance M&A transactions (i.e., where a non-U.S. company was both buyer and seller) dropped 12.4 percent to 218 in 2014 from 249 in 2013. However, the overall reported value of non-U.S. deals rose by 26.6 percent to $29.5 billion from $23.3 billion in 2013.

REPORTED GLOBAL INSURANCE-RELATED MERGERS AND ACQUISITIONS BY SECTOR, U.S. AND NON-U.S. ACQUIRERS, 2014

Sector	Number of transactions			Transaction values ($ millions)		
	U.S.[1]	Non-U.S.[2]	Total	U.S.[1]	Non-U.S.[2]	Total
Underwriting						
Property/casualty	51	66	117	$6,723	$10,250	$16,973
Life/annuity	10	22	32	7,978	17,823	25,801
Health/managed care	15	4	19	864	202	1,066
Distribution and services						
Distribution	349	112	461	2,581	773	3,354
Services	79	14	93	19,390	458	19,848
Total	**504**	**218**	**722**	**$37,536**	**$29,506**	**$67,042**

[1]Includes transactions where a U.S. company was the acquirer and/or the target.
[2]Includes transactions where a non-U.S. company was the acquirer and the target.
Source: Conning Research & Consulting, Inc. analysis.

The largest transactions of 2014 were dominated by property/casualty and life/annuity acquisitions, according to Conning research. Eight out of the top 10 largest global insurance-related M&As involved these types of companies. The 2014 transactions contrast with 2013, when three out of the top 10 transactions, including the largest, involved distribution and services.

TOP 10 GLOBAL INSURANCE-RELATED MERGERS AND ACQUISITIONS ANNOUNCED, 2014
($ millions)

Rank	Buyer (country)	Target (country)	Sector	Transaction value
1	Aviva plc (U.K.)	Friends Life Group Ltd. (U.K.)	Life/annuity	$8,519
2	Dai-Ichi Life Insurance Co. Ltd. (Japan)	Protective Life Corp. (U.S.)	Life/annuity	5,700
3	Starr Investment Holdings LLC and Partners Group (U.S.)	BC Partners and Silver Lake's MultiPlan, Inc. (U.S.)	Insurance services	4,400
4	Manulife Financial Corp. (Canada)	Standard Life plc's (U.K.) Standard Life Financial, Inc. and Standard Life Investments, Inc. (Canada)	Life/annuity	3,700
5	Kohlberg Kravis Roberts & Co. LLP (U.S.)	Stone Point Capital LLC and Hellman & Friedman LLC's Sedgwick Claims Management Services, Inc. (U.S.)	Insurance services	2,400
6	RenaissanceRe Holdings Ltd. (Bermuda)	Platinum Underwriters Holdings Ltd. (Bermuda)	Property/casualty	1,900
7	The Canada Pension Plan Investment Board (Canada)	Stone Point Capital, Kelso & Co., Vestar Capital Partners, and FFL's Wilton Re Holdings Ltd. (Bermuda)	Life/annuity	1,800
8	Helvetia Group (Switzerland)	Nationale Suisse (Switzerland)	Life/annuity	1,600
9	Desjardins Financial Corp. (Canada)	State Farm Mutual Automobile Insurance Co.'s Canadian insurance operations (U.S.)	Property/casualty	1,500
10	TPG Capital LP (U.S.)	Onex Corp.'s The Warranty Group, Inc. (Canada)	Property/casualty	1,500

Source: Conning Research & Consulting, Inc. analysis.

In 2015 all major insurance sectors were affected by blockbuster transactions:[1] property/casualty, life/annuity and health/managed care. According to Conning Research, insurance merger and acquisition (M&A) activity through the end of the third quarter in 2015 amounted to $220 billion in announced global transaction value, several times the average annual transaction value of $60 billion. Most of the activity occurred in the third quarter, accounting for $165 billion in aggregate announced value in 185 transactions worldwide, a record. The largest and most significant deal in the property/casualty sector was an announcement by ACE Ltd. that it was acquiring Chubb Corp. for $28.3 billion. The second-largest announced transaction was Exor SpA's acquisition of PartnerRe Ltd. for $6.9 billion. The largest life/annuity M&A transactions in the first three quarters of 2015 were Dai Ichi's $5.7 billion acquisition of Protective Life, Meiji Yasuda Life's announced $5 billion acquisition of StanCorp Financial and Sumitomo Life's announced $3.8 billion acquisition of Symetra Financial. However the top two M&A deals announced were in the health/managed care sector. Anthem Inc.'s announced acquisition of Cigna Corp. for $54.2 billion was the largest, followed by Aetna's acquisition of Humana for $34.1 billion.

[1] Only includes transactional activity through the third quarter of 2015.

U.S. INSURANCE-RELATED MERGERS AND ACQUISITIONS, 2005-2014[1]
($ millions)

Year	Underwriting					
	Property/casualty		Life/annuity		Health/managed care	
	Number of transactions	Transaction values	Number of transactions	Transaction values	Number of transactions	Transaction values
2005	49	$9,264	21	$21,865	22	$15,886
2006	48	35,221	23	5,055	20	646
2007	67	13,615	19	5,849	52	9,661
2008	59	16,294	14	382	19	1,691
2009	63	3,507	22	840	18	640
2010	60	6,419	20	23,848	15	692
2011	77	12,458	34	3,063	25	4,703
2012	46	4,651	21	6,083	26	18,520
2013	39	4,397	18	3,299	15	33
2014	51	6,723	10	7,978	15	864

Year	Distribution and insurance services				Total U.S. mergers and acquisitions	
	Distribution		Insurance services			
	Number of transactions	Transaction values	Number of transactions	Transaction values	Number of transactions	Transaction values
2005	180	$212	63	$3,566	335	$50,793
2006	246	944	69	1,156	406	43,022
2007	312	15,205	72	6,087	478	50,417
2008	284	5,812	94	7,256	470	31,435
2009	176	615	41	8,771	320	14,373
2010	243	1,727	98	13,823	436	46,509
2011	351	2,608	105	31,892	592	54,724
2012	323	4,225	62	9,673	478	43,152
2013	317	8,246	57	3,349	446	19,324
2014	349	2,581	79	19,390	504	37,536

[1]Includes transactions where a U.S. company was the acquirer and/or the target.

Source: Conning proprietary database.

Insurance Companies by State

An insurance company is said to be *domiciled* in the state that issued its primary license; it is *domestic* in that state. Once it receives its primary license, it may seek licenses in other states as an out-of-state insurer. These out-of-state insurers are called *foreign* insurers. An insurer incorporated in a foreign country is called an *alien* insurer in states where it is licensed.

DOMESTIC INSURANCE COMPANIES BY STATE, PROPERTY/CASUALTY AND LIFE/ANNUITIES, 2014

State	Property/ casualty	Life/ annuities	State	Property/ casualty	Life/ annuities
Alabama	20	7	Montana	3	1
Alaska	5	0	Nebraska	29	27
Arizona	39	29	Nevada	12	3
Arkansas	12	29	New Hampshire	51	1
California	107	15	New Jersey	65	3
Colorado	11	11	New Mexico	13	2
Connecticut	71	28	New York	183	79
Delaware	103	30	North Carolina	66	7
D.C.	7	0	North Dakota	13	4
Florida	122	11	Ohio	135	38
Georgia	33	14	Oklahoma	30	27
Hawaii	17	3	Oregon	15	3
Idaho	7	1	Pennsylvania	182	26
Illinois	194	56	Rhode Island	21	2
Indiana	66	26	South Carolina	24	9
Iowa	69	36	South Dakota	18	3
Kansas	26	12	Tennessee	15	18
Kentucky	8	8	Texas	203	123
Louisiana	30	35	Utah	10	16
Maine	11	3	Vermont	14	2
Maryland	38	5	Virginia	18	4
Massachusetts	51	17	Washington	10	7
Michigan	72	24	West Virginia	19	0
Minnesota	37	12	Wisconsin	1	20
Mississippi	14	15	Wyoming	2	1
Missouri	48	26	**United States**[1]	**2,370**	**879**

[1]Excludes territories, health insurers, risk retention groups, fraternals, title and other insurers. Source: Insurance Department Resources Report, 2014, published by the National Association of Insurance Commissioners (NAIC). Reprinted with permission. Further reprint or redistribution strictly prohibited without written permission of NAIC.

- According to the National Association of Insurance Commissioners, in the U.S. (including territories) there were 6,118 insurance companies in 2014, including property/casualty (P/C) (2,583), life/annuities (895), health (857), fraternal (85), title (56), risk retention groups (252) and other companies (1,390).

- Many insurance companies are part of larger organizations. According to A.M. Best, in 2014 the P/C insurance industry contained about 1,266 organizations or groups (as opposed to 2,718 companies), including 776 stock (or public) organizations, 397 mutual organizations (firms owned by their policyholders) and 70 reciprocals (a type of self-insurance). The remainder consisted of Lloyd's organizations and state funds.

Premium Taxes by State

All insurance companies pay a state tax based on their premiums. Other payments are made to states for licenses and fees, income and property taxes, sales and use taxes, unemployment compensation taxes and franchise taxes.

- Insurance companies, including life/health and property/casualty companies, paid $18.1 billion in premium taxes to the 50 states in 2014. On a per capita basis, this works out to $57 for every person living in the United States.

- Premium taxes accounted for 2.0 percent of all taxes collected by the states in 2014.

- The Bureau of the Census does not collect data on premium taxes for the District of Columbia.

- According to the Government of the District of Columbia, the District collected $77.5 million in gross revenues from insurance premiums in 2013.

PREMIUM TAXES BY STATE, PROPERTY/CASUALTY AND LIFE/HEALTH INSURANCE, 2014
($000)

State	Amount	State	Amount
Alabama	$304,441	Montana	$88,106
Alaska	62,292	Nebraska	42,746
Arizona	448,115	Nevada	264,522
Arkansas	182,092	New Hampshire	84,518
California	2,362,738	New Jersey	599,169
Colorado	239,431	New Mexico	99,832
Connecticut	205,690	New York	1,345,394
Delaware	85,735	North Carolina	476,376
Florida	702,340	North Dakota	51,047
Georgia	372,122	Ohio	510,345
Hawaii	142,051	Oklahoma	294,762
Idaho	75,205	Oregon	85,196
Ilinois	359,240	Pennsylvania	773,462
Indiana	223,072	Rhode Island	85,801
Iowa	105,532	South Carolina	214,600
Kansas	198,355	South Dakota	77,374
Kentucky	141,639	Tennessee	749,470
Louisiana	429,146	Texas	1,886,289
Maine	106,372	Utah	113,316
Maryland	475,294	Vermont	60,020
Massachusetts	346,828	Virginia	459,993
Michigan	362,397	Washington	467,351
Minnesota	403,280	West Virginia	155,021
Mississippi	263,809	Wisconsin	185,502
Missouri	302,166	Wyoming	25,310
		United States	**$18,094,904**

Source: U.S. Department of Commerce, Bureau of the Census.

Overview

Many insurance companies use a number of different channels to distribute their products. In the early days of the U.S. insurance industry, insurers hired agents, often on a part-time basis, to sign up applicants for insurance. Some agents, known nowadays as "captive" or "exclusive" agents, represented a single company. Others, the equivalent of today's independent agent, worked for a number of companies. At the same time that the two agency systems were expanding, commercial insurance brokers, who were often underwriters, began to set up shop in cities. While agents usually represented insurers, brokers represented clients who were buying insurance. These three distribution channels (captive agents, independent agents and brokers) exist in much the same form today. But with the development of information technology, which provided faster access to company representatives and made the exchange of information for underwriting purposes much easier, alternative distribution channels sprang up, including direct sales by telephone, mail and the Internet. In addition, insurers are using other types of outlets, such as banks, workplaces, associations and car dealers, to access potential policyholders.

Online Property/Casualty Insurance Sales

Insurance distribution systems have evolved to encompass many of the new ways of conducting business online. Recent studies have shown the Internet is playing an increasingly important role in the sales and servicing of auto insurance. More than half of all insurance shoppers today use the web to scout their options, and many further seek to obtain quotes online, according to J.D. Power and Associates. The company's 2013 Insurance Website Evaluation Study found that auto insurance customers indicate that using insurance company websites to service an existing policy is generally easier than using them to shop for a policy. Finding policy information and requesting a quote were found to be the hardest tasks to perform while finding company contact information was the easiest.

A 2014 study by comScore found that 46 percent of consumers shopped for auto insurance online in 2014, compared with 48 percent in 2013. Seventy-one percent of those shopping in the past year obtained a quote online in 2014, a 4 percent increase from 2013. The percentage of consumers indicating that they would be likely to purchase auto insurance online in the future continues to grow each year. In 2014, 37 percent of consumers indicated they would be likely to shop for insurance online, up from 35 percent in 2013. Forty-four percent say that price remains the most important factor when they are looking to purchase auto insurance, regardless of the channel that they use. The agent channel continues to be the most preferred method for purchasing insurance, with 30 percent of respondents saying they found it more convenient to use a website or toll-free number. In 2014 just fewer than 10 percent of consumers obtained quotes or purchased an auto insurance policy via a smartphone or tablet.

Distribution

Property/Casualty

- There were 38,500 independent agencies in the United States in 2014, about the same number as in 2012, according to the Independent Insurance Agents and Brokers of America's 2014 Agency Universe survey.

- As the number of agencies has leveled off, the IIABA notes that a growing proportion of agencies have principals over the age of 65—18 percent in 2014, versus 10 percent in 2012.

- Fifty-four percent of jumbo agencies (revenues of $10 million or more) have locations in more than one state, compared with 5 percent of all agencies.

- Almost half (46 percent) of agencies are located in large metropolitan areas.

- About one in 10 agencies (13 percent) were involved in a merger or acquisition in the past two years. Almost half (48 percent) of jumbo agencies were involved in such a transaction.

Property/Casualty Insurance Distribution

Agency writers, whose products are sold by independent agents or brokers representing several companies; and direct writers, which sell their own products through captive agents by mail, telephone, or via the Internet and other means—each account for about half of the property/casualty (P/C) market. There is a degree of overlap as many insurers use multiple channels.

A.M. Best organizes insurance into two main distribution channels: agency writers and direct writers. Its "agency writers" category includes insurers that distribute through independent agencies, brokers, general agents and managing general agents. Its "direct writers" category includes insurers that distribute through the Internet, exclusive/captive agents, direct response and affinity groups.

- In 2014 direct writers accounted for 51.2 percent of P/C insurance net premiums written and agency writers accounted for 46.6 percent, according to A.M. Best.*

- In the personal lines market, direct writers accounted for 71.0 percent of net premiums written in 2014 and agency writers accounted for 27.3 percent. Direct writers accounted for 68.4 percent of the homeowners market and agency writers accounted for 28.6 percent. Direct writers accounted for 72.1 percent of the personal auto market and agency writers accounted for 26.8 percent.*

- Agency writers accounted for 70.2 percent of commercial P/C net premiums written and direct writers accounted for 30.6 percent.*

*Unspecified distribution channels accounted for the remainder.

Life Insurance Distribution

In 2014 independent agents held 50 percent of the new individual life insurance sales market, followed by affiliated (i.e., captive) agents with 40 percent, direct marketers with 5 percent and others accounting for the remaining 5 percent, according to LIMRA, a life insurance trade association.

LIFE INDIVIDUAL MARKET SHARE BY DISTRIBUTION CHANNEL, 2005-2014
(Based on first year collected premiums)

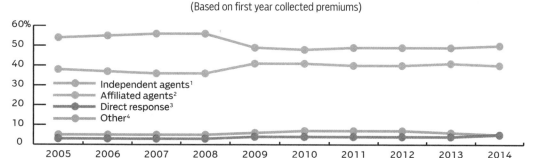

[1]Includes brokers, stockbrokers and personal producing general agents. [2]Includes career, multiline exclusive and home service agents. [3]No producers are involved. Excludes direct marketing efforts involving agents. [4]Includes financial institutions, worksite and other channels.

Source: LIMRA's *U.S. Individual Life Insurance Sales Survey* and LIMRA estimates.

Online Life Insurance Sales

Eighty-five percent of consumers say they would use the Internet to research life insurance before purchasing coverage, according to the 2015 Insurance Barometer Study by the Life and Health Insurance Foundation for Education (LIFE) and LIMRA, about the same number as a year earlier. About 90 percent of consumers between the ages of 25 and 44 would use the Internet to research life insurance. That amount falls for older age groups and was at 76 percent for consumers age 65 and older. About one quarter of consumers went online to find an agent or financial adviser and about one in three went online to find information about an agent or adviser. When it comes to purchasing life insurance, face-to-face with a financial adviser or agent was the most favored life insurance sales channel, with 52 percent preferring that method. Online was a strong second for all age groups, favored by 22 percent of respondents. About one in three respondents under the age of 45 said they preferred the online route, up from one in four a year ago. Other preferred channels were workplace sales (10 percent), mail (8 percent), phone (4 percent) and email (4 percent). About 40 percent of online shoppers went to a website with a quote engine. However, LIMRA research shows that most of these shoppers do so to obtain quick and easy price quotes—only 14 percent of online purchasers bought life insurance from a website that gives quotes, while more than half bought coverage from a company website.

Distribution

Annuities Distribution

Insurance agents, including career agents, who sell the products of a single life insurance company, and independent agents, who represent several insurers, accounted for 37 percent of annuity sales in 2014. State and federal regulators require sellers of variable annuities to register with the Financial Industry Regulatory Authority (FINRA) and the Securities and Exchange Commission.

SALES OF INDIVIDUAL ANNUITIES BY DISTRIBUTION CHANNELS, 2010 AND 2014

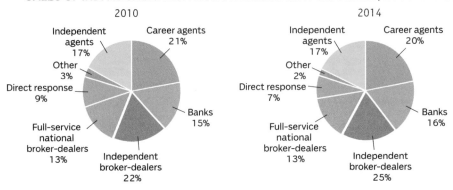

Source: *U.S. Individual Annuity Yearbook - 2014*, LIMRA Retirement Institute.

Bank Insurance Sales

The Gramm-Leach-Bliley Financial Services Modernization Act of 1999 (GLB) removed many of the Depression-era barriers that restricted affiliations between banks, securities firms and insurance companies. The arrangement that provided the major impetus for the passage of GLB, Citigroup's merger with Travelers Insurance Group, was short-lived, with Citigroup selling off its Travelers property/casualty insurance and life insurance units in 2002 and 2005, respectively. The "financial supermarkets" envisioned by GLB have not transpired. Instead, banks have tended to concentrate on distributing insurance products by buying existing agencies and brokers rather than by setting up their own agencies or purchasing insurers. For their part, insurance companies have set up thrift or banking divisions rather than buying existing banks. The 2007 to 2009 recession and resulting regulatory changes prompted some structural changes in the financial services industry, with some insurers selling their banking units.

BANK HOLDING COMPANY INSURANCE BROKERAGE, UNDERWRITING AND TOTAL INSURANCE FEE INCOME, 2010-2014[1]

	Insurance brokerage fee income[2]				
	Reporting insurance brokerage fee income		Insurance brokerage fee income ($ billions)	Average insurance brokerage fee income	Median insurance brokerage fee income[4]
Year	Number	Percent[3]			
2010	592	65.1%	$7.05	$11,916,748	$131,500
2011	606	65.2	7.70	12,702,413	119,000
2012	665	63.2	6.20	9,318,084	123,000
2013	664	62.5	6.22	9,360,139	117,500
2014	650	61.8	5.71	8,784,272	127,000

	Insurance underwriting fee income				
	Reporting insurance underwriting fee income		Insurance underwriting fee income ($ billions)	Average insurance underwriting fee income	Median insurance underwriting fee income[4]
Year	Number	Percent[3]			
2010	67	7.4%	$7.16	$106,825,388	$452,000
2011	63	6.8	5.09	80,756,651	360,000
2012	66	6.3	4.41	66,769,970	503,000
2013	60	5.7	4.00	66,645,533	581,000
2014	59	5.6	3.57	60,535,390	1,000,000

	Total insurance fee income				
	Reporting total insurance fee income		Total insurance fee income ($ billions)	Average total insurance fee income	Median total insurance fee income[4]
Year	Number	Percent[3]			
2010	594	65.3%	$14.21	$23,925,953	$156,000
2011	608	65.5	12.79	21,028,595	133,000
2012	670	63.6	10.60	15,825,887	141,000
2013	669	63.0	10.21	15,267,360	141,000
2014	655	62.3	9.28	14,170,023	150,000

[1]Bank holding companies (BHCs) own one or more banks. Excludes MetLife, Inc., which during some of these years was a financial holding company subject to reporting and supervision to the Federal Reserve Board. Other traditional insurers were similarly excluded from these findings.
[2]Income from nonunderwriting activities, mostly from insurance product sales and referrals, service charges and commissions, and fees earned from insurance and annuity sales.
[3]Percent of top-tier BHCs defined by the Federal Reserve with consolidated assets in excess of $500 million.
[4]Represents the midpoint. Half are above the median and half are below.

Source: Michael White's Bank Insurance Fee Income Report - 2015.

TOP 10 BANK HOLDING COMPANIES IN INSURANCE BROKERAGE FEE INCOME, 2013-2014[1]

($000)

Rank	Bank holding company	State	Insurance brokerage fee income				
			2013	2014	Percent change, 2013-2014	Percent of noninterest income, 2014	2014 assets
1	BB&T Corporation	North Carolina	$1,377,772	$1,504,913	9.23%	39.84%	$186,810,156
2	Wells Fargo & Company	California	1,463,000	1,317,000	-9.98	3.30	1,687,154,000
3	Citigroup Inc.	New York	733,000	721,000	-1.64	2.47	1,842,415,000
4	American Express Company	New York	184,000	184,000	[2]	0.64	158,588,000
5	Regions Financial Corporation	Alabama	114,412	124,036	8.41	6.44	119,888,669
6	Bancorpsouth, Inc.	Mississippi	98,141	115,237	17.42	45.58	13,326,530
7	Morgan Stanley	New York	99,000	76,000	-23.23	0.25	798,815,000
8	First Command Financial Services	Texas	76,736	75,599	-1.48	31.79	929,910
9	Discover Financial Services	Illinois	78,906	72,527	-8.08	4.23	82,801,232
10	First Niagara Financial Group, Inc.	New York	72,558	71,125	-1.97	24.30	38,492,000

[1]Bank holding companies own one or more banks. Includes income from nonunderwriting activities, mostly insurance product sales and referrals, service charges and commissions, and fees earned from insurance and annuity sales. [2]Less than 0.01 percent.
Source: Michael White's Bank Insurance Fee Income Report - 2015.

TOP 10 BANK HOLDING COMPANIES IN INSURANCE UNDERWRITING NET INCOME, 2014[1]

($000)

Rank	Bank holding company	State	Total insurance underwriting net income	Total net income/loss	Insurance net income as a percent of total net income	2013 assets
1	Wells Fargo & Company	California	$704,000	$23,057,000	3.05%	$1,687,154,000
2	Citigroup Inc.	New York	351,000	7,313,000	4.80	1,842,415,000
3	Ally Financial Inc.	Michigan	173,000	1,150,000	15.04	151,828,000
4	American Express Company	New York	85,000	5,885,000	1.44	158,588,000
5	BB&T Corporation	North Carolina	51,742	2,151,093	2.41	186,810,156
6	Old National Bancorp	Indiana	44,832	103,667	43.25	11,647,778
7	Bank of America Corporation	North Carolina	34,000	4,833,000	0.70	2,100,265,000
8	The PNC Financial Services Group, Inc.	Pennsylvania	18,085	4,184,251	0.43	345,243,081
9	Hilltop Holdings, Inc.	Texas	16,615	111,650	14.88	9,238,537
10	The Goldman Sachs Group, Inc.	New York	11,000	8,477,000	0.13	853,125,000

[1]Bank holding companies own one or more banks. Source: Michael White's Bank Insurance Fee Income Report - 2015.

Life/Health Sector

Whether measured by premium income or by assets, traditional life insurance is no longer the primary business of many companies in the life/health insurance industry. Today, the emphasis has shifted to the underwriting of annuities. Annuities are contracts that accumulate funds and/or pay out a fixed or variable income stream. An income stream can be for a set period of time or over the lifetimes of the contract holder or his or her beneficiaries.

Nevertheless, traditional life insurance products such as universal life and term life for individuals as well as group life remain an important part of the business, as do disability income and health insurance.

Life insurers invest primarily in corporate bonds but also significantly in corporate equities. Besides annuities and life insurance products, life insurers may offer other types of financial services such as asset management.

Life Insurance Ownership

Fifty-seven percent of all people in the United States were covered by some type of life insurance in 2014, according to LIMRA's 2015 *Insurance Barometer Study*. Nearly one-third of Americans said they need more life insurance in 2015. Other findings from the 2015 report include:

- Fifty-four percent of Americans say they are unlikely to purchase a life insurance policy within the next year. Sixty-five percent said that they have not purchased more life insurance because they think it is too expensive, yet 80 percent of consumers misjudge the price of term life insurance.
- The most common financial worry among consumers over 25 years old is being able to afford a comfortable retirement. Consumers 25 and under are more concerned with paying monthly bills.
- Only 13 percent of Americans own long-term care insurance; 26 percent own disability insurance.

2014 Financial Results

In 2014 the life insurance industry posted mixed results as it continued to face challenges from little household income growth, changing demographics, low interest rates and consumers having other financial priorities. Although premiums rose to the highest level since the Great Recession, operating results declined compared with 2013 partly because of significantly increased surrenders. The industry's net gain from operations before federal income taxes dropped to $49.0 billion in 2014 from $63.8 billion in 2013. Capital and surplus rose to $354.1 billion in 2014 from $331.8 billion in 2013, according to SNL Financial.

Investments

The life/health insurance industry's cash and invested assets totaled $3.6 trillion in 2014, according to SNL Financial.

Life/Health Financial Data

Financial Results

LIFE/HEALTH INSURANCE INDUSTRY INCOME STATEMENT, 2010-2014
($ billions, end of year)

	2010	2011	2012	2013	2014	Percent change, 2013-2014[1]
Revenue						
Life insurance premiums	$100.3	$122.8	$130.5	$126.1	$133.8	6.2%
Annuity premiums and deposits	286.3	327.0	339.9	279.4	352.8	26.3
Accident and health premiums	150.8	151.1	151.4	153.3	156.6	2.2
Credit life and credit accident and health premiums	1.6	1.6	1.6	1.4	1.4	-3.9
Other premiums and considerations	23.1	2.1	2.2	2.3	2.6	8.9
Total premiums, consideration and deposits	**$562.1**	**$604.5**	**$625.7**	**$562.6**	**$647.3**	**15.1%**
Net investment income	164.1	167.3	166.5	168.0	171.7	2.3
Reinsurance allowance	-29.3	-16.3	-30.8	-21.2	-15.0	-29.5
Separate accounts revenue	23.4	26.1	29.5	31.4	34.3	9.1
Other income	53.0	53.3	41.5	43.0	39.5	-8.0
Total revenue	**$773.3**	**$835.0**	**$832.5**	**$783.7**	**$877.9**	**12.0%**
Expense						
Benefits	231.6	239.0	241.8	250.8	251.8	0.4
Surrenders	216.8	237.3	245.7	248.7	281.5	13.2
Increase in reserves	96.2	141.2	83.8	86.2	108.7	26.1
Transfers to separate accounts	29.3	32.4	61.6	-0.8	-16.5	[2]
Commissions	48.9	51.4	52.6	53.0	52.1	-1.8
General and administrative expenses	54.7	56.4	57.2	58.5	59.0	0.8
Insurance taxes, licenses and fees	7.5	7.8	8.0	8.2	10.0	21.7
Other expenses	2.2	8.1	6.7	-0.4	65.8	[2]
Total expenses	**$687.2**	**$773.6**	**$757.4**	**$704.3**	**$812.4**	**15.4%**
Net income						
Policyholder dividends	15.0	15.1	15.2	15.7	16.4	4.9
Net gain from operations before federal income tax	53.1	28.0	59.6	63.8	49.0	-23.1
Federal income tax	8.6	4.7	9.9	8.6	10.1	18.2
Net income before capital gains	**$44.1**	**$22.9**	**$49.7**	**$55.2**	**$38.9**	**-29.5%**
Net realized capital gains (losses)	-16.0	-8.5	-9.4	-12.0	-1.3	-89.1
Net income	**$28.0**	**$14.4**	**$40.3**	**$43.2**	**$37.6**	**-12.9%**
Pre-tax operating income	53.1	28.0	59.6	63.8	49.0	-23.1

[1]Calculated from unrounded data.
[2]Not applicable.

Source: SNL Financial LC.

INVESTMENTS, LIFE/HEALTH INSURERS, 2012-2014[1]

($ billions, end of year)

Investment type	Amount			Percent of total investments		
	2012	2013	2014	2012	2013	2014
Bonds	$2,543.5	$2,601.5	$2,685.2	74.65%	74.61%	73.85%
Stocks	79.3	82.0	87.8	2.33	2.35	2.42
Preferred stock	7.8	8.3	9.1	0.23	0.24	0.25
Common stock	71.5	73.8	78.7	2.10	2.12	2.16
Mortgage loans on real estate	335.6	353.2	373.0	9.85	10.13	10.26
First lien real estate mortgage loans	333.1	350.1	368.4	9.78	10.04	10.13
Real estate loans, less first liens	2.5	3.1	4.6	0.07	0.09	0.13
Real estate	20.9	21.4	21.5	0.61	0.61	0.59
Occupied properties	5.5	5.4	5.5	0.16	0.16	0.15
Income generating properties	15.4	16.0	16.0	0.45	0.46	0.44
Properties for sale	0.5	1.0	0.4	0.02	0.03	0.01
Cash, cash equivalent and short term investments	106.6	94.8	100.0	3.13	2.72	2.75
Contract loans including premium notes	127.6	128.5	130.2	3.74	3.69	3.58
Derivatives	41.6	37.8	56.5	1.22	1.08	1.55
Other invested assets	138.6	147.7	164.2	4.07	4.23	4.51
Receivables for securities	2.1	3.2	2.2	0.06	0.09	0.06
Securities lending reinvested collateral assets	10.8	13.8	11.2	0.32	0.40	0.31
Write-ins for invested assets	-0.3	1.7	4.0	-0.01	0.05	0.11
Total cash and invested assets	**$3,407.0**	**$3,486.6**	**$3,636.2**	**100.00%**	**100.00%**	**100.00%**

[1]Data are net admitted assets of life/health insurers.

Source: SNL Financial LC.

INVESTMENTS, LIFE/HEALTH INSURERS, BOND PORTFOLIO, 2014[1]

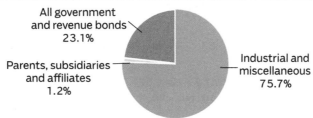

All government and revenue bonds 23.1%

Parents, subsidiaries and affiliates 1.2%

Industrial and miscellaneous 75.7%

[1]Long-term bonds with maturity dates over one year, as of December 31, 2014.

Source: SNL Financial LC.

Life/Health Financial Data

Payouts

Life insurance benefits and claims totaled $642 billion in 2014, including life insurance death benefits, annuity benefits, disability benefits and other payouts, compared with $586 billion in 2013. The largest payout, $282 billion, was for surrender benefits and withdrawals from life insurance contracts made to policyholders who terminated their policies early or withdrew cash from their policies.

LIFE INSURANCE INDUSTRY BENEFITS AND CLAIMS, 2010-2014
($000)

	2010	2011	2012	2013	2014
Death benefits	$56,507,462	$60,611,234	$61,701,263	$62,538,083	$65,961,289
Matured endowments, excluding annual pure endowments	679,242	767,092	415,088	368,210	350,488
Annuity benefits	66,781,512	70,873,226	70,296,382	74,882,585	69,583,732
Disability, accident and health benefits[1]	106,029,818	104,982,729	107,525,331	110,931,697	113,589,753
Coupons, pure endowment and similar benefits	16,264	16,075	17,179	17,222	18,992
Surrender benefits, withdrawals for life contracts	216,846,768	237,281,879	245,728,482	248,702,238	281,532,892
Group conversions	29,136	27,884	27,891	52,893	28,088
Interest and adjustments on deposit type contracts	9,541,403	9,829,729	7,321,437	8,195,240	7,749,827
Payments on supplementary contracts with life contingencies	1,578,300	1,690,841	1,809,677	1,985,919	2,237,030
Increase in aggregate reserve	86,623,332	131,335,283	76,438,193	78,024,348	100,982,446
Total benefits and claims	**$544,633,701**	**$617,415,972**	**$571,280,922**	**$585,698,435**	**$642,034,537**

[1]Excludes benefits paid by health insurance companies and property/casualty insurance companies.

Source: SNL Financial LC.

Measured by premiums written, annuities are the largest life/health product line, followed by accident and health, and life insurance. Life insurance policies can be sold on an individual, or "ordinary," basis or to groups such as employees and associations. Accident and health insurance includes medical expenses, disability income and long-term care. Other lines include credit life, which pays the balance of a loan if the borrower dies or becomes disabled, and industrial life, small policies whose premiums are generally collected by an agent on a weekly basis.

DIRECT PREMIUMS WRITTEN BY LINE, LIFE/HEALTH INSURANCE INDUSTRY, 2012-2014
($000)

Lines of insurance	2012		2013		2014	
	Direct premiums written[1]	Percent of total	Direct premiums written[1]	Percent of total	Direct premiums written[1]	Percent of total
Annuities						
Ordinary individual annuities	$192,291,621	28.1%	$198,862,072	30.7%	$205,448,744	31.0%
Group annuities	164,069,697	24.0	120,091,136	18.6	119,716,314	18.1
Total	**$356,361,318**	**52.0%**	**$318,953,208**	**49.3%**	**$325,165,057**	**49.1%**
Life						
Ordinary life	132,639,900	19.4	129,963,536	20.1	132,935,453	20.1
Group life	34,419,733	5.0	33,532,415	5.2	34,378,152	5.2
Credit life (group and individual)	1,129,433	0.2	990,170	0.2	960,229	0.1
Industrial life	165,688	[2]	146,248	[2]	142,962	[2]
Total	**$168,354,754**	**24.6%**	**$164,632,370**	**25.5%**	**$168,416,797**	**25.4%**
Accident and health[3]						
Group	90,460,090	13.2	94,590,278	14.6	98,108,859	14.8
Other	68,764,256	10.0	67,673,915	10.5	69,655,745	10.5
Credit	954,569	0.1	966,052	0.1	954,502	0.1
Total	**$160,178,916**	**23.4%**	**$163,230,245**	**25.2%**	**$168,719,106**	**25.5%**
All other lines	46	[2]	3,027	[2]	3,482	[2]
Total, all lines[4]	**$684,895,034**	**100.0%**	**$646,818,849**	**100.0%**	**$662,304,443**	**100.0%**

[1]Before reinsurance transactions.
[2]Less than 0.1 percent.
[3]Excludes accident and health premiums reported on the property/casualty and health annual statements.
[4]Excludes deposit-type funds.

Source: SNL Financial LC.

Private Health Insurance

Most private health insurance is written by insurers whose main business is health insurance. However, life/health and property/casualty insurers also write this coverage, referred to as accident and health insurance on their annual statements. Total private health insurance direct written premiums were $707.1 billion in 2014, including $533.0 billion from the health insurance segment, $168.7 billion from the life/health segment and $5.4 billion from property/casualty annual statements, according to SNL Financial.

In 2014, 33 million Americans did not have health insurance, according to the U.S. Census Bureau report, compared with 42 million in 2013. The percentage of uninsured Americans in 2014 stood at 10.4 percent, down from 13.3 percent in 2013. There is other evidence not directly comparable to the Census Bureau data of falling uninsured rates: according to the Gallup Health-Ways Well-Being Index, the percentage of Americans without health insurance fell to 11.4 percent in the second quarter of 2015, compared with 11.9 percent in the first quarter of 2015.

Other Census Bureau findings include:

- 66 percent of Americans were covered by private health insurance in 2014.
- The percentage covered by employment-based health insurance in 2014 was 55.4 percent. The percentage of people covered by government health insurance was 36.5 percent during the same period.
- The percentage of children under the age of 19 without health insurance was 6.2 percent in 2014 compared with 7.5 percent in 2013. Children under 19 are eligible for Medicaid and the Children's Health Insurance Program. Only 1.4 percent of people age 65 and older who are eligible for Medicare did not have health insurance.
- In 2014 the uninsured rate was 16.6 percent for those in households with annual income less than $25,000. This contrasts with uninsured rates of 10.7 percent for those in households with income between $50,000 and $75,000 and 5.3 percent with income of $150,000 or more.

HEALTH INSURANCE COVERAGE STATUS AND TYPE OF COVERAGE, 2014
(000)

Total U.S. population	Uninsured		Insured		
	Number of people	Percent of total population	Private health insurance	Government health insurance	Individuals with some form of insurance[1]
316,168	32,968	10.4%	66.0%	36.5%	89.6%

[1]Includes individuals with some form of insurance (government, private or a combination of both).

Source: U.S. Department of Commerce, Census Bureau.

TOP 10 HEALTH INSURANCE GROUPS BY DIRECT PREMIUMS WRITTEN, 2014

($000)

Rank	Group/company	Direct premiums written[1]	Market share
1	UnitedHealth Group Inc.	$54,968,422	10.3%
2	Anthem Inc.[2]	52,217,860	9.8
3	Humana Inc.	45,598,914	8.6
4	HealthCare Service Corp.	28,740,192	5.4
5	Aetna Inc.	23,099,513	4.3
6	Centene Corp.	13,530,755	2.5
7	Independence Health Group Inc.	12,249,432	2.3
8	Highmark Insurance Group	11,765,600	2.2
9	Kaiser Foundation Health Plan Inc.	11,173,259	2.1
10	WellCare Health Plans Inc.	11,161,715	2.1

[1]Based on health insurer annual statement data. Excludes health insurance data from the property/casualty and life/health annual statements. Excludes territories.
[2]WellPoint Inc., which was ranked first in 2013, was renamed Anthem Inc. in December 2014.

Source: SNL Financial LC.

Disability Insurance

Disability insurance pays an insured person an income when he or she is unable to work because of an accident or illness.

INDIVIDUAL DISABILITY INSURANCE, NEW ISSUES SALES, 2014[1]

	Number of policies	Percent change, 2013-2014	Annualized premiums	Percent change, 2013-2014
Noncancellable	155,148	[2]	$315,800,819	[3]
Guaranteed renewable	298,702	7%	189,975,438	4%
Total	**453,850**	**5%**	**$505,776,257**	**1%**

■ Annualized total premiums for new disability income policies rose by 1 percent in 2014, following a 1 percent decrease the previous year.

[1]Short-term and long-term individual disability income insurance. Based on a LIMRA survey of 18 personal disability insurance companies. Excludes commercial disability income.
[2]Less than one-half of 1 percent.
[3]Less than one-half of negative 1 percent.

Source: LIMRA.

INDIVIDUAL DISABILITY INSURANCE IN FORCE, 2014[1]

	Number of policies	Percent change, 2013-2014	Annualized premiums	Percent change, 2013-2014
Noncancellable	2,402,293	-1%	$4,176,776,103	1%
Guaranteed renewable	1,670,237	2	1,195,434,858	3
Total	**4,072,530**	**2**	**$5,372,210,961**	**2%**

[1]Short-term and long-term individual disability income insurance. Based on a LIMRA survey of 21 disability insurance companies. Excludes commercial disability income.
[2]Less than one half percent of 1 percent.

Source: LIMRA.

Long-Term Care Insurance

Long-term care (LTC) insurance pays for services to help individuals who are unable to perform certain activities of daily living without assistance or who require supervision due to a cognitive impairment such as Alzheimer's disease. According to the U.S. Department of Health and Human Services, about 70 percent of individuals over age 65 will require at least some type of LTC services. There were 46.2 million people age 65 and older in 2014, accounting for 14.5 percent of the U.S. population, or about one in every seven Americans, according to the U.S. Census Bureau. By 2030 the Census Bureau projects there will be about 74.1 million older people and about 88.0 million in 2050.

About 4.8 million people were covered by LTC insurance in 2014, according to LIMRA. In 2015 the average premium for a 55-year-old male ranged from $1,066 to $2,075 per year, according to the 2015-2016 Long-Term Care Sourcebook published by the American Association for Long-Term Care Insurance. For a 55-year-old woman, the premium ranged from $1,400 to $2,411. Based on 2014 buyers, 38.6 percent of new LTC insurance policies were purchased by individuals under the age of 55, and 91.9 percent of buyers were under the age of 65, according to the study. The age of new buyers has been dropping slowly. A decade or so ago the age of the average buyer was between 66 and 67 years old, whereas now the average application age for coverage is 56 years old.

INDIVIDUAL LONG-TERM CARE (LTC) INSURANCE, 2014[1]

- The number of Americans purchasing LTC insurance in 2014 fell 24 percent from 2013, and premiums declined by 22 percent, based on new business.

	Lives	Percent change, 2013-2014	Premium ($ millions)	Percent change, 2013-2014
New business	131,140	-24%	$316	-22%
In-force[2]	4,800,000	-1	10,000	1

[1]Based on LIMRA International's Individual LTC Sales survey, representing more than 95 percent of the individual LTC market.
[2]Includes estimates for non-participants.

Source: LIMRA International.

Premiums by Line by State

**LIFE/HEALTH INSURERS DIRECT PREMIUMS WRITTEN AND
ANNUITY CONSIDERATIONS BY STATE, 2014[1]**
($ millions)

State	Life insurance	Annuities	Accident and health insurance[2]	Deposit-type contract funds	Other considerations	Total
Alabama	$2,278	$2,747	$1,410	$224	$587	$7,247
Alaska	732	553	336	20	193	1,835
Arizona	2,128	5,476	3,434	321	956	12,315
Arkansas	1,025	1,539	1,011	107	215	3,897
California	15,113	23,141	13,893	2,093	7,324	61,564
Colorado	2,380	4,620	3,309	795	734	11,838
Connecticut	2,410	4,441	2,797	8,445	1,411	19,505
Delaware	1,185	2,906	568	45,525	174	50,359
D.C.	388	731	768	199	779	2,865
Florida	8,421	18,135	11,786	1,064	3,739	43,144
Georgia	4,296	5,296	4,748	572	2,653	17,564
Hawaii	724	1,354	924	59	343	3,404
Idaho	519	926	547	52	186	2,230
Illinois	6,519	10,325	6,416	1,277	2,447	26,985
Indiana	2,608	5,295	3,700	875	761	13,239
Iowa	1,717	3,040	1,276	8,214	1,985	16,231
Kansas	1,304	2,299	3,202	746	412	7,962
Kentucky	1,505	2,335	1,592	309	688	6,429
Louisiana	2,224	3,580	1,932	183	556	8,474
Maine	445	1,085	827	57	198	2,613
Maryland	2,884	5,190	3,291	631	1,004	13,000
Massachusetts	3,524	7,075	2,916	1,640	3,437	18,592
Michigan	4,121	10,864	3,366	819	1,582	20,751
Minnesota	4,024	4,492	1,540	655	1,899	12,610
Mississippi	1,171	1,518	1,628	180	167	4,664
Missouri	2,626	7,619	3,391	975	1,069	15,681
Montana	368	503	380	21	138	1,409
Nebraska	1,001	1,734	1,098	460	310	4,602

(table continues)

**LIFE/HEALTH INSURERS DIRECT PREMIUMS WRITTEN AND
ANNUITY CONSIDERATIONS BY STATE, 2014[1] (Cont'd)**

($ millions)

State	Life insurance	Annuities	Accident and health insurance[2]	Deposit-type contract funds	Other considerations	Total
Nevada	$898	$1,490	$1,068	$226	$557	$4,240
New Hampshire	577	1,591	649	181	411	3,410
New Jersey	6,261	11,568	6,533	1,401	2,567	28,330
New Mexico	619	1,011	640	78	315	2,664
New York	11,262	17,382	8,496	24,152	9,491	70,783
North Carolina	4,235	6,924	5,142	1,273	2,437	20,011
North Dakota	376	667	292	50	133	1,518
Ohio	4,856	10,022	6,373	3,890	1,879	27,020
Oklahoma	1,376	1,878	1,594	181	402	5,431
Oregon	1,162	2,390	1,835	220	833	6,439
Pennsylvania	6,256	12,695	5,979	2,987	5,924	33,842
Rhode Island	437	1,239	691	64	250	2,682
South Carolina	1,938	3,505	1,891	189	358	7,882
South Dakota	641	580	366	61	140	1,788
Tennessee	2,794	4,764	2,670	396	1,065	11,689
Texas	10,665	15,873	14,507	2,170	2,794	46,009
Utah	1,263	2,164	932	307	414	5,079
Vermont	254	528	317	45	107	1,251
Virginia	3,879	6,225	3,946	756	1,122	15,928
Washington	2,329	4,559	2,839	289	1,477	11,493
West Virginia	611	1,208	640	98	169	2,726
Wisconsin	2,476	4,843	3,544	510	1,062	12,435
Wyoming	275	424	346	22	35	1,103
United States[3]	**$143,079**	**$252,346**	**$153,376**	**$116,066**	**$69,891**	**$734,758**

[1]Direct premiums written before reinsurance transactions, excludes state funds.
[2]Excludes accident and health premiums reported on property/casualty and health annual statements.
[3]Excludes territories, dividends and other nonstate specific data.

Source: SNL Financial LC.

TOP 20 WRITERS OF LIFE INSURANCE BY DIRECT PREMIUMS WRITTEN, 2014
($000)

Rank	Group/company	Direct premiums written[1]	Market share
1	MetLife Inc.	$12,260,284	8.2%
2	Northwestern Mutual Life Insurance Co.	9,551,489	6.4
3	New York Life Insurance Group	8,271,973	5.5
4	Prudential Financial Inc.	7,760,603	5.2
5	Lincoln National Corp.	6,437,777	4.3
6	Massachusetts Mutual Life Insurance Co.	5,605,050	3.8
7	Manulife Financial Corp.	4,722,527	3.2
8	AEGON	4,445,476	3.0
9	State Farm Mutual Automobile Insurance	4,101,553	2.7
10	Aflac Inc.	3,971,656	2.7
11	Guardian Life Insurance Co. of America	3,539,161	2.4
12	American International Group (AIG)	3,459,427	2.3
13	Securian Financial Group	3,453,247	2.3
14	Pacific MHC	2,983,172	2.0
15	AXA	2,968,159	2.0
16	Voya Financial Inc.	2,677,589	1.8
17	Hartford Financial Services	2,645,617	1.8
18	Dai-ichi Life Insurance Co. Ltd.	2,377,013	1.6
19	Nationwide Mutual Group	2,173,286	1.5
20	Primerica Inc.	2,016,200	1.4

[1]Before reinsurance transactions. Based on U.S. total, includes territories. Excludes annuities, accident and health, deposit-type contract funds and other considerations.

Source: SNL Financial LC.

Life/Health Financial Data

Leading Companies

TOP 10 WRITERS OF INDIVIDUAL LIFE INSURANCE
BY DIRECT PREMIUMS WRITTEN, 2014
($000)

Rank	Group/company	Direct premiums written[1]	Market share
1	Northwestern Mutual Life Insurance Co.	$9,551,489	8.1%
2	MetLife Inc.	6,863,942	5.8
3	New York Life Insurance Group	6,501,407	5.5
4	Lincoln National Corp.	5,630,181	4.8
5	Manulife Financial Corp.	4,717,567	4.0
6	Prudential Financial Inc.	4,426,981	3.7
7	Massachusetts Mutual Life Insurance Co.	4,362,771	3.7
8	AEGON	4,104,809	3.5
9	State Farm Mutual Automobile Insurance	4,059,521	3.4
10	Aflac Inc.	3,955,899	3.3

[1]Before reinsurance transactions. Based on U.S. total, includes territories. Excludes annuities, accident and health, deposit-type contract funds and other considerations.

Source: SNL Financial LC.

TOP 10 WRITERS OF GROUP LIFE INSURANCE
BY DIRECT PREMIUMS WRITTEN, 2014
($000)

Rank	Group/company	Direct premiums written[1]	Market share
1	MetLife Inc.	$5,360,171	17.8%
2	Prudential Financial Inc.	3,333,622	11.1
3	Securian Financial Group	2,101,502	7.0
4	New York Life Insurance Group	1,770,567	5.9
5	Cigna Corp.	1,719,727	5.7
6	Unum Group	1,280,542	4.3
7	Hartford Financial Services	1,257,665	4.2
8	Massachusetts Mutual Life Insurance Co.	1,242,279	4.1
9	Aetna Inc.	1,079,745	3.6
10	Lincoln National Corp.	807,532	2.7

[1]Before reinsurance transactions. Based on U.S. total, includes territories. Excludes annuities, accident and health, deposit-type contract funds and other considerations.

Source: SNL Financial LC.

2014 Financial Results

In 2014 the property/casualty insurance industry had its second highest level of yearly profit in the post-crisis era (2013 was the only better year). Low catastrophe losses, modest premium growth, continued realized investment gains and other factors combined to deliver a return on average surplus of 8.4 percent vs. 10.2 percent in 2013, according to data compiled by ISO, a Verisk Analytics company, and the Property Casualty Insurers Association of America (PCI). The industry combined ratio in 2014 rose slightly to 97.0 from 96.2 in 2013, delivering an underwriting profit of $12.3 billion (compared to $15.2 billion in 2013). The industry's overall net income after taxes (profits) for the year tallied $55.5 billion (though down from $63.4 billion a year earlier). Net premiums written were up 4.1 percent in 2014, slightly below the 4.4 percent gain in 2013, but continuing a string of three consecutive years of growth of 4 percent or higher. Persistently low interest rates remain a challenge for the industry so that net investment income for the year slipped by $1.1 billion (down 2.3 percent). Policyholder surplus rose to a record $674.7 billion as of December 31, 2014—up $21.3 billion, or 3.2 percent, from $653.4 billion as of year-end 2013, according to data from ISO and PCI.

PROPERTY/CASUALTY INSURANCE INDUSTRY INCOME ANALYSIS, 2010-2014[1]
($ billions)

	2010	2011	2012	2013	2014
Net premiums written	$423.8	$438.0	$456.7	$477.0	$496.6
Percent change	1.3%	3.4%	4.3%	4.4%	4.1%
Premiums earned	$422.2	$434.4	$448.9	$467.4	$487.6
Losses incurred	257.7	290.8	277.7	259.4	277.4
Loss adjustment expenses incurred	52.9	53.8	55.5	55.6	57.3
Other underwriting expenses	119.8	124.2	128.9	134.6	138.1
Policyholder dividends	2.3	1.9	2.1	2.5	2.5
Net underwriting gain/loss	-10.5	-36.2	-15.4	15.2	12.3
Net investment income	47.6	49.2	48.0	47.3	46.2
Miscellaneous income/loss	1.1	2.5	2.4	1.5	-2.8
Operating income	38.2	15.4	35.0	64.1	55.6
Realized capital gains	5.9	7.0	6.2	11.4	10.1
Federal and foreign income tax	8.8	3.0	6.1	12.0	10.2
Net income after taxes	35.2	19.5	35.1	63.4	55.5

- The property/casualty insurance industry had an underwriting gain of $12.3 billion in 2014, down 19.1 percent from $15.2 billion in 2013, as catastrophe losses rose to $15.5 billion in 2014 from $12.9 billion in 2013.

[1]Data in this chart exclude state funds and other residual market insurers and may not agree with similar data shown elsewhere from different sources.

Source: ISO, a Verisk Analytics company.

Property/Casualty Financial Data

Premiums, Expenses and Combined Ratio

Insurers use various measures to gauge financial performance. The combined ratio after dividends is a measure of underwriting profitability. It reflects the percentage of each premium dollar an insurer spends on claims and expenses. The combined ratio does not take investment income into account. A combined ratio above 100 indicates an underwriting loss.

NET PREMIUMS WRITTEN AND COMBINED RATIO, PROPERTY/CASUALTY INSURANCE, 2005-2014
($ billions)

Year	Net premiums written[1]	Annual percent change	Combined ratio after dividends[2]	Annual point change[3]	Year	Net premiums written[1]	Annual percent change	Combined ratio after dividends[2]	Annual point change[3]
2005	$422.4	-0.7%	100.7	2.2 pts.	2010	$425.9	0.6%	102.5	2.1 pts.
2006	447.8	6.0	92.4	-8.2	2011	441.6	3.7	108.3	5.8
2007	446.2	-0.4	95.6	3.2	2012	460.5	4.3	103.1	-5.2
2008	440.3	-1.3	105.2	9.5	2013	481.3	4.5	96.3	-6.8
2009	423.5	-3.8	100.4	-4.8	2014	502.6	4.4	97.2	0.8

[1]After reinsurance transactions, excludes state funds. [2]After dividends to policyholders. A drop in the combined ratio represents an improvement; an increase represents a deterioration. [3]Calculated from unrounded numbers.

Source: SNL Financial LC.

PROPERTY/CASUALTY INSURANCE INDUSTRY UNDERWRITING EXPENSES, 2014[1]

Expense	Percent of premiums
LOSSES AND RELATED EXPENSES[2]	
Loss and loss adjustment expense (LAE) ratio	**69.0%**
Incurred losses	57.2
Defense and cost containment expenses incurred	4.4
Adjusting and other expenses incurred	7.4
UNDERWITING EXPENSES[3]	
Expense ratio	**27.7%**
Net commissions and brokerage expenses incurred	10.7
Taxes, licenses and fees	2.5
Other acquisition and field supervision expenses incurred	7.6
General expenses incurred	6.9
DIVIDENDS TO POLICYHOLDERS[2]	**0.6%**
COMBINED RATIO AFTER DIVIDENDS[4]	**97.2%**

[1]After reinsurance transactions.
[2]As a percent of net premiums earned ($493.3 billion in 2014).
[3]As a percent of net premium written ($502.6 billion in 2014).
[4]Sum of loss and LAE, expense and dividends ratios.

Source: SNL Financial LC.

Profitability: Insurance and Other Selected Industries

Profitability of property/casualty (P/C) insurance companies using generally accepted accounting principles (GAAP) lags other industries. The median return on shareholders' equity for the Fortune 500 Combined Industrial and Service Businesses for the years 2005 to 2014 exceeded that of the P/C industry in every year. Insurers are required to use statutory accounting principles (SAP), which are more conservative than GAAP, when filing annual financial reports with state regulators and the Internal Revenue Service. Insurers outside the United States use standards that differ from SAP and GAAP. Some insurers support a move toward uniform global standards. The P/C industry's GAAP rate of return in 2014 was 7.5 percent, down from 8.9 percent in 2013.

ANNUAL RATE OF RETURN:
NET INCOME AFTER TAXES AS A PERCENT OF EQUITY, 2005-2014

Year	Property/casualty[1]		Life/health		Selected other industries[2]			Fortune 500 combined industrials and service[8]
	Statutory accounting[3]	GAAP accounting[4]	Life/health insurance[5]	Healthcare insurance[6]	Diversified financial[7]	Commercial banks	Electric and gas utilities	
2005	10.8%	9.6%	13.0%	16.2%	15.0%	16.0%	10.0%	14.9%
2006	14.4	12.7	12.0	19.0	15.0	15.0	11.0	15.4
2007	12.4	10.9	11.0	19.0	-1.0	11.0	11.0	15.2
2008	0.6	0.1	1.0	11.0	8.0	3.0	13.0	13.1
2009	5.9	5.0	4.0	14.0	9.0	4.0	9.0	10.5
2010	6.6	5.6	7.0	12.0	10.0	8.0	10.0	12.7
2011	3.5	3.0	8.0	15.0	12.0	8.0	10.0	14.5
2012	6.1	5.3	7.0	12.0	18.0	9.0	8.0	15.0
2013	10.2	8.9	7.0	13.0	18.0	9.0	9.0	13.7
2014	8.4	7.5	9.0	12.0	22.0	9.0	10.0	14.2

[1]Excludes state funds for workers compensation and other residual market carriers.
[2]Return on equity on a GAAP accounting basis, Fortune.
[3]Statutory net income after taxes, divided by the average of current and prior year-end policyholders' surplus. Calculated by ISO. Statutory accounting is used by insurers when preparing the Annual Statements they submit to regulators.
[4]Estimated from statutory data. Equals GAAP net income divided by the average of current and prior-year-end GAAP net worth. Calculated by ISO.
[5]Return on equity on a GAAP accounting basis, Fortune. Combined stock and mutual companies, calculated by the Insurance Information Institute.
[6]Healthcare insurance and managed care.
[7]Companies whose major source of revenue comes from providing diversified financial services. These companies are not specifically chartered as insurance companies, banks or savings institutions, or brokerage or securities companies, but they may earn revenue from these sources.
[8]Fortune 500 Combined Industrial and Service Businesses median return on shareholders' equity.

Source: SNL Financial LC; ISO, a Verisk Analytics company; Fortune.

Property/Casualty Insurance Cycle

Most industries are cyclical to some extent. The property/casualty (P/C) insurance industry cycle is characterized by periods of soft market conditions, in which premium rates are stable or falling and insurance is readily available, and by periods of hard market conditions, where rates rise, coverage may be more difficult to find and insurers' profits increase.

A dominant factor in the P/C insurance cycle is intense competition within the industry. Premium rates drop as insurance companies compete vigorously to increase market share. As the market softens to the point that profits diminish or vanish completely, the capital needed to underwrite new business is depleted. In the up phase of the cycle, competition is less intense, underwriting standards become more stringent, the supply of insurance is limited due to the depletion of capital and, as a result, premiums rise. The prospect of higher profits draws more capital into the marketplace, leading to more competition and the inevitable down phase of the cycle.

The chart below shows the real, or inflation-adjusted, growth of P/C net premiums written over four decades and three hard markets. Premiums can be accounted for in several ways. This chart uses net premiums written, which reflect premium amounts after deductions for reinsurance transactions.

During the last three hard markets, inflation-adjusted net premiums written grew 7.7 percent (1975 to 1978), 10.0 percent (1984 to 1987) and 6.3 percent (2001 to 2004).

PERCENT CHANGE FROM PRIOR YEAR, NET PREMIUMS WRITTEN, P/C INSURANCE, 1975-2014[1]

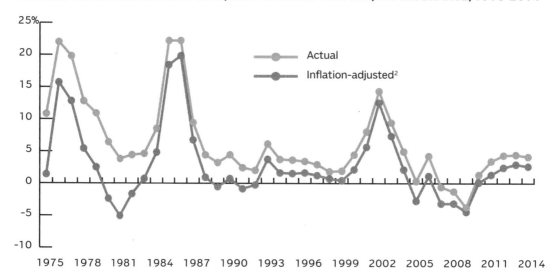

[1]Excludes state funds and other residual market insurers.
[2]Adjusted for inflation by ISO using the GDP implicit price deflator.

Source: ISO, a Verisk Analytics company.

Operating Results

In many years the insurance industry does not generate profits from its underwriting operations. Investment income from a number of sources—including capital and surplus accounts, money set aside as loss reserves and unearned premium reserves—generally offsets these losses. Underwriting results were favorable in 2006, 2007 and 2009, according to SNL Financial. The industry posted underwriting losses in 2010 through 2012, including 2011's $35.3 billion loss, the largest since 2001's $50.3 billion loss. Results for 2014 showed an underwriting gain of $14.3 billion, about $3.3 billion less than a year earlier.

OPERATING RESULTS, PROPERTY/CASUALTY INSURANCE, 2005-2014[1]
($ millions)

Year	Net underwriting gain/loss	Net investment income earned	Net realized capital gain/loss	Policyholder dividends	Taxes[2]	Net income after taxes[3]
2005	-$3,152	$49,960	$11,933	$1,974	$10,642	$47,198
2006	34,753	55,719	3,670	3,611	22,651	67,479
2007	21,637	56,320	8,817	2,814	19,857	63,138
2008	-19,810	53,430	-19,609	2,211	7,730	4,446
2009	1,579	48,640	-7,895	2,141	8,481	32,492
2010	-8,422	48,833	8,003	2,709	8,951	37,716
2011	-35,305	51,000	6,891	2,315	3,026	19,532
2012	-13,827	49,605	8,525	2,656	6,267	37,565
2013	17,528	48,781	17,193	3,018	11,948	70,039
2014	14,267	54,914	11,747	2,933	10,396	64,704

[1]Excludes state funds. [2]Includes federal and foreign taxes. [3]Does not equal the sum of the columns shown due to the omission of miscellaneous income.

Source: SNL Financial LC.

OPERATING RESULTS, PROPERTY/CASUALTY INSURANCE, 2005-2014[1]
($ billions)

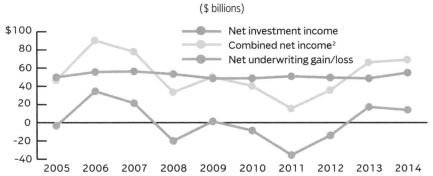

Net investment income
Combined net income[2]
Net underwriting gain/loss

[1]Excludes state funds. [2]Net underwriting gain/loss plus net investment income.

Source: SNL Financial LC.

Policyholders' Surplus

A property/casualty insurer must maintain a certain level of surplus to underwrite risks. This financial cushion is known as *capacity*. When the industry is hit by high losses, such as a major hurricane, capacity is diminished. It can be restored by increases in net income, favorable investment returns, reinsuring more risk and/or raising additional capital.

CONSOLIDATED ASSETS AND POLICYHOLDERS' SURPLUS, P/C INSURANCE, 2005-2014
($ millions)

Year	Net admitted assets	Annual percent change	Statutory liabilities	Annual percent change	Policyholders' surplus	Annual percent change	Total net premiums written[1]	Annual percent change
2005	$1,386,853	6.6%	$951,719	6.1%	$435,135	7.8%	$426,671	-0.1%
2006	1,549,509	11.7	1,045,931	9.9	503,578	15.7	448,967	5.2
2007	1,468,776	-5.2	940,758	-10.1	528,016	4.9	446,378	-0.6
2008	1,405,742	-4.3	943,732	0.3	462,006	-12.5	440,681	-1.3
2009	1,456,852	3.6	936,261	-0.8	520,591	12.7	423,545	-3.9
2010	1,514,190	3.9	947,390	1.2	566,800	8.9	426,380	0.7
2011	1,537,222	1.5	974,699	2.9	562,522	-0.8	441,925	3.6
2012	1,594,419	3.7	996,473	2.2	597,946	6.3	460,930	4.3
2013	1,682,079	5.5	1,014,676	1.8	667,402	11.6	481,505	4.5
2014	1,736,422	3.2	1,046,285	3.1	690,137	3.4	502,842	4.4

[1]After reinsurance transactions, excludes state funds. May not match total premiums written shown elsewhere in this book because of the use of different exhibits from SNL Financial.

Source: SNL Financial LC.

PERCENT CHANGE FROM PRIOR YEAR, NET PREMIUMS WRITTEN AND POLICYHOLDERS' SURPLUS, P/C INSURANCE, 2005-2014[1]

- Policyholders' surplus dropped substantially in 2008, reflecting the deterioration in global financial markets.

- Policyholders' surplus reached a record $690.1 billion in 2014, rising 3.4 percent from 2013.

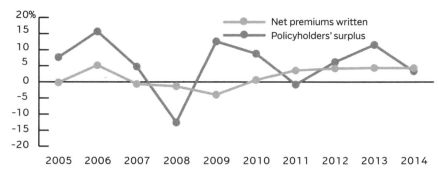

[1]After reinsurance transactions, excludes state funds.

Source: SNL Financial LC.

The Combined Ratio

The combined ratio represents the percentage of each premium dollar an insurer spends on claims and expenses. The following chart shows the components of the combined ratio, a measure of the industry's underwriting performance.

The combined ratio is the sum of the loss ratio and the expense ratio. The loss ratio expresses the relationship between losses and premiums in percentage terms. The expense ratio expresses the relationship between underwriting expenses and premiums.

COMPONENTS OF THE COMBINED RATIO, PROPERTY/CASUALTY INSURANCE, 2005-2014[1]

Year	Loss ratio[2]	Expense ratio[3]	Combined ratio	Dividends to policyholders[4]	Combined ratio after dividends
2005	74.6	25.8	100.4	0.4	100.9
2006	65.2	26.4	91.6	0.8	92.4
2007	67.7	27.3	94.9	0.6	95.5
2008	77.1	27.5	104.6	0.4	105.0
2009	72.5	28.0	100.5	0.5	101.0
2010	73.6	28.3	101.8	0.5	102.4
2011	79.3	28.4	107.7	0.4	108.1
2012	74.2	28.2	102.5	0.5	102.9
2013	67.4	28.2	95.6	0.5	96.2
2014	68.7	27.8	96.5	0.5	97.0

[1]Excludes state funds and other residual insurers.
[2]Incurred loss and loss adjustment expenses as a percent of earned premiums.
[3]Other underwriting expenses as a percent of written premiums.
[4]Dividends to policyholders as a percent of earned premiums.

Source: ISO, a Verisk Analytics company.

PROPERTY/CASUALTY INSURANCE COMBINED RATIO, 1975-2014[1]

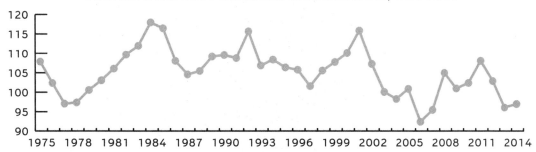

[1]Excludes state funds and other residual insurers.
Source: ISO, a Verisk Analytics company.

Property/Casualty Financial Data

Investments

Cash and invested assets of property/casualty insurance companies totaled $1.53 trillion in 2014. This represents 88 percent of total assets, which were $1.74 trillion. Most of these assets were invested in highly liquid securities (high-quality stocks and bonds, for example, rather than real estate), which can be sold quickly to pay claims in the event of a major catastrophe.

INVESTMENTS, PROPERTY/CASUALTY INSURERS, 2012-2014[1]

($ millions, end of year)

Investment type	Amount			Percent of total investments		
	2012	2013	2014	2012	2013	2014
Bonds	$907,304	$925,895	$941,934	65.21%	62.45%	61.45%
Stocks	268,125	329,486	345,760	19.27	22.22	22.56
Preferred	11,943	11,539	14,630	0.86	0.78	0.95
Common	256,182	317,947	331,131	18.41	21.44	21.60
Mortgage loans on real estate	5,681	7,972	10,008	0.41	0.54	0.65
First liens	5,427	7,765	9,820	0.39	0.52	0.64
Other than first liens	254	207	188	0.02	0.01	0.01
Real estate	10,388	9,966	10,162	0.75	0.67	0.66
Properties occupied by company	8,962	8,475	8,598	0.64	0.57	0.56
Properties held for income production	1,228	1,249	1,286	0.09	0.08	0.08
Properties held for sale	198	243	278	0.01	0.02	0.02
Cash, cash equivalent and short-term investments	82,502	83,552	90,749	5.93	5.64	5.92
Derivatives	592	578	637	0.04	0.04	0.04
Other invested assets	109,321	118,316	126,582	7.86	7.98	8.26
Receivable for securities	956	1,491	1,104	0.07	0.10	0.07
Securities lending reinvested collateral assets	2,640	2,637	2,681	0.19	0.18	0.17
Aggregate write-in for invested assets	3,873	2,776	3,282	0.28	0.19	0.21
Total cash and invested assets	**$1,391,380**	**$1,482,670**	**$1,532,899**	**100.00%**	**100.00%**	**100.00%**

[1]Includes cash and net admitted assets of property/casualty insurers.

Source: SNL Financial LC.

Bonds

Property/casualty insurers invest primarily in safe, liquid securities, mainly bonds. These provide stability against underwriting results, which can vary considerably from year to year. The vast majority of bonds are government-issued or are high-grade corporates. Bonds in or near default accounted for less than 1 percent (0.13 percent) of all short- and long-term bonds owned by insurers at the end of 2014, according to SNL Financial.

INVESTMENTS, PROPERTY/CASUALTY INSURERS, 2014

INVESTMENTS BY TYPE[1]

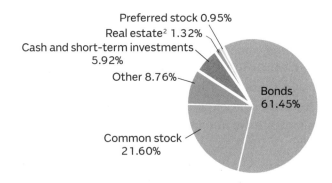

Preferred stock 0.95%
Real estate[2] 1.32%
Cash and short-term investments 5.92%
Other 8.76%
Bonds 61.45%
Common stock 21.60%

BOND PORTFOLIO	**COMMON STOCK PORTFOLIO**
(Represents 61.5% of total investments)	(Represents 21.6% of total investments)

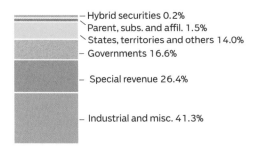

Hybrid securities 0.2%
Parent, subs. and affil. 1.5%
States, territories and others 14.0%
Governments 16.6%
Special revenue 26.4%
Industrial and misc. 41.3%

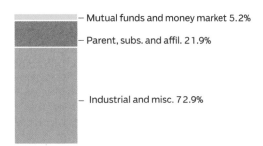

Mutual funds and money market 5.2%
Parent, subs. and affil. 21.9%
Industrial and misc. 72.9%

[1]Cash and invested net admitted assets, as of December 31, 2014.
[2]Includes mortgage loans on real estate.
Source: SNL Financial LC.

Surplus Lines

The surplus lines market exists to assume risks that licensed companies decline to insure or will only insure at a very high price, with many exclusions or with a very high deductible. To be eligible to seek coverage in the surplus lines market, a diligent effort must have been made to place insurance with an admitted company, usually defined by a certain number of *declinations*, or rejections, by licensed insurers, typically three to five. Many states provide an *export list* of risks that can be insured in the surplus lines market. This obviates the diligent search requirement.

The terms applied to the surplus lines market—nonadmitted, unlicensed and unauthorized—do not mean that surplus lines companies are barred from selling insurance in a state or are unregulated. They are just less regulated. Each state has surplus lines regulations, and each surplus lines company is overseen for solvency by its home state. More than half of the states maintain a list of eligible surplus lines companies and some a list of those that are not eligible to do business in that state.

In a number of states, surplus lines companies are also monitored by surplus lines organizations, known as *Stamping Offices*, which assist their state's department of insurance in the regulation and oversight of surplus lines insurers. They also evaluate insurers for eligibility to do business in the state and review insurance policies obtained by surplus lines agents or brokers for their clients. Surplus lines companies thrive in hard markets, when certain kinds of coverages may be more difficult to obtain.

The 2010 Dodd-Frank Wall Street and Consumer Protection Act streamlined the regulation of surplus lines insurance through state-based reforms, including a requirement that multistate transactions be subject to regulatory oversight by a single state—the home state of the insured.

- Surplus lines gross premiums rose 7.2 percent in 2014, after rising 9.7 percent the previous year.

- At $11.41 billion in 2014, nonadmitted direct premiums written for the top ten surplus lines insurers rose 10.1 percent from 2013.

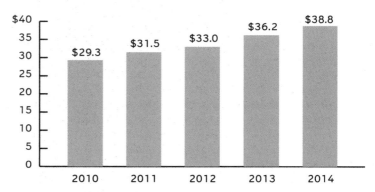

SURPLUS LINES GROSS PREMIUMS WRITTEN, 2010-2014
($ billions)

Source: 2012 to 2014 premiums from Business Insurance August 31, 2015; earlier premiums from other issues.

TOP 10 U.S.-BASED SURPLUS LINES INSURANCE COMPANIES
BY NONADMITTED DIRECT PREMIUMS WRITTEN, 2014

Rank	Company	Parent	Nonadmitted direct premiums
1	Lexington Insurance Co.	American International Group Inc.	$3,814,636,188
2	Scottsdale Insurance Co.	Nationwide Mutual Insurance Co.	1,541,509,541
3	Steadfast Insurance Co	Zurich Insurance Group Ltd.	1,065,950,654
4	Ironshore Specialty Insurance Co.	Ironshore Inc.	901,226,373
5	AIG Specialty Insurance Co.	American International Group Inc.	899,743,943
6	Columbia Casualty Co.	CNA Financial Corp.	746,194,802
7	Indian Harbor Insurance Co.	XL Group P.L.C.	727,864,465
8	Axis Surplus Insurance Co.	Axis Capital Holdings Ltd.	591,636,313
9	Westchester Surplus Lines Insurance Co.	Ace Ltd.	577,206,821
10	Arch Specialty Insurance Co.	Arch Capital Group Ltd.	545,949,763

Source: Business Insurance, August 31, 2015.

Concentration

According to ISO, concentration in the property/casualty insurance sector as measured by the Herfindahl-Hirschman Index increased from 229 in 1980 to 357 in 2008, and then fell, albeit irregularly, to 344 in 2014. The U.S. Department of Justice classifies any market with an HHI under 1,500 as unconcentrated and any market with an HHI over 2,500 as highly concentrated.

MARKET SHARE TRENDS BY SIZE OF INSURER, 1994-2014[1]

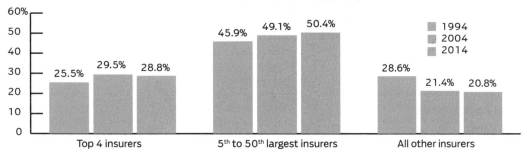

[1]Based on net premiums written. Excludes state funds and other residual market carriers.

Source: ISO, a Verisk Analytics company.

Property/Casualty Financial Data

Reinsurance

Reinsurance is essentially insurance for insurance companies. It is a way for primary insurers to protect against unforeseen or extraordinary losses. Reinsurance also serves to limit liability on specific risks, to increase individual insurers' capacity to write business and to help insurers stabilize their business in the face of the wide swings in profit and loss margins which are inherent in the insurance business.

NET PREMIUMS WRITTEN, U.S. PROPERTY/CASUALTY REINSURERS, 2005-2014
($000)

Year	Net premiums written	Annual percent change	Combined ratio[1]	Annual point change
2005	$26,520,474	-11.8%	126.0	20.5 pts.
2006	26,625,918	0.4	94.2	-31.8
2007	24,548,841	-7.8	93.5	-0.7
2008	26,440,426	7.7	100.4	6.9
2009	25,548,851	-3.4	92.3	-8.1
2010	25,722,426	0.7	94.5	2.2
2011	27,897,553	8.5	107.1	12.6
2012	31,649,616	13.4	96.2	-10.9
2013	29,144,853	-7.9	86.8	-9.4
2014	50,012,241[2]	71.6	91.0	4.2

[1]After dividends to policyholders. [2]Includes National Indemnity Co.'s loss portfolio and quota share agreements with affiliated GEICO companies. Source: Reinsurance Association of America.

TOP 10 U.S. PROPERTY/CASUALTY REINSURERS OF U.S. BUSINESS BY GROSS PREMIUMS WRITTEN, 2014
($000)

Rank	Company[1]	Country of parent company	Gross premiums written
1	National Indemnity Company (Berkshire Hathaway)[2]	U.S.	$26,447,145
2	QBE Re America	Australia	5,288,813
3	Everest Reinsurance Company	Bermuda	4,995,249
4	Swiss Reinsurance America Corporation	Switzerland	4,491,990
5	Munich Re America	Germany	4,162,336
6	XL Reinsurance America	Ireland	3,603,590
7	Transatlantic Reinsurance	U.S.	3,143,029
8	Odyssey Reinsurance Group	Canada	2,551,797
9	Partner Reinsurance Company of the U.S.	Bermuda	1,721,966
10	AXIS Reinsurance Company	Bermuda	1,269,884

[1]See Reinsurance Underwriting Report footnotes posted at www.reinsurance.org for list of affiliated companies included.
[2]Underwriting results exclude assumptions from affiliated General Re Group; includes National Indemnity Co.'s loss portfolio and quota share agreements with affiliated GEICO companies.Source: Reinsurance Association of America.

Direct Premiums Written by State

Direct premiums written represent premium amounts before reinsurance transactions. This contrasts with charts based on net premiums written, i.e., premium amounts after reinsurance transactions.

DIRECT PREMIUMS WRITTEN, P/C INSURANCE BY STATE, 2014[1]
($000)

State	Total, all lines	State	Total, all lines
Alabama	$7,508,361	Montana	$2,155,997
Alaska	1,738,802	Nebraska	4,304,681
Arizona	9,115,864	Nevada	4,283,885
Arkansas	4,621,804	New Hampshire	2,223,994
California	65,688,674	New Jersey	19,672,071
Colorado	9,989,820	New Mexico	2,979,849
Connecticut	8,015,041	New York	41,811,445
Delaware	2,201,194	North Carolina	13,697,735
D.C.	1,687,749	North Dakota	2,510,676
Florida	42,946,719	Ohio	15,048,210
Georgia	16,059,027	Oklahoma	7,706,380
Hawaii	2,300,890	Oregon	5,910,395
Idaho	2,294,633	Pennsylvania	22,289,367
Illinois	23,046,613	Rhode Island	2,120,517
Indiana	10,193,768	South Carolina	7,871,399
Iowa	6,012,397	South Dakota	2,308,430
Kansas	6,060,539	Tennessee	10,138,502
Kentucky	6,681,634	Texas	47,448,589
Louisiana	10,797,349	Utah	3,885,193
Maine	2,028,986	Vermont	1,395,653
Maryland	10,325,057	Virginia	12,224,198
Massachusetts	13,189,338	Washington	10,122,238
Michigan	17,571,288	West Virginia	2,873,244
Minnesota	10,545,874	Wisconsin	9,493,999
Missouri	10,240,479	Wyoming	1,083,314
Missouri	9,842,171	**United States**	**$561,189,111**

[1]Before reinsurance transactions, includes some state funds, excludes territories.

Source: SNL Financial LC.

- In 2014 California accounted for the largest amount of direct premiums written, followed by Texas, Florida, New York and Illinois.

- Among the states with the most premiums, Texas experienced the highest increase in 2014 (6.6 percent), followed by California, with a 6.4 percent increase. Premiums rose 4.1 percent in New York, and 3.7 percent in both Florida and Illinois.

- Nationally, direct premiums written rose 4.4 percent in 2014.

Incurred Losses by State

Property/casualty (P/C) insurers pay out billions of dollars each year to settle claims. Many of the payments go to businesses, such as auto repair companies, that help claimants get their lives back together after an accident, fire, windstorm or other incident that caused the injury or property damage. Insurance claim payments support local businesses, enabling them to provide jobs and pay taxes that support the local economy. When P/C insurance claims are paid, funds flow to the industries that supply claimants with the goods and services necessary for their recovery. The chart below shows incurred losses, i.e., losses occurring during a fixed period, whether or not adjusted or paid during the same period.

INCURRED LOSSES BY STATE, PROPERTY/CASUALTY INSURANCE, 2014[1]
($000)

State	Incurred losses	State	Incurred losses	State	Incurred losses
Alabama	$4,070,408	Louisiana	$5,316,056	Oklahoma	$3,802,954
Alaska	663,414	Maine	1,072,569	Oregon	2,827,460
Arizona	5,378,513	Maryland	5,834,877	Pennsylvania	13,781,591
Arkansas	2,524,482	Massachusetts	6,530,654	Rhode Island	1,116,666
California	35,481,617	Michigan	12,848,751	South Carolina	4,518,529
Colorado	7,161,207	Minnesota	6,206,780	South Dakota	1,355,990
Connecticut	4,253,526	Mississippi	2,714,133	Tennessee	5,230,236
Delaware	1,394,543	Missouri	5,684,459	Texas	24,840,655
D.C.	623,950	Montana	1,521,779	Utah	1,871,508
Florida	19,737,799	Nebraska	3,969,364	Vermont	657,928
Georgia	9,636,088	Nevada	2,338,136	Virginia	6,250,994
Hawaii	926,077	New Hampshire	1,055,290	Washington	5,611,684
Idaho	1,263,675	New Jersey	11,117,524	West Virginia	1,339,350
Illinois	13,306,216	New Mexico	1,607,417	Wisconsin	5,527,664
Indiana	5,524,122	New York	23,061,180	Wyoming	580,718
Iowa	5,115,332	North Carolina	6,771,999		
Kansas	3,325,967	North Dakota	1,373,347		
Kentucky	3,723,405	Ohio	7,372,566	**United States**	**$309,821,148**

[1]Losses occurring within a fixed period whether or not adjusted or paid during the same period, on a direct basis before reinsurance.
Source: SNL Financial LC.

Guaranty Funds

All 50 states, Washington, D.C., Puerto Rico, and the Virgin Islands have procedures under which solvent property/casualty (P/C) insurance companies cover claims against insolvent insurers. New York has a pre-assessment system, under which estimates are made annually of how much will be needed in the coming year to fulfill the system's obligations to pay the claims of insolvent insurers. Some states—including New Jersey, New York and Pennsylvania—have separate pre-assessment funds for workers compensation. Florida has a post-assessment fund, which covers the claims of insolvent workers compensation insurers and self-insurers.

The P/C lines of insurance covered by guaranty funds and the maximum amount paid on any claim vary from state to state. Assessments are used to pay claims against companies that became insolvent in the past as well as for current insolvencies. A similar system for life and health insurers is coordinated by the National Organization of Life and Health Insurance Guaranty Associations.

PROPERTY/CASUALTY GUARANTY FUND NET ASSESSMENTS, 2005-2014

Year	Net assessments[1]
2005	$836,130,812
2006[2]	1,344,487,899
2007	943,164,094
2008	368,451,899
2009	522,881,688
2010	171,159,059
2011	281,991,694
2012[3]	311,694,359
2013	455,103,717
2014	477,572,306
Total, inception-2014[4]	**$16,147,709,494**

[1]Assessments less refunds and abatements (cancellations of uncalled portions of assessments when funds on hand are sufficient to pay claims).
[2]Includes New York and New York Workers Compensation after 2005.
[3]Includes Arizona Workers Compensation after 2011.
[4]Includes pre-1978 net assessments.

Source: National Conference of Insurance Guaranty Funds.

- At $478 million, guaranty fund net assessments in 2014 were up 4.9 percent from $455 million in 2013.

- Net assessments in 2014 were at their highest level since 2009, when they totaled $523 million.

PROPERTY/CASUALTY GUARANTY FUND NET ASSESSMENTS BY STATE, 2014

State	Net assessments[1]	State	Net assessments[1]
Alabama	$6,674,581	Montana	0
Alaska	6,062,671	Nebraska	$4,400,000
Arizona	0	Nevada	0
Arkansas	0	New Hampshire	0
California	186,360,109	New Jersey	152,766,848
Colorado	0	New Mexico	0
Connecticut	16,126,349	New York	0
Delaware	0	North Carolina	7,800,000
D.C.	0	North Dakota	0
Florida	0	Ohio	0
Georgia	0	Oklahoma	13,496,078
Hawaii	36,780,002	Oregon	0
Idaho	0	Pennsylvania	-27,200,000
Illinois	58,161,260	Rhode Island	-679,509
Indiana	1,603,000	South Carolina	6,109,061
Iowa	0	South Dakota	0
Kansas	0	Tennessee	0
Kentucky	-1,488,012	Texas	0
Louisiana	0	Utah	0
Maine	1,541,526	Vermont	0
Maryland	0	Virginia	6,000,000
Massachusetts	0	Washington	558,342
Michigan	0	West Virginia	2,500,000
Minnesota	0	Wisconsin	0
Mississippi	0	Wyoming	0
Missouri	0	**United States**	**$477,572,306**

[1]Assessments less refunds and abatements (cancellations of uncalled portions of assessments when funds on hand are sufficient to pay claims). Negative numbers represent net refunds.

Source: National Conference of Insurance Guaranty Funds.

Premiums by Line

Premiums can be accounted for in two major ways: net premiums written, which reflect premium amounts after deductions for reinsurance, and direct premiums written, which are calculated before reinsurance transactions.

PREMIUMS WRITTEN BY LINE, PROPERTY/CASUALTY INSURANCE, 2014

($ billions)

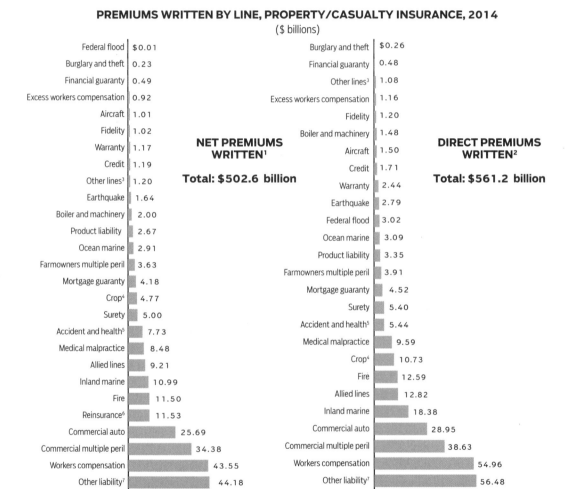

NET PREMIUMS WRITTEN[1]

Total: $502.6 billion

Federal flood	$0.01
Burglary and theft	0.23
Financial guaranty	0.49
Excess workers compensation	0.92
Aircraft	1.01
Fidelity	1.02
Warranty	1.17
Credit	1.19
Other lines[3]	1.20
Earthquake	1.64
Boiler and machinery	2.00
Product liability	2.67
Ocean marine	2.91
Farmowners multiple peril	3.63
Mortgage guaranty	4.18
Crop[4]	4.77
Surety	5.00
Accident and health[5]	7.73
Medical malpractice	8.48
Allied lines	9.21
Inland marine	10.99
Fire	11.50
Reinsurance[6]	11.53
Commercial auto	25.69
Commercial multiple peril	34.38
Workers compensation	43.55
Other liability[7]	44.18
Homeowners multiple peril	77.91
Private passenger auto	183.42

DIRECT PREMIUMS WRITTEN[2]

Total: $561.2 billion

Burglary and theft	$0.26
Financial guaranty	0.48
Other lines[3]	1.08
Excess workers compensation	1.16
Fidelity	1.20
Boiler and machinery	1.48
Aircraft	1.50
Credit	1.71
Warranty	2.44
Earthquake	2.79
Federal flood	3.02
Ocean marine	3.09
Product liability	3.35
Farmowners multiple peril	3.91
Mortgage guaranty	4.52
Surety	5.40
Accident and health[5]	5.44
Medical malpractice	9.59
Crop[4]	10.73
Fire	12.59
Allied lines	12.82
Inland marine	18.38
Commercial auto	28.95
Commercial multiple peril	38.63
Workers compensation	54.96
Other liability[7]	56.48
Homeowners multiple peril	86.29
Private passenger auto	188.91

[1]After reinsurance transactions; excludes state funds. [2]Before reinsurance transactions; includes some state funds. [3]Includes international and miscellaneous coverages. [4]Includes federally sponsored multiple peril crop and private market crop-hail. [5]Premiums from certain insurers that write health insurance but file financial statements with state regulators on a property/casualty rather than life/health basis. [6]Only includes nonproportional reinsurance, an arrangement in which a reinsurer makes payments to an insurer whose losses exceed a predetermined amount. [7]Coverages protecting against legal liability resulting from negligence, carelessness or failure to act.

Source: SNL Financial LC.

Property/Casualty Insurance by Line

Personal vs. Commercial

The property/casualty (P/C) insurance industry is divided into two main segments: personal lines and commercial lines. Personal lines include coverage for individuals, mainly auto and homeowners. Commercial lines include the many kinds of insurance products designed for businesses. In 2014 private passenger auto insurance was the largest line of insurance, based on net premiums written, making up 37 percent of all P/C insurance (commercial and personal combined) and 70 percent of personal insurance. Homeowners multiple peril insurance is the second largest line. Other liability is the largest commercial line and third-largest P/C line. It accounted for 9 percent of all P/C net premiums and 18 percent of all commercial premiums.

NET PREMIUMS WRITTEN, PERSONAL AND COMMERCIAL LINES, 2014

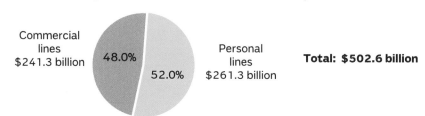

Commercial lines
$241.3 billion
48.0%

Personal lines
$261.3 billion
52.0%

Total: $502.6 billion

Source: SNL Financial LC.

NET PREMIUMS WRITTEN BY LINE, PROPERTY/CASUALTY INSURANCE, 2012-2014[1]
($ millions)

Lines of insurance	2012	2013	2014	Percent change from prior year			Percent of total, 2014
				2012	2013	2014	
Private passenger auto	$168,049.3	$174,899.0	$183,416.0	2.9%	4.1%	4.9%	36.5%
Liability	103,429.7	107,446.4	112,328.9	3.0	3.9	4.5	22.4
Collision and comprehensive	64,619.7	67,452.7	71,087.1	2.7	4.4	5.4	14.1
Commercial auto	22,084.0	23,890.9	25,685.0	5.0	8.2	7.5	5.1
Liability	16,984.6	18,354.8	19,570.6	3.7	8.1	6.6	3.9
Collision and comprehensive	5,099.4	5,536.2	6,114.4	9.7	8.6	10.4	1.2
Fire	10,795.6	11,229.4	11,500.4	4.6	4.0	2.4	2.3
Allied lines	8,161.3	9,251.9	9,209.8	4.6	13.4	-0.5	1.8
Crop[2]	5,321.8	4,942.5	4,772.6	-2.5	-7.1	-3.4	0.9
Federal flood[3]	0.4	5.1	8.5	-98.2	1,110.4	67.3	[4]
Farmowners multiple peril	3,277.4	3,511.7	3,628.1	11.8	7.1	3.3	0.7

(table continues)

NET PREMIUMS WRITTEN BY LINE, PROPERTY/CASUALTY INSURANCE, 2012-2014[1] (Cont'd)

($ millions)

Lines of insurance	2012	2013	2014	Percent change from prior year			Percent of total, 2014
				2012	2013	2014	
Homeowners multiple peril	$67,847.0	$72,773.2	$77,908.8	5.8%	7.3%	7.1%	15.5%
Commercial multiple peril	31,502.7	33,244.7	34,375.1	5.0	5.5	3.4	6.8
Mortgage guaranty	3,965.9	4,329.9	4,180.0	-6.5	9.2	-3.5	0.8
Ocean marine	2,704.7	2,863.5	2,910.4	-2.0	5.9	1.6	0.6
Inland marine	9,603.7	10,147.0	10,990.0	9.5	5.7	8.3	2.2
Financial guaranty	692.5	710.5	488.5	-28.5	2.6	-31.2	0.1
Medical malpractice	8,713.6	8,530.7	8,475.5	-1.4	-2.1	-0.6	1.7
Earthquake	1,593.5	1,587.0	1,641.8	8.6	-0.4	3.5	0.3
Accident and health[5]	7,941.1	7,538.6	7,732.4	3.3	-5.1	2.6	1.5
Workers compensation	38,747.6	40,921.6	43,546.7	8.6	5.6	6.4	8.7
Excess workers compensation	815.8	844.1	920.2	-0.1	3.5	9.0	0.2
Product liability	2,575.2	2,718.9	2,674.2	11.0	5.6	-1.6	0.5
Other liability[6]	38,307.7	42,053.4	44,181.3	4.9	9.8	5.1	8.8
Aircraft	1,160.5	1,067.7	1,005.7	3.4	-8.0	-5.8	0.2
Fidelity	1,096.4	1,124.2	1,165.3	-0.2	2.5	3.7	0.2
Surety	4,695.8	4,868.8	5,000.4	-3.2	3.7	2.7	1.0
Burglary and theft	220.8	205.2	226.2	13.4	-7.1	10.2	4
Boiler and machinery	1,887.6	1,979.5	1,999.0	4.2	4.9	1.0	0.4
Credit	1,457.8	1,167.3	1,191.0	-2.2	-19.9	2.0	0.2
Warranty	1,386.4	1,155.3	1,020.2	-18.2	-16.7	-11.7	0.2
International	105.8	113.2	125.1	14.0	6.9	10.6	4
Reinsurance[7]	14,673.9	12,458.6	11,532.9	11.2	-15.1	-7.4	2.3
Other lines[8]	1,100.2	1,132.4	1,073.0	13.4	2.9	-5.2	0.2
Total, all lines[9]	**$460,486.3**	**$481,266.0**	**$502,584.4**	**4.3%**	**4.5%**	**4.4%**	**100.0%**

[1]After reinsurance transactions, excludes state funds. [2]Includes federally sponsored multiple peril crop and crop-hail provided by the private market. [3]Provided by the Federal Emergency Management Agency through participating private insurers.
[4]Less than 0.1 percent. [5]Premiums from certain insurers that write health insurance but file financial statements with state regulators on a property/casualty basis. [6]Coverages protecting against legal liability resulting from negligence, carelessness or failure to act.
[7]Only includes nonproportional reinsurance, an arrangement in which a reinsurer makes payments to an insurer whose losses exceed a predetermined amount. [8]Includes miscellaneous coverages. [9]May not match total premiums shown elsewhere in this book because of the use of different exhibits from SNL Financial.

Source: SNL Financial LC.

DIRECT PREMIUMS WRITTEN, PROPERTY/CASUALTY INSURANCE BY STATE BY LINE, 2014[1]
($000)

State	Private passenger auto		Commercial auto		Homeowners multiple peril
	Liability	Coll./comp.	Liability	Coll./comp.	
Alabama	$1,436,654	$1,204,084	$305,083	$101,977	$1,618,502
Alaska	274,845	172,420	51,458	18,411	160,018
Arizona	2,263,737	1,515,364	324,794	87,433	1,445,309
Arkansas	870,319	737,811	214,831	93,891	839,419
California	12,492,912	9,284,710	2,262,548	650,389	7,239,213
Colorado	2,007,642	1,323,833	322,555	121,242	1,889,910
Connecticut	1,613,720	984,269	301,383	71,485	1,379,750
Delaware	515,788	217,928	85,769	17,457	230,180
D.C.	154,725	137,609	33,971	7,105	144,502
Florida	10,778,248	3,779,196	1,574,264	305,579	8,716,736
Georgia	3,780,723	2,457,798	663,374	181,424	2,696,701
Hawaii	404,104	261,437	81,941	20,706	357,518
Idaho	437,096	300,259	96,911	44,538	298,686
Illinois	3,530,480	2,774,645	913,208	280,419	3,313,866
Indiana	1,782,991	1,319,937	417,384	172,932	1,776,409
Iowa	740,461	745,785	213,554	135,985	693,101
Kansas	812,450	781,451	168,475	111,692	1,049,641
Kentucky	1,676,841	846,372	278,264	94,927	1,068,606
Louisiana	2,316,772	1,385,826	512,862	104,676	1,805,758
Maine	348,958	284,510	88,638	36,332	381,334
Maryland	2,503,889	1,641,254	392,998	104,152	1,548,800
Massachusetts	2,578,738	1,900,941	553,813	176,078	2,072,114
Michigan	5,077,222	2,697,919	586,435	259,352	2,553,593
Minnesota	1,790,538	1,304,118	332,036	164,083	1,930,257
Mississippi	879,528	706,645	233,262	82,405	926,736
Missouri	1,760,949	1,411,336	383,458	155,519	1,841,778
Montana	332,959	276,981	95,629	53,402	276,527
Nebraska	551,429	483,762	136,041	98,233	591,466
Nevada	1,269,532	568,716	191,321	32,505	505,468
New Hampshire	383,774	350,646	85,954	31,293	373,119
New Jersey	4,833,988	2,123,504	996,112	181,458	2,479,828
New Mexico	742,819	423,997	133,102	44,969	468,730
New York	7,547,168	3,934,340	1,825,315	305,467	5,110,113
North Carolina	2,708,801	2,179,089	519,694	164,346	2,314,547
North Dakota	202,614	239,529	92,613	78,054	187,514
Ohio	3,244,114	2,494,895	622,924	223,547	2,686,484
Oklahoma	1,294,432	1,022,190	294,279	132,780	1,524,715
Oregon	1,607,407	680,903	231,823	66,294	714,520
Pennsylvania	4,360,505	3,215,115	942,909	343,286	3,173,062
Rhode Island	507,094	251,901	75,949	19,535	353,593
South Carolina	1,860,363	1,161,048	265,117	79,116	1,536,483
South Dakota	220,993	237,116	63,609	46,213	203,614
Tennessee	1,885,763	1,482,846	378,117	167,801	1,839,623
Texas	9,087,961	7,226,551	2,104,839	680,766	7,860,674
Utah	922,720	547,045	168,705	62,937	463,877
Vermont	170,833	162,296	45,809	20,348	184,161
Virginia	2,709,520	2,019,469	455,350	131,363	2,073,201
Washington	2,813,566	1,379,962	391,687	113,891	1,521,728
West Virginia	675,861	497,781	121,854	41,365	414,178
Wisconsin	1,499,900	1,155,022	357,961	155,290	1,287,145
Wyoming	171,778	181,768	56,404	33,146	170,125
United States	**$114,436,227**	**$74,473,930**	**$22,046,388**	**$6,907,591**	**$86,292,932**

[1]Includes some state funds.
Source: SNL Financial LC.

DIRECT PREMIUMS WRITTEN, PROPERTY/CASUALTY INSURANCE BY STATE BY LINE, 2014[1]

($000)

Farmowners multiple peril	Commercial multiple peril	Workers compensation	Excess workers compensation	Medical malpractice	Product liability
$73,607	$571,143	$331,235	$22,486	$118,649	$30,752
578	112,520	283,324	4,719	23,403	4,363
15,750	606,051	818,076	12,074	219,733	38,132
27,732	318,399	253,233	7,607	62,262	16,925
205,910	4,494,223	11,418,599	215,993	753,609	428,837
76,273	718,217	956,260	12,860	155,718	66,126
5,493	635,253	868,249	22,621	168,004	52,752
5,295	298,109	187,541	1,232	34,308	6,995
0	162,465	158,453	2,789	30,437	4,895
23,065	2,115,298	2,569,884	58,707	592,577	193,200
116,138	963,658	1,348,560	38,362	253,950	77,226
410	171,676	243,495	4,555	29,360	10,107
56,587	190,233	342,901	1,831	31,227	11,650
165,917	1,682,816	2,753,626	57,626	527,348	145,029
194,441	784,664	847,794	15,587	119,974	73,375
182,514	363,228	748,622	10,462	68,254	42,142
223,083	379,269	492,644	10,903	59,338	37,229
154,189	507,333	513,768	21,004	107,636	27,055
13,270	536,885	868,836	53,502	101,396	48,458
4,252	215,973	207,994	3,081	41,673	7,180
26,243	624,967	931,390	12,035	273,066	48,336
3,007	1,099,653	1,081,253	20,451	307,108	104,521
138,742	1,049,293	1,194,278	34,404	191,888	91,884
137,437	690,799	924,773	1,333	79,039	88,254
21,956	330,106	379,457	12,637	49,762	18,587
163,417	751,307	895,556	32,796	144,441	57,608
65,619	164,541	283,617	5,885	41,458	10,938
199,918	257,987	382,304	5,705	34,629	22,519
7,636	301,692	344,269	17,726	74,044	18,061
2,907	226,109	271,488	3,597	38,281	11,769
2,544	1,434,577	2,385,005	34,877	456,507	198,421
24,727	219,686	291,389	7,255	51,929	9,341
39,591	3,711,941	5,261,029	54,605	1,733,437	250,192
56,495	935,112	1,430,889	29,060	184,651	96,335
109,201	143,396	6,663	0	12,022	17,013
157,722	1,237,066	21,036	75,115	293,799	112,429
149,369	525,855	893,482	31,724	100,774	47,497
62,706	451,558	664,456	12,438	91,246	35,085
100,465	1,699,468	2,644,800	42,855	648,924	138,274
238	151,397	199,677	1,384	38,623	10,880
11,976	467,215	701,687	10,051	64,576	37,071
108,196	127,096	176,184	1,406	17,088	10,074
141,631	681,707	861,022	19,853	233,906	54,920
256,717	2,601,838	2,843,768	37,376	306,108	309,613
12,446	248,455	411,695	4,272	58,208	29,770
14,238	177,611	185,193	1,319	17,373	6,197
73,610	764,637	925,675	24,074	196,403	54,065
68,760	775,983	23,499	31,551	176,092	48,906
13,467	199,140	318,516	8,055	72,175	12,172
165,101	654,978	1,803,581	9,092	78,656	72,839
33,477	96,906	5,489	249	23,563	5,752
$3,914,066	**$38,629,497**	**$54,956,211**	**$1,161,184**	**$9,588,629**	**$3,351,753**

[1]Includes some state funds.
Source: SNL Financial LC.

(table continues)

DIRECT PREMIUMS WRITTEN, PROPERTY/CASUALTY INSURANCE BY STATE BY LINE, 2014[1] (Cont'd)
($000)

State	Other liability	Fire	Allied lines	Inland marine	Ocean marine	Surety
Alabama	$577,909	$222,718	$197,823	$250,230	$37,669	$61,838
Alaska	148,248	59,217	35,071	205,939	40,428	33,888
Arizona	751,236	129,121	122,406	286,837	18,375	91,096
Arkansas	329,244	151,103	120,712	194,092	17,875	38,585
California	6,899,860	1,241,465	785,228	2,364,701	278,657	701,545
Colorado	1,044,735	134,388	155,321	311,303	13,117	101,788
Connecticut	973,757	142,656	124,768	254,596	52,181	66,618
Delaware	280,015	27,990	24,332	64,974	7,547	17,388
D.C.	369,825	36,597	28,522	99,971	2,582	133,443
Florida	3,846,364	1,303,270	3,124,280	1,093,858	320,011	335,491
Georgia	1,397,936	337,220	270,301	516,220	53,555	127,539
Hawaii	286,733	69,786	95,837	86,879	14,296	45,520
Idaho	165,313	29,966	29,521	72,805	4,904	20,246
Illinois	3,366,337	381,240	340,008	704,790	90,765	223,654
Indiana	844,839	313,413	192,422	291,276	25,409	68,361
Iowa	519,436	106,820	123,189	196,343	7,673	45,012
Kansas	425,287	105,100	148,767	168,430	9,495	47,782
Kentucky	425,379	132,077	107,079	231,050	23,115	74,668
Louisiana	876,778	347,851	480,241	405,403	211,190	107,256
Maine	149,005	42,716	39,773	62,076	25,003	15,133
Maryland	987,352	150,002	133,116	305,375	93,278	154,708
Massachusetts	1,676,746	299,564	222,833	414,071	84,699	128,298
Michigan	1,233,828	322,715	181,711	467,794	54,331	77,402
Minnesota	1,030,887	186,063	278,067	297,888	27,986	85,466
Mississippi	304,206	144,452	126,336	159,017	18,145	47,225
Missouri	907,903	218,254	182,258	311,748	34,954	73,361
Montana	151,659	29,105	27,993	67,962	3,122	27,431
Nebraska	319,066	57,637	73,778	145,681	5,201	36,807
Nevada	398,311	84,848	77,640	136,313	6,073	68,712
New Hampshire	186,474	37,419	31,386	74,751	11,154	16,009
New Jersey	2,240,190	387,830	343,522	507,068	133,880	167,357
New Mexico	211,355	39,133	43,336	97,820	1,774	45,378
New York	6,649,898	849,193	593,643	1,400,482	452,773	343,033
North Carolina	1,078,272	278,872	274,915	492,329	43,464	122,751
North Dakota	184,147	32,760	51,918	74,455	1,411	30,064
Ohio	1,541,440	390,869	247,926	527,614	52,915	129,033
Oklahoma	588,044	179,320	190,560	243,896	20,012	64,067
Oregon	461,737	92,218	75,286	207,476	30,680	56,058
Pennsylvania	2,339,132	436,485	299,847	623,104	56,773	220,583
Rhode Island	204,142	49,870	42,327	72,151	35,283	13,069
South Carolina	451,225	207,488	191,727	276,011	26,887	66,953
South Dakota	110,398	25,237	30,694	52,311	1,040	32,175
Tennessee	882,109	260,004	176,571	335,565	57,069	79,097
Texas	4,785,315	1,717,079	1,781,380	1,900,148	332,014	496,402
Utah	354,011	93,784	52,101	130,759	9,045	49,688
Vermont	102,289	23,177	15,861	32,515	12,042	7,908
Virginia	1,150,660	222,847	186,061	398,722	69,207	151,116
Washington	1,032,915	202,204	141,872	408,343	123,631	131,446
West Virginia	198,968	63,526	36,937	71,344	3,453	34,191
Wisconsin	935,780	170,606	141,556	239,970	36,355	60,873
Wyoming	106,212	25,528	21,162	47,759	821	30,381
United States	**$56,482,906**	**$12,592,805**	**$12,819,922**	**$18,382,213**	**$3,093,318**	**$5,403,893**

[1]Includes some state funds.
Source: SNL Financial LC.

DIRECT PREMIUMS WRITTEN, PROPERTY/CASUALTY INSURANCE BY STATE BY LINE, 2014[1]
($000)

Fidelity	Burglary and theft	Boiler and machinery	Financial guaranty	Aircraft	Earthquake	Federal flood
$14,297	$2,656	$26,528	$1,924	$16,803	$7,721	$28,298
2,358	594	10,107	126	33,330	24,676	2,076
12,096	3,137	22,427	577	47,914	9,087	17,973
10,786	1,947	15,429	1,220	21,069	29,855	11,299
120,537	32,005	142,189	45,997	136,814	1,656,283	164,916
22,262	4,044	19,848	3,472	43,157	10,231	14,895
24,639	4,302	18,559	1,481	36,724	8,428	47,559
3,614	2,150	3,958	23,108	14,865	1,259	16,179
14,379	2,484	4,629	158	2,305	2,882	1,290
62,805	16,234	62,134	4,258	97,207	25,280	875,332
31,965	7,872	35,802	724	67,613	16,627	54,543
5,192	567	6,221	4,297	10,053	12,303	33,024
3,003	655	7,560	226	12,956	4,164	3,601
63,988	14,585	68,332	13,475	66,136	67,095	29,738
17,919	3,584	61,805	798	22,065	37,968	17,909
16,164	2,118	21,918	3,312	11,847	5,121	11,231
12,461	2,105	19,494	878	18,217	6,738	7,161
10,543	1,954	22,106	761	6,945	41,818	15,883
12,960	3,800	27,588	2,102	50,690	6,487	264,913
3,832	706	7,878	410	3,466	1,836	8,504
26,493	4,439	21,498	5,487	16,221	11,039	38,056
41,986	6,512	32,892	6,056	12,627	21,873	65,300
33,921	6,564	52,767	32,066	26,931	8,488	16,835
28,288	4,848	34,119	6,363	27,366	6,470	7,382
8,150	1,812	13,748	415	11,519	17,634	33,947
23,999	4,706	26,061	4,728	23,207	91,893	17,855
3,244	603	5,427	0	9,861	4,258	3,282
7,949	1,418	12,489	338	12,020	2,722	8,001
6,995	1,981	11,201	1,030	26,111	19,694	7,201
3,442	870	5,779	322	6,415	2,617	7,856
45,055	8,932	44,717	12,528	19,713	19,339	204,308
4,395	777	6,811	573	6,459	2,381	9,373
142,868	28,724	106,112	255,101	55,356	50,597	172,769
34,820	5,087	34,625	1,628	26,589	13,427	92,985
2,799	354	9,129	0	7,818	821	6,243
41,890	10,289	56,719	1,648	58,010	30,550	27,626
10,924	2,230	20,015	69	17,075	16,437	9,287
10,670	2,374	16,277	208	26,512	69,684	20,323
53,804	11,197	63,534	6,431	32,091	17,316	56,874
4,763	755	5,020	394	13,766	2,681	19,132
10,632	2,290	19,371	682	10,759	37,147	116,712
3,018	382	5,806	7	6,682	858	3,594
18,441	6,283	27,218	142	24,485	75,402	19,459
79,234	22,994	119,318	26,956	174,600	35,820	300,205
6,635	1,580	9,078	523	23,147	41,122	2,195
4,194	438	3,896	1,372	2,383	28,361	4,732
32,433	7,117	29,149	669	41,128	17,921	65,644
18,046	4,376	33,783	840	31,936	162,245	29,606
4,234	639	6,986	169	3,227	1,474	13,426
23,841	4,537	38,932	292	17,969	5,820	10,187
1,571	254	6,344	250	5,363	2,982	1,470
$1,204,536	**$262,865**	**$1,483,332**	**$476,595**	**$1,497,526**	**$2,794,930**	**$3,018,188**

[1] Includes some state funds.
Source: SNL Financial LC.

(table continues)

Property/Casualty Insurance by Line

Premiums

DIRECT PREMIUMS WRITTEN, PROPERTY/CASUALTY INSURANCE BY STATE BY LINE, 2014[1] (Cont'd)
($000)

State	Credit	Warranty	Accident and health	Crop[2]	Mortgage guaranty	Misc.
Alabama	$21,914	$7,845	$64,238	$63,041	$66,367	$24,371
Alaska	4,514	4,375	10,117	91	15,960	1,629
Arizona	21,398	15,701	84,982	19,710	95,933	19,404
Arkansas	14,052	4,177	44,497	134,842	30,421	8,170
California	131,682	154,175	458,320	420,309	427,044	80,002
Colorado	18,634	21,280	77,539	200,414	126,520	16,237
Connecticut	31,365	11,716	45,504	5,100	57,222	4,889
Delaware	15,106	6,535	59,852	11,084	19,357	1,279
D.C.	12,620	205	100,760	0	36,968	1,180
Florida	74,826	379,476	198,455	99,381	217,913	103,387
Georgia	39,731	35,754	149,292	138,020	168,506	31,892
Hawaii	6,338	1,821	13,466	1,066	20,286	1,894
Idaho	3,880	3,790	16,695	74,611	26,463	2,352
Illinois	64,083	169,360	244,603	746,425	206,981	40,039
Indiana	27,427	45,265	224,040	380,684	98,935	14,161
Iowa	11,560	2,336	69,651	862,337	46,950	5,268
Kansas	15,260	129,358	67,052	701,633	43,298	5,851
Kentucky	31,897	12,250	49,241	153,970	40,157	4,746
Louisiana	25,866	8,198	61,446	80,659	57,982	17,699
Maine	6,308	4,131	10,803	10,108	16,164	1,209
Maryland	18,284	18,008	70,993	33,625	119,708	10,246
Massachusetts	39,804	16,596	84,592	3,318	121,256	12,636
Michigan	99,087	526,456	188,860	185,637	148,357	32,528
Minnesota	19,262	39,653	129,186	749,859	129,263	14,290
Mississippi	18,597	4,791	54,648	119,550	26,544	15,430
Missouri	34,167	34,472	160,598	400,130	82,872	9,145
Montana	4,439	1,047	22,297	171,326	13,526	1,859
Nebraska	6,130	4,089	60,477	754,181	27,086	5,619
Nevada	20,483	6,031	27,478	12,519	37,122	3,171
New Hampshire	5,853	5,836	17,910	686	27,046	3,233
New Jersey	68,533	25,841	135,304	6,805	147,284	27,045
New Mexico	5,167	4,197	22,654	27,048	26,051	7,224
New York	154,365	100,275	419,568	45,745	172,301	45,441
North Carolina	50,497	44,958	127,171	189,049	142,818	24,458
North Dakota	1,613	1,013	8,189	998,980	9,359	985
Ohio	57,280	41,771	186,879	274,111	157,518	44,991
Oklahoma	26,024	14,802	51,075	182,671	40,646	12,130
Oregon	29,182	6,877	57,393	39,671	65,896	23,435
Pennsylvania	71,911	75,064	347,995	58,950	172,449	36,165
Rhode Island	3,750	526	24,145	87	16,589	1,794
South Carolina	23,719	7,347	77,214	64,272	75,072	11,187
South Dakota	2,147	4,654	21,781	784,301	10,276	1,480
Tennessee	38,505	43,702	143,250	104,300	84,629	15,081
Texas	194,631	266,053	482,466	921,578	360,662	135,486
Utah	17,839	24,731	57,127	4,611	73,470	3,618
Vermont	7,664	4,673	5,342	3,637	9,282	140,507
Virginia	54,824	22,075	112,426	68,366	149,196	17,268
Washington	28,075	44,860	88,722	133,878	138,167	21,668
West Virginia	6,581	3,345	31,164	2,885	12,802	3,330
Wisconsin	18,699	26,736	149,791	268,681	94,364	9,444
Wyoming	1,705	658	18,565	20,532	12,494	606
United States	**$1,707,280**	**$2,438,883**	**$5,435,817**	**$10,734,473**	**$4,523,530**	**$1,077,157**

[1]Includes some state funds. [2]Includes federally sponsored multiple peril crop and crop-hail provided by the private market.
Source: SNL Financial LC.

TOTAL AUTO PREMIUMS BY SECTOR, 2014
($ billions, net premiums written)

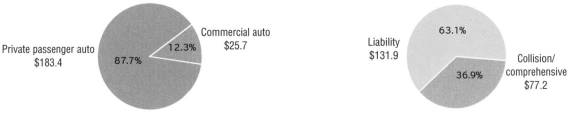

Commercial auto $25.7 — 12.3%
Private passenger auto $183.4 — 87.7%

Liability $131.9 — 63.1%
Collision/comprehensive $77.2 — 36.9%

AUTO SHARE OF P/C INDUSTRY, 2014
($ billions, net premiums written)

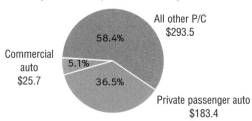

All other P/C $293.5 — 58.4%
Commercial auto $25.7 — 5.1%
Private passenger auto $183.4 — 36.5%

Source: SNL Financial LC.

PRIVATE PASSENGER AUTOMOBILE INSURANCE, 2005-2014
($000)

Year	Liability				Collision/comprehensive			
	Net premiums written[1]	Annual percent change	Combined ratio[2]	Annual point change[3]	Net premiums written[1]	Annual percent change	Combined ratio[2]	Annual point change[3]
2005	$94,384,329	1.6%	98.4	-0.4 pts.	$64,882,303	0.3%	90.7	3.7 pts.
2006	95,325,685	1.0	98.6	0.2	65,125,977	0.4	91.4	0.7
2007	94,974,640	-0.4	101.8	3.1	64,700,792	-0.7	93.4	2.0
2008	94,545,647	-0.5	103.5	1.7	64,054,581	-1.0	95.8	2.4
2009	94,990,682	0.5	106.2	2.7	62,630,693	-2.2	93.0	-2.8
2010	97,672,826	2.8	105.9	-0.3	62,595,851	-0.1	93.4	0.4
2011	100,369,441	2.8	103.8	-2.1	62,948,280	0.6	99.6	6.3
2012	103,429,677	3.0	103.2	-0.6	64,619,667	2.7	100.2	0.6
2013	107,446,382	3.9	103.6	0.4	67,452,663	4.4	98.7	-1.5
2014	112,328,916	4.5	103.8	0.2	71,087,058	5.4	100.2	1.5

[1]After reinsurance transactions, excludes state funds.
[2]After dividends to policyholders. A drop in the combined ratio represents an improvement; an increase represents a deterioration.
[3]Calculated from unrounded data.

Source: SNL Financial LC.

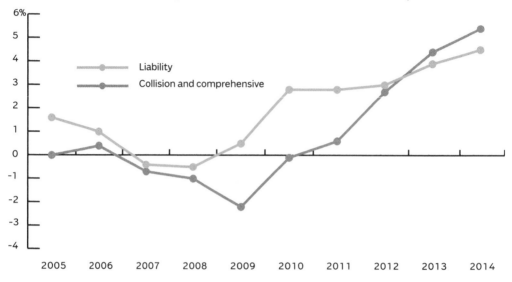

**PERCENT CHANGE FROM PRIOR YEAR,
NET PREMIUMS WRITTEN, PRIVATE PASSENGER AUTO INSURANCE, 2005-2014**

Liability

Collision and comprehensive

Source: SNL Financial LC.

TOP 10 WRITERS OF PRIVATE PASSENGER AUTO INSURANCE
BY DIRECT PREMIUMS WRITTEN, 2014
($000)

Rank	Group/company	Direct premiums written[1]	Market share[2]
1	State Farm Mutual Automobile Insurance	$35,588,209	18.7%
2	Berkshire Hathaway Inc.	20,520,188	10.8
3	Allstate Corp.	19,000,663	10.0
4	Progressive Corp.	16,566,932	8.7
5	USAA Insurance Group	9,843,321	5.2
6	Farmers Insurance Group of Companies[3]	9,701,153	5.1
7	Liberty Mutual	9,499,538	5.0
8	Nationwide Mutual Group	7,337,880	3.9
9	American Family Mutual	3,530,595	1.9
10	Travelers Companies Inc.	3,153,507	1.7

[1]Before reinsurance transactions, includes state funds.
[2]Based on U.S. total, includes territories.
[3]Data for Farmers Insurance Group of Companies and Zurich Financial Group (which owns Farmers' management company) are reported separately by SNL Financial.

Source: SNL Financial LC.

COMMERCIAL AUTOMOBILE INSURANCE, 2005-2014
($000)

Year	Liability				Collision/comprehensive			
	Net premiums written[1]	Annual percent change	Combined ratio[2]	Annual point change[3]	Net premiums written[1]	Annual percent change	Combined ratio[2]	Annual point change[3]
2005	$19,766,618	1.0%	92.0	-4.9 pts.	$6,929,335	-3.1%	88.1	5.1 pts.
2006	19,704,282	-0.3	95.7	3.7	6,949,388	0.3	88.4	0.3
2007	18,803,425	-4.6	95.4	-0.3	6,630,652	-4.6	91.0	2.5
2008	17,833,085	-5.2	97.4	2.0	5,989,108	-9.7	94.7	3.7
2009	16,581,981	-7.0	100.6	3.1	5,347,981	-10.7	96.9	2.3
2010	16,249,433	-2.0	97.1	-3.5	4,870,380	-8.9	101.6	4.7
2011	16,382,082	0.8	101.1	4.0	4,647,376	-4.6	112.0	10.4
2012	16,984,612	3.7	106.6	5.5	5,099,427	9.7	109.2	-2.9
2013	18,354,752	8.1	107.2	0.7	5,536,173	8.6	105.2	-3.9
2014	19,570,622	6.6	103.7	-3.5	6,114,388	10.4	103.0	-2.2

[1]Ater reinsurance transactions, excludes state funds.
[2]After dividends to policyholders. A drop in the combined ratio represents an improvement; an increase represents a deterioration.
[3]Calculated from unrounded numbers.

Source: SNL Financial LC.

TOP 10 WRITERS OF COMMERCIAL AUTO INSURANCE BY DIRECT PREMIUMS WRITTEN, 2014
($000)

Rank	Group/company	Direct premiums written[1]	Market share[2]
1	Travelers Companies Inc.	$1,969,790	6.7%
2	Progressive Corp.	1,910,682	6.5
3	Nationwide Mutual Group	1,665,217	5.7
4	Liberty Mutual	1,526,578	5.2
5	Zurich Insurance Group[3]	1,313,106	4.5
6	American International Group (AIG)	1,118,789	3.8
7	Old Republic International Corp.	977,453	3.3
8	Berkshire Hathaway Inc.	863,112	3.0
9	Auto-Owners Insurance Co.	610,600	2.1
10	Tokio Marine Group	572,975	2.0

[1]Before reinsurance transactions, includes state funds.
[2]Based on U.S. total, includes territories.
[3]Data for Farmers Insurance Group of Companies and Zurich Financial Group (which owns Farmers' management company) are reported separately by SNL Financial.

Source: SNL Financial LC.

Property/Casualty Insurance by Line

Auto: Costs/Expenditures

AAA's 2015 Your Driving Costs study found that the average cost to own and operate an average sedan was $8,698 in 2014, down 2 percent from $8,876 in 2013. The decline reflects reduced gasoline and finance costs offsetting increases in other areas. Average insurance costs for sedans rose 9 percent, or $92, to $1,115 in 2014 from $1,023 in 2013. AAA insurance cost estimates are based on a full coverage policy for a 47-year-old male with a clean driving record for a policy with $100,000/$300,000 bodily injury liability coverage with a $500 deductible for collision and a $100 deductible for comprehensive coverage. Figures are not comparable with the National Association of Insurance Commissioners' Auto Expenditures data below.

- Average expenditures for auto insurance are projected to have risen 2.6 percent in 2013 to $836 and 2.9 percent in 2014 to $860, according to the Insurance Information Institute (I.I.I.).

- 77 percent of insured drivers purchase comprehensive coverage in addition to liability insurance, and 72 percent buy collision coverage, based on an I.I.I. analysis of 2012 NAIC data.

AVERAGE EXPENDITURES FOR AUTO INSURANCE, UNITED STATES, 2003-2012

Year	Average expenditure	Percent change
2003	$830	5.6%
2004	843	1.6
2005	832	-1.3
2006	818	-1.7
2007	799	-2.3
2008	791	-1.0
2009	787	-0.5
2010	792	0.6
2011	798	0.8
2012	815	2.1

Source: © 2014 National Association of Insurance Commissioners (NAIC).

Auto Insurance Expenditures, by State

The tables on the following pages show estimated average expenditures for private passenger automobile insurance by state from 2008 to 2012, providing approximate measures of the relative cost of automobile insurance to consumers in each state. To calculate average expenditures the National Association of Insurance Commissioners (NAIC) assumes that all insured vehicles carry liability coverage but not necessarily collision or comprehensive coverage. The average expenditure measures what consumers actually spend for insurance on each vehicle. It does not equal the sum of liability, collision and comprehensive expenditures because not all policyholders purchase all three coverages.

Expenditures are affected by the coverages purchased and other factors. In states with a healthy economy, people are more likely to purchase new cars. Since new car owners are more likely to purchase physical damage coverages, these states will have a higher average expenditure.

The NAIC notes that urban population, traffic density and per capita income have a significant impact on premiums. The latest report shows that high premium states tend also to be highly urban, with higher wage and price levels and greater traffic density. Tort liability and other auto laws, auto repair costs, liability coverage requirements, theft rates and other factors can also affect auto insurance prices.

TOP 10 MOST EXPENSIVE AND LEAST EXPENSIVE STATES FOR AUTOMOBILE INSURANCE, 2012[1]

Rank	Most expensive states	Average expenditure	Rank	Least expensive states	Average expenditure
1	New Jersey	$1,219.93	1	Idaho	$534.56
2	D.C.	1,154.91	2	South Dakota	556.51
3	New York	1,152.45	3	Iowa	561.26
4	Florida	1,127.93	4	North Dakota	576.08
5	Louisiana	1,112.53	5	Maine	582.43
6	Delaware	1,065.37	6	Wisconsin	598.84
7	Michigan	1,048.87	7	North Carolina	611.48
8	Rhode Island	1,034.50	8	Nebraska	616.78
9	Connecticut	986.73	9	Wyoming	618.81
10	Massachusetts	976.65	10	Kansas	632.07

[1]Based on average automobile insurance expenditures. Source: © 2014 National Association of Insurance Commissioners (NAIC).

TOP 10 MOST EXPENSIVE AND LEAST EXPENSIVE CITIES FOR AUTOMOBILE INSURANCE, 2014[1]

Rank	Most expensive cities	Average car insurance prices	Rank	Least expensive cities	Average car insurance prices
1	Detroit, MI	$10,723	1	Winston-Salem, NC	$969
2	New Orleans, LA	4,310	2	Greensboro, NC	1,090
3	Grand Rapids, MI	4,042	3	Raleigh, NC	1,098
4	Newark, NJ	3,525	4	Durham, NC	1,101
5	Baton Rouge, LA	3,364	5	Charlotte, NC	1,123
6	Hialeah, FL	3,272	6	Boise, ID	1,222
7	Jersey City, NJ	3,267	7	Rochester, NY	1,249
8	Louisville, KY	3,256	8	Fayetteville, NC	1,295
9	Miami, FL	3,169	9	Spokane, WA	1,308
10	Philadelphia, PA	2,931	10	Montgomery, AL	1,376

[1]Based on a 26-year-old male without any history of accidents, insuring a 2012 Toyota Camry. Assumes $100,000/$300,000/$50,000 liability limits with a $500 deductible. To calculate city averages, NerdWallet used only ZIP codes within city limits and not in the city's metro area. Source: NerdWallet.

AVERAGE EXPENDITURES FOR AUTO INSURANCE BY STATE, 2008-2012

| State | 2012 | | | | |
	Liability	Collision	Comprehensive	Average expenditure	Rank[1]
Alabama	$359.88	$287.59	$140.60	$659.06	37
Alaska	544.66	365.92	142.96	873.15	13
Arizona	473.30	245.64	180.97	781.71	18
Arkansas	371.02	295.68	175.90	679.46	35
California[3]	442.17	348.63	98.13	749.79	22
Colorado	449.65	252.40	147.69	737.95	25
Connecticut	626.47	334.23	121.35	986.73	9
Delaware	759.04	286.06	108.49	1,065.37	6
D.C.	624.34	437.18	227.97	1,154.91	2
Florida	855.87	234.51	105.65	1,127.93	4
Georgia	454.76	316.13	151.16	768.34	20
Hawaii	453.47	289.26	101.41	735.19	27
Idaho	326.00	205.64	107.55	534.56	51
Illinois	422.27	273.16	110.56	731.22	28
Indiana	376.18	233.60	113.30	637.37	40
Iowa	290.46	201.45	164.52	561.26	49
Kansas	329.67	244.10	211.94	632.07	42
Kentucky	516.40	247.95	124.11	759.70	21
Louisiana	698.21	372.20	204.69	1,112.53	5
Maine	331.91	241.06	90.66	582.43	47
Maryland	594.28	319.30	143.13	966.29	11
Massachusetts	578.75	343.43	125.88	976.65	10
Michigan	660.93	368.51	142.50	1,048.87	7
Minnesota	428.63	205.12	166.49	718.61	29
Mississippi	424.58	291.79	186.58	748.44	23
Missouri	390.04	253.12	155.98	683.82	34
Montana	383.76	247.30	190.62	658.42	38
Nebraska	340.33	218.30	192.56	616.78	44
Nevada	619.84	289.97	114.48	906.00	12
New Hampshire	390.55	265.72	96.21	716.84	30
New Jersey	860.54	356.36	117.64	1,219.93	1
New Mexico	441.11	262.06	163.02	695.09	32
New York	779.96	345.99	147.33	1,152.45	3
North Carolina	356.81	248.84	115.08	611.48	45
North Dakota	272.71	216.62	225.42	576.08	48
Ohio	326.96	243.00	107.30	634.89	41
Oklahoma	426.30	289.80	185.01	737.02	26
Oregon	527.64	203.52	86.92	741.51	24
Pennsylvania	495.05	296.19	124.06	827.61	16
Rhode Island	702.48	357.12	116.41	1,034.50	8
South Carolina	485.27	239.32	156.18	772.09	19
South Dakota	281.04	195.84	214.07	556.51	50
Tennessee	387.40	280.82	126.31	673.90	36
Texas	485.05	345.29	189.72	858.54	14
Utah	454.35	247.80	103.18	713.20	31
Vermont	339.97	269.36	111.99	642.39	39
Virginia	401.50	254.02	125.87	691.80	33
Washington	547.11	241.32	102.61	809.56	17
West Virginia	503.05	313.43	189.20	846.74	15
Wisconsin	346.74	200.37	119.69	598.84	46
Wyoming	298.94	285.60	234.27	618.81	43
United States	**$503.88**	**$289.66**	**$134.04**	**$814.99**	

[1]Ranked highest to lowest by average expenditure. [2]Less than 0.1 Percent. [3]Preliminary. Note: Average expenditure=Total written premium/liability car years. A car year is equal to 365 days of insured coverage for a single vehicle. The NAIC does not rank state

AVERAGE EXPENDITURES FOR AUTO INSURANCE BY STATE, 2008-2012

2011 Average expenditure	Rank[1]	Average expenditure percent change, 2011-2012	Average expenditure 2010	Average expenditure 2009	Average expenditure 2008	State
$653.37	37	0.9%	$651.22	$652.07	$662.76	Alabama
873.11	13	[2]	890.35	896.74	904.12	Alaska
776.56	18	0.7	804.97	842.21	863.81	Arizona
665.49	35	2.1	662.44	657.13	651.26	Arkansas
740.11	24	1.3	746.77	756.63	780.20	California[3]
723.61	27	2.0	730.42	741.28	728.67	Colorado
969.41	9	1.8	965.22	952.36	950.16	Connecticut
1,048.03	6	1.7	1,030.98	1,021.42	1,007.32	Delaware
1,139.43	2	1.4	1,133.87	1,127.72	1,126.56	D.C.
1,090.58	5	3.4	1,037.36	1,006.20	1,054.89	Florida
754.06	19	1.9	748.89	754.61	760.58	Georgia
748.46	20	-1.8	765.83	786.33	816.21	Hawaii
535.11	51	-0.1	548.03	554.80	562.76	Idaho
727.33	25	0.5	733.45	727.82	713.97	Illinois
621.38	41	2.6	624.27	620.31	611.21	Indiana
551.72	48	1.7	546.59	530.96	518.48	Iowa
625.91	40	1.0	625.17	622.16	622.14	Kansas
744.53	22	2.0	722.70	698.85	698.93	Kentucky
1,110.63	3	0.2	1,121.44	1,100.09	1,104.62	Louisiana
577.38	47	0.9	582.29	597.87	600.46	Maine
956.14	10	1.1	947.74	928.92	922.01	Maryland
942.12	11	3.7	890.83	860.49	903.27	Massachusetts
983.82	8	6.6	954.75	913.28	905.82	Michigan
696.00	31	3.2	693.08	692.08	697.09	Minnesota
740.14	23	1.1	745.17	737.77	749.38	Mississippi
674.60	34	1.4	678.03	668.29	656.33	Missouri
654.56	36	0.6	657.42	655.61	666.69	Montana
602.39	44	2.4	592.56	575.26	561.46	Nebraska
904.91	12	0.1	930.43	944.16	970.31	Nevada
705.88	30	1.6	706.24	717.56	727.15	New Hampshire
1,184.99	1	2.9	1,157.30	1,100.66	1,081.28	New Jersey
691.74	32	0.5	703.64	717.96	730.27	New Mexico
1,109.94	4	3.8	1,078.88	1,057.82	1,044.04	New York
600.04	46	1.9	599.90	609.80	595.48	North Carolina
549.73	49	4.8	528.81	509.72	503.18	North Dakota
619.73	43	2.4	619.45	616.33	616.51	Ohio
716.21	28	2.9	703.03	677.71	662.64	Oklahoma
723.72	26	2.5	724.47	722.85	726.64	Oregon
812.77	16	1.8	812.15	811.15	816.65	Pennsylvania
1,004.13	7	3.0	984.95	969.02	985.89	Rhode Island
748.26	21	3.2	737.77	737.74	749.30	South Carolina
538.49	50	3.3	525.16	512.47	512.12	South Dakota
649.98	38	3.7	641.17	634.24	639.00	Tennessee
842.58	14	1.9	848.11	860.42	853.55	Texas
712.74	29	0.1	716.97	717.28	708.70	Utah
633.51	39	1.4	630.11	645.79	653.47	Vermont
679.60	33	1.8	673.72	667.51	662.72	Virginia
806.02	17	0.4	815.29	826.59	839.23	Washington
834.04	15	1.5	830.10	815.00	807.49	West Virginia
600.23	45	-0.2	613.41	590.54	581.42	Wisconsin
619.88	42	-0.2	621.15	624.10	632.92	Wyoming
$797.61		**2.2%**	**$791.93**	**$786.71**	**$790.66**	**United States**

average expenditures and does not endorse any conclusion drawn from these data.

Source: © 2014 National Association of Insurance Commissioners (NAIC).

Auto Insurance Claims and Expenses

The combined ratio after dividends is a measure of underwriting profitability. It reflects the percentage of each premium dollar an insurer spends on claims (the claims ratio) and percentage of each premium dollar that goes toward expenses (the expense ratio). The combined ratio does not take investment income into account. The private passenger auto combined ratio after dividends was 102.4 in 2014, reflecting a claims ratio of 77.4 percent and an expense ratio of 24.5 percent. A combined ratio above 100 indicates an underwriting loss.

PRIVATE PASSENGER AUTO INSURANCE INDUSTRY UNDERWRITING EXPENSES, 2014[1]

Expense	Percent of premiums
LOSSES AND RELATED EXPENSES[2]	
Loss and loss adjustment expense (LAE) ratio	**77.4%**
Incurred losses	65.0
Defense and cost containment expenses incurred	2.8
Adjusting and other expenses incurred	9.6
OPERATING EXPENSES[3]	
Expense ratio	**24.5%**
Net commissions and brokerage expenses incurred	8.9
Taxes, licenses and fees	2.2
Other acquisition and field supervision expenses incurred	8.1
General expenses incurred	5.3
DIVIDENDS TO POLICYHOLDERS[2]	**0.5%**
COMBINED RATIO AFTER DIVIDENDS[4]	**102.4%**

[1]After reinsurance transactions.

[2]As a percent of net premiums earned ($180.6 billion in 2014).

[3]As a percent of net premiums written ($183.4 billion in 2014).

[4]Sum of loss and LAE, expense and dividends ratios.

Source: SNL Financial LC.

Liability insurance pays for the policyholder's legal responsibility to others for bodily injury or property damage. Collision and comprehensive insurance cover property damage and theft to the policyholder's car.

PRIVATE PASSENGER AUTO INSURANCE LOSSES, 2005-2014[1]

	Liability			
	Bodily injury[2]		Property damage[3]	
Year	Claim frequency[4]	Claim severity[5,6]	Claim frequency[4]	Claim severity[5,6]
2005	1.04	$12,282	3.55	$2,717
2006	0.98	12,907	3.40	2,796
2007	0.90	13,361	3.46	2,847
2008	0.91	14,067	3.42	2,903
2009	0.89	13,891	3.49	2,869
2010	0.91	14,406	3.53	2,881
2011	0.92	14,848	3.56	2,958
2012	0.95	14,690	3.50	3,073
2013	0.95	15,441	3.55	3,231
2014	0.87	16,640	3.65	3,290

	Physical damage[7]			
	Collision		Comprehensive[8]	
Year	Claim frequency[4]	Claim severity[5]	Claim frequency[4]	Claim severity[5]
2005	5.04	$3,067	2.38	$1,457
2006	4.87	3,194	2.40	1,528
2007	5.20	3,109	2.48	1,524
2008	5.35	3,005	2.57	1,551
2009	5.48	2,869	2.75	1,389
2010	5.69	2,778	2.62	1,476
2011	5.75	2,861	2.79	1,490
2012	5.57	2,950	2.62	1,585
2013	5.71	3,144	2.57	1,621
2014	5.95	3,160	2.80	1,567

[1]For all limits combined. Data are for paid claims.
[2]Excludes Massachusetts and most states with no-fault automobile insurance laws.
[3]Excludes Massachusetts, Michigan and New Jersey.
[4]Claim frequency is claims per 100 earned car years. A car year is equal to 365 days of insured coverage for one vehicle.
[5]Claim severity is the size of the loss.
[6]Includes loss adjustment expenses.
[7]Excludes Massachusetts, Michigan and Puerto Rico. Based on coverage with a $500 deductible.
[8]Excludes wind and water losses.

Source: ISO, a Verisk Analytics company.

- In 2014 less than 1 percent of people with liability insurance had a bodily injury liability claim, while 3.7 percent of those with liability insurance had a property damage liability claim, according to ISO.

- In 2014, 6.0 percent of collision insurance policyholders had a claim, while 2.8 percent of people with comprehensive coverage had a claim.

- In 2014 the average auto liability claim for property damage was $3,290; the average auto liability claim for bodily injury was $16,640.

- In 2014 the average collision claim was $3,160; the average comprehensive claim was $1,567.

Auto: Claims/High-Risk Markets

INCURRED LOSSES FOR AUTO INSURANCE, 2010-2014[1]
($000)

	2010	2011	2012	2013	2014
Private passenger auto					
Liability	$64,110,267	$64,310,776	$65,135,976	$67,879,783	$72,027,357
Physical damage	36,454,102	40,589,159	41,275,620	41,754,861	45,313,540
Commercial auto					
Liability	8,798,119	9,363,647	10,515,806	11,305,679	11,933,884
Physical damage	2,911,013	3,164,880	3,250,740	3,255,581	3,627,601
Total	**$112,273,501**	**$117,428,462**	**$120,178,142**	**$124,195,904**	**$132,902,382**

[1]Losses occurring within a fixed period, whether or not adjusted or paid during the same period, after reinsurance transactions.
Source: SNL Financial LC.

Auto: High-Risk Markets

The Shared/Residual Market

All states and the District of Columbia use special systems to guarantee that auto insurance is available to those who cannot obtain it in the private market. These systems are commonly known as assigned risk plans, although that term technically applies to only one type of plan. The assigned risk and other plans are known in the insurance industry as the shared, or residual, market. Policyholders in assigned risk plans are assigned to various insurance companies doing business in the state. In the voluntary, or regular market, auto insurers are free to select policyholders.

The percentage of vehicles insured in the shared market is dropping, in part because of the evolution of the nonstandard sector of the voluntary market. The nonstandard market is a niche market for drivers who have a worse than average driving record or drive specialized cars such as high-powered sports cars or custom-built cars. It is made up of both small specialty companies, whose only business is the nonstandard market, and well-known auto insurance companies with nonstandard divisions.

Insured Vehicles

In 2013, 195 million private passenger vehicles were insured in the United States, up from 192 million in 2012, according to AIPSO. The figures include cars insured by private auto insurers in the voluntary market as well as those insured in the so-called shared or residual markets set up by states to cover hard-to-insure risks. In 2013 California had the most insured private passenger cars (25.6 million), followed by Florida (11.8 million) and New York (9.3 million), including vehicles in the voluntary and residual markets.

PRIVATE PASSENGER CARS INSURED IN THE SHARED AND VOLUNTARY MARKETS, 2013

State	Voluntary market	Shared market	Total	Shared market as a percent of total
Alabama	3,707,397	3	3,707,400	1
Alaska	488,441	8	488,449	0.002%
Arizona	4,349,856	0	4,349,856	1
Arkansas	2,123,674	2	2,123,676	1
California	25,608,562	437	25,608,999	0.002
Colorado	3,910,852	0	3,910,852	1
Connecticut	2,488,334	166	2,488,500	0.007
Delaware	637,051	0	637,051	1
D.C.	239,003	108	239,111	0.045
Florida	11,814,855	1,580	11,816,435	0.013
Georgia	7,169,005	0	7,169,005	1
Hawaii	851,080	3,436	854,516	0.402
Idaho	1,279,285	1	1,279,286	1
Illinois	8,097,584	456	8,098,040	0.006
Indiana	4,742,354	8	4,742,362	1
Iowa	2,466,459	11	2,466,470	1
Kansas	2,286,626	1,756	2,288,382	0.077
Kentucky	3,166,468	292	3,166,760	0.009
Louisiana	3,016,602	2	3,016,604	1
Maine	1,029,950	9	1,029,959	0.001
Maryland	3,965,105	40,500	4,005,605	1.011
Massachusetts	4,241,492	85,074	4,326,566	1.966
Michigan	6,349,461	5,896	6,355,357	0.093
Minnesota	3,913,423	4	3,913,427	1
Mississippi	1,915,778	11	1,915,789	0.001
Missouri	4,295,237	4	4,295,241	1
Montana	843,192	19	843,211	0.002
Nebraska	1,532,765	2	1,532,767	1
Nevada	1,855,120	0	1,855,120	1
New Hampshire	924,285	207	924,492	0.022
New Jersey	5,391,537	29,318	5,420,855	0.541

(table continues)

- From 2009 to 2013 about 1 percent of vehicles were insured in the shared market annually, compared with 3.6 percent in 1995 and 1.4 percent in 2000 (excluding Texas).

- In 2013 the number of vehicles in the shared market nationwide rose by about 92,000 vehicles, or 4.9 percent, compared with the previous year.

- In 2013 North Carolina had the highest percentage of cars in the shared market, 23.5 percent, followed by Massachusetts, 2.0 percent, and Rhode Island, 1.9 percent.

- In 2013 the number of cars in shared market plans rose 8.8 percent in North Carolina and 27.2 percent in Rhode Island. The number fell 17.5 percent in Massachusetts.

PRIVATE PASSENGER CARS INSURED IN THE SHARED AND VOLUNTARY MARKETS, 2013 (Cont'd)

State	Voluntary market	Shared market	Total	Shared market as a percent of total
New Mexico	1,533,578	3	1,533,581	[1]
New York	9,342,253	47,326	9,389,579	0.504%
North Carolina	5,621,890	1,727,112	7,349,002	23.501
North Dakota	659,146	4	659,150	0.001
Ohio	8,204,330	0	8,204,330	[1]
Oklahoma	2,782,165	15	2,782,180	0.001
Oregon	2,739,065	0	2,739,065	[1]
Pennsylvania	8,713,520	6,952	8,720,472	0.080
Rhode Island	667,321	12,663	679,984	1.862
South Carolina	3,553,729	1	3,553,730	[1]
South Dakota	732,450	0	732,450	[1]
Tennessee	4,432,482	9	4,432,491	[1]
Texas[2]	NA	NA	NA	NA
Utah	1,904,888	6	1,904,894	[1]
Vermont	490,665	42	490,707	0.009
Virginia	6,265,373	453	6,265,826	0.007
Washington	4,742,977	0	4,742,977	[1]
West Virginia	1,332,456	10	1,332,466	0.001
Wisconsin	4,077,674	1	4,077,675	[1]
Wyoming	536,326	0	536,326	[1]
United States	**193,033,121**	**1,963,907**	**194,997,028**	**1.007%**

[1] Less than 0.001 percent.
[2] Texas information is longer available.

NA=Data not available.

Source: AIPSO.

Uninsured Motorists

Uninsured and underinsured motorist coverage reimburses policyholders in an accident involving an uninsured, underinsured or hit-and-run driver. Twenty states and the District of Columbia have mandatory requirements for uninsured or underinsured motorist coverage. More than half of the states have passed laws and begun to develop and implement online auto insurance verification systems to identify uninsured motorists.

In 2012, 12.6 percent of motorists, or about one in eight drivers, was uninsured, according to a 2014 study by the Insurance Research Council (IRC). The percentage has been declining in recent years. Oklahoma had the highest percentage of uninsured motorists, 26 percent, and Massachusetts had the lowest, 4 percent. IRC measures the number of uninsured motorists based on insurance claims, using a ratio of insurance claims made by people who were injured by uninsured drivers relative to the claims made by people who were injured by insured drivers.

ESTIMATED PERCENTAGE OF UNINSURED MOTORISTS, 1992-2012[1]

Year	Percent	Year	Percent	Year	Percent
1992	15.6%	1999	12.8%	2006	14.3%
1993	16.0	2000	13.4	2007	13.8
1994	15.1	2001	14.2	2008	14.3
1995	14.2	2002	14.5	2009	13.8
1996	13.8	2003	14.9	2010	12.3
1997	13.2	2004	14.6	2011	12.2
1998	13.0	2005	14.6	2012	12.6

[1]Percentage of uninsured drivers, as measured by the ratio of uninsured motorists (UM) claims to bodily injury (BI) claim frequencies.

Source: Insurance Research Council.

TOP 10 HIGHEST AND LOWEST STATES BASED ON ESTIMATED PERCENTAGE OF UNINSURED MOTORISTS, 2012[1]

Rank	Highest	Percent uninsured	Rank	Lowest	Percent uninsured
1	Oklahoma	25.9%	1	Massachusetts	3.9%
2	Florida	23.8	2	Maine	4.7
3	Mississippi	22.9	3	New York	5.3
4	New Mexico	21.6	4	Utah	5.8
5	Michigan	21.0	5	North Dakota	5.9
6	Tennessee	20.1	6	Pennsylvania	6.5
7	Alabama	19.6	7	Nebraska	6.7
8	Rhode Island	17.0	8	Idaho	6.7
9	Colorado	16.2	9	South Carolina	7.7
10	Washington	16.1	10	South Dakota	7.8

[1]Percentage of uninsured drivers, as measured by the ratio of uninsured motorists (UM) claims to bodily injury (BI) claim frequencies.

Source: Insurance Research Council.

ESTIMATED PERCENTAGE OF UNINSURED MOTORISTS BY STATE, 2012[1]

State	Uninsured	Rank[2]	State	Uninsured	Rank[2]	State	Uninsured	Rank[2]
Alabama	19.6%	7	Kentucky	15.8%	12	North Dakota	5.9%	47
Alaska	13.2	21	Louisiana	13.9	16	Ohio	13.5	17
Arizona	10.6	29	Maine	4.7	50	Oklahoma	25.9	1
Arkansas	15.9	11	Maryland	12.2	22	Oregon	9.0	36
California	14.7	13	Massachusetts	3.9	51	Pennsylvania	6.5	46
Colorado	16.2	9	Michigan	21.0	5	Rhode Island	17.0	8
Connecticut	8.0	41	Minnesota	10.8	28	South Carolina	7.7	43
Delaware	11.5	27	Mississippi	22.9	3	South Dakota	7.8	42
D.C.	11.9	24	Missouri	13.5	18	Tennessee	20.1	6
Florida[3]	23.8	2	Montana	14.1	15	Texas	13.3	19
Georgia	11.7	26	Nebraska	6.7	44	Utah	5.8	48
Hawaii	8.9	37	Nevada	12.2	23	Vermont	8.5	39
Idaho	6.7	45	New Hampshire	9.3	34	Virginia	10.1	31
Illinois	13.3	20	New Jersey	10.3	30	Washington	16.1	10
Indiana	14.2	14	New Mexico	21.6	4	West Virginia	8.4	40
Iowa	9.7	32	New York	5.3	49	Wisconsin	11.7	25
Kansas	9.4	33	North Carolina	9.1	35	Wyoming	8.7	38

[1]Percentage of uninsured drivers, as measured by the ratio of uninsured motorists (UM) claims to bodily injury (BI) claim frequencies.
[2]Rank calculated from unrounded data.
[3]In Florida, compulsory auto laws apply to personal injury protection (PIP) and physical damage, but not to third party bodily injury coverage.

Source: Insurance Research Council.

Auto: Laws

Automobile Financial Responsibility Laws

Most states require motor vehicle owners to buy a minimum amount of bodily injury and property damage liability insurance before they can legally drive their vehicles. All states have financial responsibility laws, which means that people involved in an accident will be required to furnish proof of financial responsibility up to a certain amount. To comply with these laws, most drivers purchase liability insurance. Despite these laws a significant percentage of drivers are uninsured.

Motorcycle insurance is compulsory in every state except Hawaii, Montana, New Hampshire and Washington. Minimum auto liability limits and the insurance required by state law are the same for motorcycles as for autos and other motor vehicles.

The chart below shows mandatory requirements for bodily injury (BI), property damage (PD) liability, no-fault personal injury protection (PIP), and uninsured (UM) and underinsured (UIM) motorists coverage. It also indicates which states have only financial responsibility (FR) laws.

AUTOMOBILE FINANCIAL RESPONSIBILITY LIMITS BY STATE

State	Insurance required	Minimum liability limits[1]
Alabama	BI & PD Liab	25/50/25
Alaska	BI & PD Liab	50/100/25
Arizona	BI & PD Liab	15/30/10
Arkansas	BI & PD Liab, PIP	25/50/25
California	BI & PD Liab	15/30/5[2]
Colorado	BI & PD Liab	25/50/15
Connecticut	BI & PD Liab, UM, UIM	20/40/10
Delaware	BI & PD Liab, PIP	15/30/10
D.C.	BI & PD Liab, PIP, UM	25/50/10
Florida	PD Liab, PIP	10/20/10[3]
Georgia	BI & PD Liab	25/50/25
Hawaii	BI & PD Liab, PIP	20/40/10
Idaho	BI & PD Liab	25/50/15
Illinois	BI & PD Liab, UM, UIM	25/50/20
Indiana	BI & PD Liab	25/50/10
Iowa	BI & PD Liab	20/40/15
Kansas	BI & PD Liab, PIP	25/50/10
Kentucky	BI & PD Liab, PIP	25/50/10[3]
Louisiana	BI & PD Liab	15/30/25
Maine	BI & PD Liab, UM	50/100/25[4]
Maryland	BI & PD Liab, PIP, UM, UIM	30/60/15
Massachusetts	BI & PD Liab, PIP, UM	20/40/5
Michigan	BI & PD Liab, PIP	20/40/10
Minnesota	BI & PD Liab, PIP, UM, UIM	30/60/10
Mississippi	BI & PD Liab	25/50/25
Missouri	BI & PD Liab, UM	25/50/10
Montana	BI & PD Liab	25/50/20
Nebraska	BI & PD Liab, UM, UIM	25/50/25

(table continues)

AUTOMOBILE FINANCIAL RESPONSIBILITY LIMITS BY STATE (Cont'd)

State	Insurance required	Minimum liability limits[1]
Nevada	BI & PD Liab	15/30/10
New Hampshire	FR only, UM	25/50/25[4]
New Jersey	BI & PD Liab, PIP, UM, UIM	15/30/5[5]
New Mexico	BI & PD Liab	25/50/10
New York	BI & PD Liab, PIP, UM	25/50/10[6]
North Carolina	BI & PD Liab, UM, UIM[7]	30/60/25
North Dakota	BI & PD Liab, PIP, UM, UIM	25/50/25
Ohio	BI & PD Liab	25/50/25
Oklahoma	BI & PD Liab	25/50/25
Oregon	BI & PD Liab, PIP, UM, UIM	25/50/20
Pennsylvania	BI & PD Liab, PIP	15/30/5
Rhode Island	BI & PD Liab	25/50/25[3]
South Carolina	BI & PD Liab, UM	25/50/25
South Dakota	BI & PD Liab, UM, UIM	25/50/25
Tennessee	BI & PD Liab	25/50/15[3]
Texas	BI & PD Liab	30/60/25
Utah	BI & PD Liab, PIP	25/65/15[3]
Vermont	BI & PD Liab	25/50/10
Virginia	BI & PD Liab[8], UM, UIM	25/50/20
Washington	BI & PD Liab	25/50/10
West Virginia	BI & PD Liab, UM	25/50/25
Wisconsin	BI & PD Liab, UM	25/50/10
Wyoming	BI & PD Liab	25/50/20

[1]The first two numbers refer to bodily injury (BI) liability limits and the third number to property damage (PD) liability. For example, 20/40/10 means coverage up to $40,000 for all persons injured in an accident, subject to a limit of $20,000 for one individual, and $10,000 coverage for property damage. [2]Low-cost policy limits for low-income drivers in the California Automobile Assigned Risk Plan are 10/20/3. [3]Instead of policy limits, policyholders can satisfy the requirement with a combined single limit policy. Amounts vary by state. [4]In addition, policyholders must carry coverage for medical payments. Amounts vary by state. [5]Basic policy (optional) limits are 10/10/5. Uninsured and underinsured motorist coverage not available under the basic policy but uninsured and underinsured motorist coverage is required under the standard policy. Special Automobile Insurance Policy available for certain drivers which only covers emergency treatment and a $10,000 death benefit. [6]In addition, policyholders must have 50/100 for wrongful death coverage. [7]UIM mandatory in policies with UM limits exceeding 30/60. [8]Compulsory to buy insurance or pay an uninsured motorists vehicle (UMV) fee to the state Department of Motor Vehicles.

Source: Property Casualty Insurers Association of America; state departments of insurance.

State Auto Insurance Laws Governing Liability Coverage

State auto insurance laws governing liability coverage fall into four broad categories: no-fault, choice no-fault, tort liability and add-on. The major differences are whether there are restrictions on the right to sue and whether the policyholder's own insurer pays first-party (i.e., the insured's) benefits, up to the state maximum amount, regardless of who is at fault in the accident.

- **No-fault:** The no-fault system is intended to lower the cost of auto insurance by taking small claims out of the courts. Each insurance company compensates its own policyholders for the cost of minor injuries regardless of who was at fault in the accident. These first-party benefits, known as personal injury protection (PIP), are a mandatory coverage in no-fault states but benefits vary by state. In states with the most extensive benefits, a policyholder receives compensation for medical fees, lost wages, funeral costs and other out-of-pocket expenses. The term *no-fault* can be confusing because it is often used to denote any auto insurance system in which each driver's own insurance company pays for certain losses, regardless of fault. In its strict form, the term no-fault applies only to states where insurance companies pay first-party benefits and where there are restrictions on the right to sue.

    Drivers in no-fault states may sue for severe injuries if the case meets certain conditions. These conditions are known as the tort liability threshold, and may be expressed in verbal terms such as death or significant disfigurement (verbal threshold) or in dollar amounts of medical bills (monetary threshold).

- **Choice no-fault:** In choice no-fault states, drivers may select one of two options: a no-fault auto insurance policy, usually with a verbal threshold, or a traditional tort liability policy.

- **Tort liability:** In traditional tort liability states, there are no restrictions on lawsuits. A policyholder at fault in a car crash can be sued by the other driver and by the other driver's passengers for the pain and suffering the accident caused as well as for out-of-pocket expenses such as medical costs.

- **Add-on:** In add-on states, drivers can purchase medical coverage and other first-party benefits from their own insurance company as they do in no-fault states but there are no restrictions on lawsuits. The term add-on is used because in these states first-party benefits have been added on to the traditional tort liability system. In add-on states, first-party coverage may not be mandatory and the benefits may be lower than in true no-fault states.

Auto: Laws

STATE AUTO INSURANCE LAWS GOVERNING LIABILITY COVERAGE

- In the following 28 states auto liability is based on the traditional tort liability system. In these states, there are no restrictions on lawsuits:

True no-fault	First-party benefits (PIP)[1]		Restrictions on lawsuits		Thresholds for lawsuits	
	Compulsory	Optional	Yes	No	Monetary	Verbal
Florida	X		X			X
Hawaii	X		X		X	
Kansas	X		X		X	
Kentucky	X		X	X[2]	X[2]	
Massachusetts	X		X		X	
Michigan	X		X			X
Minnesota	X		X		X	
New Jersey	X		X	X[2]		X[2,3]
New York	X		X			X
North Dakota	X		X		X	
Pennsylvania	X		X	X[2]		X[2]
Puerto Rico	X		X		X	
Utah	X		X		X	
Add-on						
Arkansas	X			X		
Delaware	X			X		
D.C.		X	X[4]	X[4]		
Maryland	X			X		
New Hampshire		X		X		
Oregon	X			X		
South Dakota		X		X		
Texas		X		X		
Virginia		X		X		
Washington		X		X		
Wisconsin		X		X		

Alabama
Alaska
Arizona
California
Colorado
Connecticut
Georgia
Idaho
Illinois
Indiana
Iowa
Louisiana
Maine
Mississippi
Missouri
Montana
Nebraska
Nevada
New Mexico
North Carolina
Ohio
Oklahoma
Rhode Island
South Carolina
Tennessee
Vermont
West Virginia
Wyoming

[1] Personal injury protection.
[2] Choice no-fault state. Policyholder can choose a policy based on the no-fault system or traditional tort liability.
[3] Verbal threshold for the Basic Liability Policy, the Special Policy and the Standard Policy where the policyholder chooses no-fault. The Basic and Special Policies contain lower amounts of coverage.
[4] The District of Columbia is neither a true no-fault nor add-on state. Drivers are offered the option of no-fault or fault-based coverage, but in the event of an accident a driver who originally chose no-fault benefits has 60 days to decide whether to receive those benefits or file a claim against the other party.

Source: Property Casualty Insurers Association of America.

Seatbelt Laws

Thirty-four states and the District of Columbia have a primary seatbelt enforcement law, which allows law enforcement officers to stop a car for noncompliance with seatbelt laws. The other states have secondary laws; officials can only issue seatbelt violations if they stop motorists for other infractions. New Hampshire, the only state that does not have a seatbelt law that applies to adults, has a child restraint law. Seatbelts were in use 87 percent of the time nationwide in 2014; states with primary seatbelt laws had an average 90 percent usage rate, 11 points higher than the 79 percent in states with secondary laws.

STATE SEATBELT USE LAWS

State	2013 usage rate	Primary/ secondary enforcement[1]	Age requirements	Maximum fine, first offense	Damages reduced[2]
Alabama	97.3%	P	15+ yrs. in front seat	$25	
Alaska	86.1	P	16+ yrs. in all seats	15	X
Arizona	84.7	S	8+ yrs. in front seat; 8-15 in all seats	10	X
Arkansas	76.7	P	15+ yrs. in front seat	25	
California	97.4	P	16+ yrs. in all seats	20	X
Colorado	82.1	S	16+ yrs. in front seat	71	X
Connecticut	86.6	P	7+ yrs. in front seat	15	
Delaware	92.2	P	16+ yrs. in all seats	25	
D.C.	87.5	P	16+ yrs. in all seats	50	
Florida	87.2	P	6+ yrs. in front seat; 6-17 yrs. in all seats	30	X
Georgia	95.5	P	8-17 yrs. in all seats; 18+ yrs. in front seat	15	
Hawaii	94.0	P	8+ yrs. in all seats	45	
Idaho	81.6	S	7+ yrs. in all seats	10	
Illinois	93.7	P	16+ yrs. in all seats	25	
Indiana	91.6	P	16+ yrs. in all seats	25	
Iowa	91.9	P	18+ yrs. in front seat	25	X
Kansas	80.7	P	14+ yrs. in all seats	10-60	
Kentucky	85.0	P	7 and younger and more than 57 inches tall in all seats; 8+ yrs. in all seats	25	X
Louisiana	82.5	P	13+ yrs. in all seats	25-45	
Maine	83.0	P	18+ yrs. in all seats	50	
Maryland	90.7	P	16+ yrs. in all seats	50	
Massachusetts	74.8	S	13+ yrs. in all seats	25	
Michigan	93.0	P	16+ yrs. in front seat	25	X
Minnesota	94.8	P	7 and younger and more than 57 inches tall in all seats; 8+ in all seats	25	

(table continues)

STATE SEATBELT USE LAWS (Cont'd)

State	2013 usage rate	Primary/ secondary enforcement[1]	Age requirements	Maximum fine, first offense	Damages reduced[2]
Mississippi	74.4%	P	7+ yrs. in front seat	$25	
Missouri	80.1	3	16+ yrs. in front seat	10	X
Montana	74.0	S	6+ yrs. in all seats	20	
Nebraska	79.1	S	18+ yrs. in front seat	25	X
Nevada	94.8	S	6+ yrs. in all seats	25	
New Hampshire	73.0	No law for adults			
New Jersey	91.0	P[4]	7 yrs. and younger and more than 57 inches.; 8+ yrs. in all seats	20	X
New Mexico	92.0	P	18+ yrs. in all seats	25	
New York	91.1	P	16+ yrs. in front seat	50	X
North Carolina	88.6	P[4]	16+ yrs. in all seats	25	
North Dakota	77.7	S	18+ yrs. in front seat	20	X
Ohio	84.5	S	8-14 yrs. in all seats; 15+ yrs. in front seat	30 driver/20 passenger	X
Oklahoma	83.6	P	9+ yrs. in front seat	20	
Oregon	98.2	P	16+ yrs. in all seats	110	X
Pennsylvania	84.0	3	8-17 yrs. in all seats; 18+ yrs. in front seat	10	
Rhode Island	85.6	P	18+ yrs. in all seats	40	
South Carolina	91.7	P	6+ yrs. in all seats	25	
South Dakota	68.7	S	18+ yrs. in front seat	20	
Tennessee	84.8	P	16+ yrs. in front seat	25	
Texas	90.3	P	7 yrs. and younger who are 57 inches or taller; 8+ yrs. in all seats	200	
Utah	82.4	P	16+ yrs. in all seats	45	
Vermont	84.9	S	18+ yrs. in all seats	25	
Virginia	79.7	S	18+ yrs. in front seat	25	
Washington	94.5	P	16+ yrs. in all seats	124	
West Virginia	82.2	P	8+ yrs. in front seat; 8-17 yrs. in all seats	25	X
Wisconsin	82.4	P	8+ yrs. in all seats	10	X
Wyoming	81.9	S	9+ yrs. in all seats	25 driver/ 10 passenger	
United States	**87.0%**				

[1]Primary enforcement means police may stop a vehicle and issue a fine for noncompliance with seatbelt laws. Secondary enforcement means that police may issue a fine for not wearing a seatbelt only if the vehicle has been stopped for other traffic violations. [2]Court awards for compensation for injury may be reduced if seatbelt laws were violated. [3]Primary enforcement for children; ages vary. [4]Secondary for rear seat occupants.

Source: U.S. Department of Transportation, National Highway Traffic Safety Administration (NHTSA); Insurance Institute for Highway Safety.

Drunk Driving Laws

In 2013, 10,076 people died in the United States in alcohol-impaired crashes, down 2.5 percent from 10,336 in 2012, according to the National Highway Traffic Safety Administration. In 2013 alcohol-impaired crash fatalities accounted for 31 percent of all crash fatalities, the same proportion as in 2012. A major factor in the long-term downward trend in alcohol-impaired deaths is the enactment, beginning in the 1980s, of state laws designed to deter drunk driving. By 2004 every state and the District of Columbia had lowered the limit defining drunk driving from a 0.10 percent blood alcohol concentration to 0.08 percent. All states have enacted more stringent restrictions for drivers under the legal drinking age (21 years old in all states).

STATE LAWS CURBING DRUNK DRIVING

State	License revocation — Admin. license rev./susp.[2]	License revocation — Mandatory 90-day license rev./susp.[3]	Open container law[4]	Mandatory ignition interlocks[1] — All offenders	First offenders — All	First offenders — High-BAC offenders only[5]	Repeat offenders
Alabama	X	X	X	X	X		X
Alaska	X	X	X	X	X		X
Arizona	X	X	X	X	X		X
Arkansas	X	X		X	X		X
California	X	X	X	X	In 4 counties		X
Colorado	X	X	X	X	X		X
Connecticut	X			X	X		X
Delaware	X	X		X	X		X
D.C.	X		X				
Florida	X	X	X			X	X
Georgia	X	X	X				X
Hawaii	X	X	X	X	X		X
Idaho	X	X	X				X
Illinois	X	X	X	X	X		X
Indiana	X	X	X				
Iowa	X	X	X			X	X
Kansas	X		X	X	X		X
Kentucky			X			X	X
Louisiana	X	X	X	X	X		X
Maine	X	X	X	X	X		X
Maryland	X		X			X	X
Massachusetts	X		X				X
Michigan			X			X	X

(table continues)

STATE LAWS CURBING DRUNK DRIVING (Cont'd)

State	License revocation		Open container law⁴	Mandatory ignition interlocks[1]			
	Admin. license rev./susp.[2]	Mandatory 90-day license rev./susp.[3]		All offenders	First offenders		Repeat offenders
					All	High-BAC offenders only[5]	
Minnesota	X	X	X				X	X
Mississippi	X	X		X	X			X
Missouri	X			X	X			X
Montana			X					
Nebraska	X	X	X	X	X			X
Nevada	X	X	X				X	X
New Hampshire	X	X	X			X	X	X
New Jersey			X				X	X
New Mexico	X	X	X	X	X			X
New York	6		X	X	X			X
North Carolina	X		X				X	X
North Dakota	X	X	X					
Ohio	X	X	X					X
Oklahoma	X	X	X				X	X
Oregon	X	X	X	X	X			X
Pennsylvania			X					X
Rhode Island			X				X	X
South Carolina			X				X	X
South Dakota			X					
Tennessee			X	X	X			X
Texas	X	X	X	X	X			X
Utah	X	X	X	X	X			X
Vermont	X	X	X	X	X			X
Virginia	X		X	X	X			X
Washington	X	X	X	X	X			X
West Virginia	X	X	X	X	X			X
Wisconsin	X	X	X				X	X
Wyoming	X	X	X				X	X

[1]Ignition interlock devices analyze a driver's breath for alcohol and disable the ignition if a driver has been drinking. States identified mandate the devices on offenders' vehicles. [2]On-the-spot drivers license suspension or revocation if blood alcohol concentration (BAC) is over the legal limit or the driver refuses to take a BAC test. [3]Mandatory penalty for violation of the implied consent law, which means that drivers who refuse to take a breath alcohol test when stopped or arrested for drunk driving will have their license revoked or suspended. [4]Prohibits unsealed alcohol containers in motor vehicle passenger compartments for all occupants. Arresting officer not required to witness consumption. [5]Usually 0.15 percent BAC or higher. [6]Administrative license suspension lasts until prosecution is complete.

Source: Insurance Institute for Highway Safety; Property Casualty Insurers Association of America.

Alcohol Server Liability Laws

Most states have enacted liquor liability laws that hold businesses and/or people who serve liquor liable for the damage a drunk driver causes.

STATUTES OR COURT CASES HOLDING ALCOHOLIC BEVERAGE SERVERS LIABLE

State	Commercial servers Statute[1]	Court[2]	Social hosts Statute[3]	Court	State	Commercial servers Statute[1]	Court[2]	Social hosts Statute[3]	Court
Alabama	X		X	X	Montana	X	X	X	
Alaska	X		X		Nebraska			X	
Arizona	X	X	X	X	Nevada			X[4]	
Arkansas	X	X			New Hampshire	X		X	X
California	X		X		New Jersey	X		X	X
Colorado	X	X	X		New Mexico	X		X	X
Connecticut	X	X		X[4,5]	New York	X		X	
Delaware					North Carolina	X	X	X	X[4]
D.C.		X[4]			North Dakota	X		X	
Florida	X		X	X	Ohio	X	X	X	X[4]
Georgia	X		X		Oklahoma	X	X		
Hawaii		X	X		Oregon	X		X	
Idaho	X	X	X		Pennsylvania	X	X		X[4]
Illinois	X		X	X	Rhode Island	X			
Indiana	X	X	X	X	South Carolina	X	X	X	X[4]
Iowa	X	X	X	X[4]	South Dakota				
Kansas					Tennessee	X			
Kentucky	X	X		X[4]	Texas	X	X	X	X
Louisiana	X	X	X	X	Utah	X		X	X
Maine	X		X		Vermont	X		X	X
Maryland					Virginia				
Massachusetts	X	X	X	X	Washington	X	X	X	X[4]
Michigan	X		X	X[4]	West Virginia	X	X[4]		
Minnesota	X		X	X	Wisconsin	X	X	X	X
Mississippi	X	X	X	X	Wyoming	X		X	X[4]
Missouri	X								

[1]Indicates some form of liability is permitted by statute. [2]States where common-law liability has not been specifically overruled by statute or where common-law actions are specifically recognized in addition to statutory liability. [3]Indicates that language is capable of being read broadly enough to include noncommercial servers. [4]For guests under the age of 21. [5]Only if host purveyed or supplied alcohol.

Source: Property Casualty Insurers Association of America.

Property/Casualty Insurance by Line

Auto: Laws

Older Drivers

In 2013, 14 percent of the total U.S. resident population (44.7 million people) were 65 years old and older. In 2013, 5,671 people age 65 and older were killed in traffic crashes, accounting for 17 percent of all traffic fatalities that year. Recognizing the need for older drivers to retain their mobility and independence, some states issue restricted licenses. Depending on ability, older drivers may be limited to driving during daylight hours or on non-freeway types of roads. In most states restrictions such as these can be placed on anyone's drivers license regardless of age, if his or her medical condition warrants it.

STATE DRIVERS LICENSE RENEWAL LAWS INCLUDING REQUIREMENTS FOR OLDER DRIVERS

State	Length of regular renewal cycle (years)	Renewal for older drivers		Require older drivers to pass tests		Require doctors to report medical conditions[1]	Age limits on mail renewal
		Length (years)	Age	Age	Type of test		
Alabama	4						
Alaska	5			69	Vision		69
Arizona	12	5	65	65	Vision[2]		70
Arkansas	8						
California	5			70	Vision	X[3]	70
Colorado	5						66
Connecticut	6						
Delaware	8					X	
D.C.	8			70	Medical		70
Florida	8	6	80	80	Vision		
Georgia	8	5	59	64	Vision	X	65
Hawaii	8	2	72				
Idaho	4 or 8	4	63				70
Illinois	4	2	81[4]	75	Road, vision		75
Indiana	6	3	75[4]				75
Iowa	8	2	72	70	Vision		70
Kansas	6	4	65				
Kentucky	4						
Louisiana	6			70	Vision		70
Maine	6	4	65	40 and 62	Vision		62
Maryland	8			40 70	Vision; medical		
Massachusetts	5			75	Vision		75
Michigan	4						
Minnesota	4						

(table continues)

STATE DRIVERS LICENSE RENEWAL LAWS INCLUDING REQUIREMENTS FOR OLDER DRIVERS (Cont'd)

State	Length of regular renewal cycle (years)	Renewal for older drivers		Require older drivers to pass tests		Require doctors to report medical conditions[1]	Age limits on mail renewal
		Length (years)	Age	Age	Type of test		
Mississippi	4 or 8						
Missouri	6	3	70				
Montana	8	4	75				
Nebraska	5			72	Vision		72
Nevada	4 or 8	4	65	70 72	Medical[2]; vision	X	
New Hampshire	5						
New Jersey	4					X	
New Mexico	4 or 8	4	67[4]				75
New York	8						
North Carolina	8	5	66				
North Dakota	6	4	78				
Ohio	4						
Oklahoma	4						
Oregon	8			50	Vision	X	
Pennsylvania	4					X	
Rhode Island	5	2	75				
South Carolina	10	5	65	65	Vision		
South Dakota	5			65	Vision		
Tennessee	8*						
Texas	6	2	85	79	Vision		79
Utah	5			65	Vision	X	
Vermont	4						
Virginia	8	5	75	75	Vision		75
Washington	6						70
West Virginia	8					X	
Wisconsin	8						
Wyoming	4						

[1]Physicians must report physical conditions that might impair driving skills.

[2]If renewing by mail.

[3]Specifically requires doctors to report a diagnosis of dementia.

[4]These states have special renewal requirements for other age groups. Illinois (1 year for drivers 87 and older); Indiana (2 years for drivers 85 and older); Missouri (3 years for drivers age 21 and younger); and New Mexico (1 year for drivers 75 and older).

Note: Specific requirements vary by state; contact state department of motor vehicles for more information.

Source: Insurance Institute for Highway Safety.

Cellphone Laws

Most states have passed laws to address the problem of using a cellphone while driving. Fourteen states—California, Connecticut, Delaware, Hawaii, Illinois, Maryland, Nevada, New Hampshire, New Jersey, New York, Oregon, Vermont, Washington, West Virginia—and the District of Columbia have a law banning the use of handheld cellphones behind the wheel for all drivers. The use of all cellphones by novice drivers is restricted in 37 states and the District of Columbia, according to the Insurance Institute for Highway Safety. Washington state was the first state to ban the practice of texting with a cellphone while driving. Text messaging is now banned for all drivers in 45 states and the District of Columbia.

Young Driver Laws

Young drivers account for a disproportionate number of motor vehicle crashes. States are increasingly adopting laws to help lower the crash rate. One approach has been to lower blood alcohol concentration (BAC) limits so those young drivers who drink even small amounts of alcohol will be penalized. Another has been to require a more rigorous learning period before granting young drivers the privilege of a drivers license. This requires young drivers between the ages of 15 and 18 to apply for a graduated drivers license (GDL) to help them improve their driving skills and habits before receiving full driving privileges.

Graduated licensing as defined by the National Highway Traffic Safety Administration consists of three stages. Stage 1 (learners permit) requirements and recommendations include a vision test, a road knowledge test, driving accompanied by a licensed adult, seatbelt use by all vehicle occupants, a zero BAC level, and six months with no crashes or convictions for traffic violations. Stage 2 (intermediate license) includes the completion of Stage 1, a behind-the-wheel road test, advanced driver education training, driving accompanied by a licensed adult at night and 12 consecutive months with no crashes or convictions for traffic offenses before reaching Stage 3 (full license).

Driverless Cars

As automotive technology has advanced, a number of companies have begun working on proto-types of driverless cars, in which the vehicle goes from point to point without guidance. In May 2012 Nevada became the first state to approve a license to test self-driving cars on public roads. California, Florida, Michigan and the District of Columbia have passed similar laws and other states are considering them.

STATE YOUNG DRIVER LAWS[1]

State	Learners permit required for a minimum period	Graduated licensing		Driver may not operate a cellphone in learner and/ or intermediate stages[4]
		Intermediate phase		
		Restrictions on night driving[2]	Passenger restrictions[3]	
Alabama	6 months	X	X	Talk
Alaska	6 months	X	X	
Arizona	6 months	X	X	
Arkansas	6 months	X	X	Talk
California	6 months	X	X	Talk
Colorado	12 months	X	X	Talk
Connecticut	6 months	X	X	Talk
Delaware	6 months	X	X	Talk
D.C.	6 months	X	X	Talk
Florida	12 months	X		
Georgia	12 months	X	X	Talk
Hawaii	6 months	X	X	Talk
Idaho	6 months	X	X	
Illinois	9 months	X	X	Talk
Indiana	6 months	X	X	Talk
Iowa	12 months	X		Talk
Kansas	12 months	X	X	Talk
Kentucky	6 months	X	X	Talk
Louisiana	6 months	X	X	Talk
Maine	6 months	X	X	Talk
Maryland	9 months	X	X	Talk
Massachusetts	6 months	X	X	Talk
Michigan	6 months	X	X	Talk
Minnesota	6 months	X	X	Talk
Mississippi	12 months	X		
Missouri	6 months	X	X	Text
Montana	6 months	X	X	
Nebraska	6 months	X	X	Talk
Nevada	6 months	X	X	
New Hampshire	none[5]	X	X	Talk
New Jersey	6 months	X	X	Talk
New Mexico	6 months	X	X	Talk

(table continues)

STATE YOUNG DRIVER LAWS[1] (Cont'd)

State	Learners permit required for a minimum period	Graduated licensing		Driver may not operate a cellphone in learner and/ or intermediate stages[4]
		Intermediate phase		
		Restrictions on night driving[2]	Passenger restrictions[3]	
New York	6 months	X	X	
North Carolina	12 months	X	X	Talk
North Dakota	6-12 months[6]	X		Talk
Ohio	6 months	X	X	Talk
Oklahoma	6 months	X	X	Talk[7]
Oregon	6 months	X	X	Talk
Pennsylvania	6 months	X	X	
Rhode Island	6 months	X	X	Talk
South Carolina	6 months	X	X	
South Dakota	6 months	X		Talk
Tennessee	6 months	X	X	Talk
Texas	6 months	X	X	Talk, text
Utah	6 months	X	X	Talk
Vermont	12 months		X	Talk
Virginia	9 months	X	X	Talk
Washington	6 months	X	X	Talk
West Virginia	6 months	X	X	Talk
Wisconsin	6 months	X	X	Talk
Wyoming	10 days	X	X	

[1]Designed to aid young novice drivers between the ages of 15 and 18 gain driving experience. To date they apply only to drivers under the age of 18. All states have lower blood alcohol content laws for under-21 drivers which range from none to 0.02 percent, in contrast with 0.08 percent for drivers over the age of 21 in all states. Includes graduated licensing as defined by the National Highway Traffic Safety Administration. Every state has a graduated licensing law.

[2]Intermediate stage; varies by state with regard to age of driver, night hours that driving is restricted, who must accompany driver during night hours and how long and what stage the restrictions are lifted. Exceptions may be made for work, school or religious activities and emergencies.

[3]Intermediate stage; limits the number of teenage passengers a young driver may have in the vehicle.

[4]Only includes states with restrictions on the use of cellphones for talking or texting by young drivers. Does not reference cellphone laws such as bans on handheld cellphones that apply to all drivers in some states.

[5]New Hampshire does not issue learners permits.

[6]Under age 16: 12 months; 16-18: 6 months.

[7]Banned for non-life-threatening purposes.

Source: Insurance Institute for Highway Safety; U.S. Department of Transportation, National Highway Traffic Safety Administration; National Conference of State Legislatures; Insurance Information Institute.

Homeowners Insurance

Homeowners insurance accounts for 15.5 percent of all property/casualty (P/C) insurance premiums and 29.8 percent of personal property/casualty lines insurance.

Homeowners insurance is a package policy, providing both property and personal liability insurance. The typical policy covers the house, garage and other structures on the property—as well as personal property inside the house—against a wide variety of perils, such as fire, windstorm, vandalism and accidental water damage. The typical homeowners policy includes theft coverage on personal property anywhere in the world and liability coverage for accidental harm caused to others. It also reimburses the policyholder for the additional cost of living elsewhere while his or her house is being repaired or rebuilt after a fire or other disaster.

Earthquake damage and flood damage caused by external flooding are not covered by standard homeowners policies but special policies can be purchased separately. Flood coverage is provided by the federal government's National Flood Insurance Program and some private insurers.

HOMEOWNERS PREMIUMS AS A PERCENT OF ALL P/C PREMIUMS, 2014

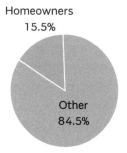

Homeowners
15.5%

Other
84.5%

Source: SNL Financial LC.

HOMEOWNERS MULTIPLE PERIL INSURANCE, 2005-2014
($000)

Year	Net premiums written[1]	Annual percent change	Combined ratio[2]	Annual point change[3]
2005	$53,010,922	6.1%	105.1	8.9 pts.
2006	55,822,275	5.3	89.5	-15.6
2007	57,053,137	2.2	93.9	4.4
2008	57,375,139	0.6	115.4	21.5
2009	58,478,195	1.9	105.7	-9.7
2010	61,659,466	5.4	106.0	0.3
2011	64,131,058	4.0	121.0	15.0
2012	67,847,033	5.8	103.0	-18.1
2013	72,773,216	7.3	89.6	-13.4
2014	77,908,777	7.1	91.6	2.0

[1]After reinsurance transactions, excludes state funds.
[2]After dividends to policyholders. A drop in the combined ratio represents an improvement; an increase represents a deterioration.
[3]Calculated from unrounded data.

Source: SNL Financial LC.

Property/Casualty Insurance by Line

Homeowners: Premiums/High-Risk Markets

TOP 10 WRITERS OF HOMEOWNERS INSURANCE BY DIRECT PREMIUMS WRITTEN, 2014
($000)

Rank	Group/company	Direct premiums written[1]	Market share[2]
1	State Farm Mutual Automobile Insurance	$17,631,832	20.3%
2	Allstate Corp.	7,712,425	8.9
3	Liberty Mutual	5,712,724	6.6
4	Farmers Insurance Group of Companies[3]	5,153,641	5.9
5	USAA Insurance Group	4,696,925	5.4
6	Travelers Companies Inc.	3,305,761	3.8
7	Nationwide Mutual Group	3,206,155	3.7
8	American Family Mutual	2,428,167	2.8
9	Chubb Corp.	2,049,106	2.4
10	Erie Insurance Group	1,368,426	1.6

[1]Before reinsurance transactions, includes state funds.
[2]Based on U.S. total, includes territories.
[3]Data for Farmers Insurance Group of Companies and Zurich Financial Group (which owns Farmers' management company) are reported separately by SNL Financial.

Source: SNL Financial LC.

Homeowners: High-Risk Markets

TOP 10 STATES, BY POPULATION CHANGE IN COASTAL COUNTIES, 1960-2010

■ The Atlantic Coast, the Gulf of Mexico and the Hawaiian Islands are home to the U.S. counties most vulnerable to hurricanes. These counties accounted for nearly two-thirds of the nation's coastline population in 2008, according to the U.S. Census Bureau.

	By number change			By percent change	
Rank	State	Number change	Rank	State	Percent change
1	California	13,130,000	1	Florida	270.1%
2	Florida	10,360,000	2	Alaska	239.8
3	Texas	3,732,000	3	New Hampshire	198.0
4	Washington	2,578,000	4	Texas	161.9
5	Virginia	1,903,000	5	Virginia	150.8
6	New York	1,400,000	6	Washington	144.4
7	New Jersey	1,275,000	7	South Carolina	125.1
8	Maryland	938,000	8	Hawaii	115.2
9	Massachusetts	826,000	9	North Carolina	114.4
10	Hawaii	728,000	10	California	107.2

Source: U.S. Department of Commerce, Census Bureau.

From 1960 to 2008, five of the 11 most hurricane-prone counties were in Louisiana; three were in Florida and three were in North Carolina. In Florida, 75.7 percent of the state's population resides in coastal counties, compared with 32.3 percent in Louisiana and 9.9 percent in North Carolina. In the United States as a whole, 52 percent of the population resides in coastal counties outside of Alaska, according to the U.S. Census Bureau. The population of most counties along the Pacific, Atlantic and Gulf coasts grew between 2000 and 2010, creating an almost unbroken chain of coastal counties with population densities of 319 people per square mile or more running from New Hampshire through northern Virginia, according to the U.S. Census Bureau.

TOP COASTAL COUNTIES MOST FREQUENTLY HIT BY HURRICANES: 1960 TO 2008

County	State	Coastline region	Number of hurricanes	Percent change in population, 1960 to 2008
Monroe County	Florida	Gulf of Mexico	15	50.8%
Lafourche Parish	Louisiana	Gulf of Mexico	14	67.2
Carteret County	North Carolina	Atlantic	14	104.3
Dare County	North Carolina	Atlantic	13	465.9
Hyde County	North Carolina	Atlantic	13	10.1
Jefferson Parish	Louisiana	Gulf of Mexico	12	108.9
Palm Beach County	Florida	Atlantic	12	454.7
Miami-Dade County	Florida	Atlantic	11	156.5
St. Bernard Parish	Louisiana	Gulf of Mexico	11	17.2
Cameron Parish	Louisiana	Gulf of Mexico	11	4.8
Terrebonne Parish	Louisiana	Gulf of Mexico	11	78.7

Source: U.S. Department of Commerce, Census Bureau, Decennial Census of Population and Housing: 1960 to 2000; Population Estimates Program: 2008.

Coastal Area Growth

A report by AIR Worldwide on the insured value of properties in coastal areas of the United States (the cost of rebuilding) shows that over the past five years the compound annual growth rate slowed from 7 percent to 4 percent, due to the sharp decrease in the number of housing starts which, in turn, kept the cost of labor and building materials in check. But as the economy recovers, particularly the demand for new housing, AIR expects the growth rate to accelerate. Among the 18 coastal states studied, New York has the highest coastal property values, but Florida has the largest proportion of total value in coastal counties, at 79 percent, compared with 62 percent for New York. The total insured value of residential and commercial properties in U.S. coastal counties exceeds $10 trillion, with New York and Florida accounting for nearly $3 trillion each. Of the $10.6 trillion in insured coastal properties, $4.7 trillion, or 44 percent, were residential and $5.9 trillion, or 56 percent, were commercial.

VALUE OF INSURED RESIDENTIAL COASTAL EXPOSURE, 2012
($ billions)

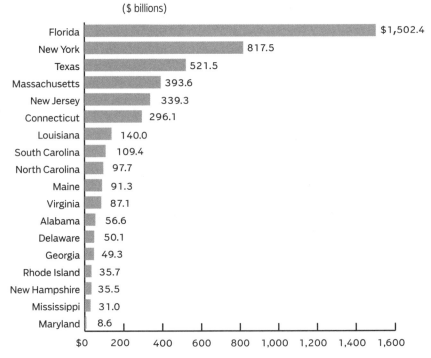

- Total U.S. insured residential coastal exposure totaled $4.7 trillion in 2012.

State	Value ($ billions)
Florida	$1,502.4
New York	817.5
Texas	521.5
Massachusetts	393.6
New Jersey	339.3
Connecticut	296.1
Louisiana	140.0
South Carolina	109.4
North Carolina	97.7
Maine	91.3
Virginia	87.1
Alabama	56.6
Delaware	50.1
Georgia	49.3
Rhode Island	35.7
New Hampshire	35.5
Mississippi	31.0
Maryland	8.6

Source: AIR Worldwide.

ESTIMATED VALUE OF INSURED COASTAL PROPERTIES VULNERABLE TO HURRICANES BY STATE, 2012[1]

($ billions)

Rank	State	Coastal	Total exposure[2]	Coastal as a percent of total
1	New York	$2,923.1	$4,724.2	62%
2	Florida	2,862.3	3,640.1	79
3	Texas	1,175.3	4,580.7	26
4	Massachusetts	849.6	1,561.4	54
5	New Jersey	713.9	2,129.9	34
6	Connecticut	567.8	879.1	65
7	Louisiana	293.5	823.0	36
8	South Carolina	239.3	843.6	28
9	Virginia	182.3	1,761.7	10
10	Maine	164.6	285.5	58
11	North Carolina	163.5	1,795.1	9
12	Alabama	118.2	917.8	13
13	Georgia	106.7	1,932.2	6
14	Delaware	81.9	208.9	39
15	New Hampshire	64.0	278.7	23
16	Mississippi	60.6	468.5	13
17	Rhode Island	58.3	207.5	28
18	Maryland	17.3	1,293.4	1
	Total, states shown	**$10,642.2**	**$28,331.4**	**38%**
	Total, United States	**$10,642.2**	**$64,624.3**	**16%**

- The insured value of properties in coastal areas in the United States totaled $10.6 trillion in 2012, according to AIR Worldwide.

[1]Includes residential and commercial properties, as of December 31, 2012. Ranked by value of insured coastal property.
[2]Total exposure is an estimate of the actual total value of all property in the state that is insured or can be insured, including the full replacement value of structures and their contents, additional living expenses and the time value of business interruption coverage.

Source: AIR Worldwide.

VALUE OF INSURED COMMERCIAL COASTAL EXPOSURE, 2012

($ billions)

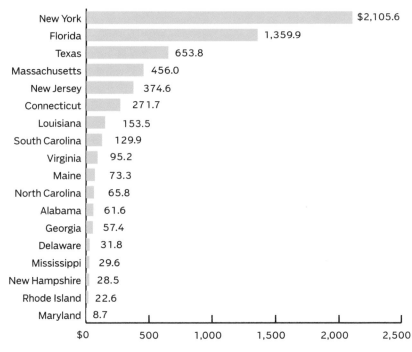

- Total U.S. insured commercial exposure totaled $5.9 trillion in 2012.

State	Value
New York	$2,105.6
Florida	1,359.9
Texas	653.8
Massachusetts	456.0
New Jersey	374.6
Connecticut	271.7
Louisiana	153.5
South Carolina	129.9
Virginia	95.2
Maine	73.3
North Carolina	65.8
Alabama	61.6
Georgia	57.4
Delaware	31.8
Mississippi	29.6
New Hampshire	28.5
Rhode Island	22.6
Maryland	8.7

Source: AIR Worldwide.

Residual Market Property Plans

A myriad of different programs in place across the United States provide insurance to high-risk policyholders who may have difficulty obtaining coverage from the standard market. So called residual, shared or involuntary market programs make basic insurance coverage more readily available. Today, property insurance for the residual market is provided by Fair Access to Insurance Requirements (FAIR) Plans, Beach and Windstorm Plans, and two state-run insurance companies in Florida and Louisiana: Florida's Citizens Property Insurance Corp. and Louisiana's Citizens Property Insurance Corp. Established in the late 1960s to ensure the continued provision of insurance in urban areas, FAIR Plans often provide property insurance in both urban and coastal areas, while Beach and Windstorm Plans cover predominantly wind-only risks in designated coastal areas. Exposure to loss in both FAIR Plans and Beach and Windstorm Plans fell from $703 billion in 2009 to $620 billion in 2014. The number of policies in force grew from 2.48 million to 2.78 million during the same period.

INSURANCE PROVIDED BY FAIR PLANS, FISCAL YEARS 2005-2014[1]

Year	Number of policies			Exposure[2] ($000)	Direct premiums written ($000)
	Habitational	Commercial	Total		
2005	1,928,292	117,942	2,046,234	$387,780,124	$2,234,493
2006	2,389,299	172,070	2,561,369	601,859,916	4,063,324
2007	2,412,252	114,053	2,526,305	684,829,667	4,431,381
2008	2,190,189	90,876	2,281,065	612,749,753	3,727,311
2009	2,043,969	86,575	2,130,544	614,905,551	3,038,712
2010	2,378,736	83,243	2,461,979	662,633,180	3,448,576
2011	2,658,662	51,657	2,710,319	715,289,876	3,942,021
2012	2,518,808	71,776	2,590,584	635,705,150	4,059,446
2013	2,484,816	64,359	2,549,175	445,635,335	3,685,283
2014	2,015,536	61,285	2,076,821	424,732,706	3,029,772

[1]Includes the Texas FAIR Plan; Florida's Citizens Property Insurance Corp., which includes FAIR and Beach Plans; the Louisiana Citizens Property Insurance Corp., which includes FAIR and Beach Plans for 2005 and premiums written after 2007; and North Carolina after 2010.
[2]Exposure is the estimate of the aggregate value of all insurance in force in all FAIR Plans in all lines (except liability, where applicable, and crime) for 12 months ending September through December.

Source: Property Insurance Plans Service Office (PIPSO).

INSURANCE PROVIDED BY FAIR PLANS BY STATE, FISCAL YEAR 2014[1]

State	Number of policies			Exposure[2] ($000)	Direct premiums written ($000)
	Habitational	Commercial	Total		
California	123,729	5,045	128,774	$43,958,244	$73,384
Connecticut	2,779	103	2,882	532,514	3,842
Delaware	1,800	71	1,871	285,049	623
D.C.	303	79	382	107,000	349
Florida[3]	943,284	38,515	981,799	201,957,396	2,083,870
Georgia	28,768	1,638	30,406	4,066,259	26,869
Illinois	6,386	94	6,480	711,340	7,344
Indiana	2,284	54	2,338	175,625	2,458
Iowa	1,274	44	1,318	94,488	971
Kansas	16,095	183	16,278	968,312	8,678
Kentucky	11,748	534	12,282	604,164	7,881
Louisiana[3]	113,624	4,335	117,959	17,059,256	168,069

(table continues)

INSURANCE PROVIDED BY FAIR PLANS BY STATE, FISCAL YEAR 2014[1] (Cont'd)

State	Number of policies		Total	Exposure[2] ($000)	Direct premiums written ($000)
	Habitational	Commercial			
Maryland	2,004	86	2,090	$391,000	$1,337
Massachusetts	215,087	391	215,478	78,739,414	278,865
Michigan	22,230	387	22,617	2,887,324	24,137
Minnesota	5,711	42	5,753	956,310	4,146
Mississippi	11,393	4	11,393	711,411	8,669
Missouri	3,912	173	4,085	246,539	2,317
New Jersey	16,977	458	17,435	2,436,351	10,697
New Mexico	10,991	288	11,279	93,491	4,484
New York	50,935	3,348	54,283	14,169,172	35,488
North Carolina	151,822	2,613	154,435	13,571,310	61,679
Ohio	28,454	514	28,968	6,820,948	24,804
Oregon	2,594	51	2,645	272,000	889
Pennsylvania	19,057	1,415	20,472	1,646,337	8,052
Rhode Island	17,135	122	17,257	4,209,288	22,233
Texas	164,954	4	164,954	21,944,279	133,206
Virginia	33,975	531	34,506	4,671,246	21,028
Washington	64	21	85	25,406	171
West Virginia	534	65	599	34,719	360
Wisconsin	5,633	85	5,718	386,514	2,872
Total	**2,015,536**	**61,285**	**2,076,821**	**$424,732,706**	**$3,029,772**

[1]Excludes the FAIR Plans of Arkansas and Hawaii.
[2]Exposure is the estimate of the aggregate value of all insurance in force in all FAIR Plans in all lines (except liability, where applicable, and crime) for 12 months ending September through December.
[3]Citizens Property Insurance Corp., which combined the FAIR and Beach Plans.
[4]The Mississippi and Texas FAIR Plans do not offer a commercial policy.

Source: Property Insurance Plans Service Office (PIPSO).

Insurance Provided by Beach and Windstorm Plans

Beach and Windstorm Plans ensure that insurance is available against damage from hurricanes and other windstorms. In Georgia, Massachusetts and New York, FAIR Plans provide wind and hail coverage for certain coastal communities. These states do not have Beach and Windstorm Plans.

Homeowners: High-Risk Markets/Costs/Expenditures

INSURANCE PROVIDED BY BEACH AND WINDSTORM PLANS, FISCAL YEAR 2014[1]

State	Number of policies			Exposure[2] ($000)	Direct premiums written ($000)
	Habitational	Commercial	Total		
Alabama	31,893	103	31,996	$5,558,923	$43,973
Mississippi	71,367	3,693	75,060	6,711,829	75,123
North Carolina	247,227	12,393	259,620	91,107,419	407,092
South Carolina	37,672	781	38,453	13,568,982	84,428
Texas	278,038	15,767	293,805	78,763,326	494,036
Total	**666,197**	**32,737**	**698,934**	**$195,710,479**	**$1,104,652**

[1]The Florida and Louisiana Beach Plans merged with their FAIR Plans, see chart on page 101. [2]Exposure is the estimate of the aggregate value of all insurance in force in each state's Beach and Windstorm Plan in all lines (except liability, where applicable, and crime) for 12 months ending September through December.

Source: Property Insurance Plans Service Office (PIPSO).

Homeowners: Costs/Expenditures

The average homeowners insurance premium rose by 5.6 percent in 2012, following a 7.7 percent increase in 2011, according to a February 2015 study by the National Association of Insurance Commissioners. The average renters insurance premium was unchanged in 2012, after rising 1.1 percent the previous year.

AVERAGE PREMIUMS FOR HOMEOWNERS AND RENTERS INSURANCE, UNITED STATES, 2004-2012

Year	Homeowners[1]	Percent change	Renters[2]	Percent change
2004	$729	9.1%	$195	1.6%
2005	764	4.8	193	-1.0
2006	804	5.2	189	-2.1
2007	822	2.2	182	-3.7
2008	830	1.0	182	[3]
2009	880	6.0	184	1.1
2010	909	3.3	185	0.5
2011	979	7.7	187	1.1
2012	1,034	5.6	187	[3]

[1]Based on the HO-3 homeowner package policy for owner-occupied dwellings, one- to four-family units. Provides all risks coverage (except those specifically excluded in the policy) on buildings and broad named-peril coverage on personal property, and is the most common package written. [2]Based on the HO-4 renters insurance policy for tenants. Includes broad named-peril coverage for the personal property of tenants. [3]Less than 0.1 percent.

Source: © 2015 National Association of Insurance Commissioners (NAIC). Reprinted with permission. Further reprint or distribution strictly prohibited without written permission of NAIC.

- A 2015 Insurance Information Institute poll conducted by ORC International found that 95 percent of homeowners had homeowners insurance but only 40 percent of renters had renters insurance.

- The U.S. homeownership rate was 63.4 percent in second-quarter 2015, down from 64.7 percent a year ago to the lowest rate since 1967, according to the U.S. Census Bureau. The 2010 Census showed that in some of the largest cities renters outnumbered owners, including New York, where 69.0 percent of households were occupied by renters, followed by Los Angeles (61.8 percent), Chicago (55.1 percent) and Houston (54.6 percent).

AVERAGE HOMEOWNERS INSURANCE PREMIUMS RANKED BY STATE, 2012[1]

Rank[2]	State	Average premium	Rank[2]	State	Average premium
1	Florida	$2,084	27	Kentucky	$916
2	Louisiana	1,742	28	Illinois	881
3	Texas[3]	1,661	29	Montana	871
4	Oklahoma	1,501	30	New Hampshire	848
5	Mississippi	1,314	31	New Mexico	844
6	Alabama	1,248	32	Virginia	843
7	Rhode Island	1,233	33	Indiana	840
8	Kansas	1,213	34	Maryland	837
9	Connecticut	1,160	35	Wyoming	821
10	New York	1,158	36	Pennsylvania	804
11	Massachusetts	1,150	37	Michigan	802
12	Minnesota	1,140	38	South Dakota	789
13	South Carolina	1,134	39	Vermont	782
14	D.C.	1,103	40	Iowa	779
15	Arkansas	1,096	41	West Virginia	771
16	Missouri	1,091	42	Maine	741
17	Nebraska	1,040	43	Ohio	721
18	Colorado	1,038	44	Arizona	691
18	North Dakota	1,038	45	Delaware	678
20	Tennessee	1,008	46	Nevada	674
21	New Jersey	981	47	Washington	648
22	California[4]	980	48	Wisconsin	631
23	Georgia	975	49	Utah	580
24	Hawaii	957	50	Oregon	567
25	Alaska	942	51	Idaho	538
26	North Carolina	927			

[1]Includes policies written by Citizens Property Insurance Corp. (Florida) and Louisiana Citizens Property Insurance Corp., Alabama Insurance Underwriting Association, Mississippi Windstorm Underwriting Association and Residential Property Insurance Underwriting Association, North Carolina Joint Underwriting Association and South Carolina Wind and Hail Underwriting Association. Other southeastern states have wind pools in operation and their data may not be included in this chart. Based on the HO-3 homeowner package policy for owner-occupied dwellings, one- to four-family units. Provides all risks coverage (except those specifically excluded in the policy) on buildings and broad named-peril coverage on personal property and is the most common package written.
[2]States with the same premium receive the same rank.
[3]The Texas Department of Insurance developed home insurance policy forms that are similar but not identical to the standard forms. In addition, due to the Texas Windstorm Insurance Association (which writes wind-only policies) classifying HO-1, 2 and 5 premiums as HO-3, the average premium for homeowners insurance is artificially high.
[4]Data provided by the California Department of Insurance.

Note: Average premium=Premiums/exposure per house years. A house year is equal to 365 days of insured coverage for a single dwelling. The NAIC does not rank state average expenditures and does not endorse any conclusions drawn from this data.

Source: © 2015 National Association of Insurance Commissioners (NAIC). Reprinted with permission. Further reprint or distribution strictly prohibited without written permission of NAIC.

AVERAGE PREMIUMS FOR HOMEOWNERS AND RENTERS INSURANCE BY STATE, 2012[1]

State	Homeowners Average premium[2]	Rank[3]	Renters Average premium[4]	Rank[3]	State	Homeowners Average premium[2]	Rank[3]	Renters Average premium[4]	Rank[3]
Alabama	$1,248	6	$239	3	Montana	$871	29	$145	46
Alaska	942	25	161	33	Nebraska	1,040	17	150	41
Arizona	691	44	195	17	Nevada	674	46	193	18
Arkansas	1,096	15	215	9	New Hampshire	848	30	150	41
California[5]	980	22	207	12	New Jersey	981	21	166	31
Colorado	1,038	18	169	29	New Mexico	844	31	183	20
Connecticut	1,160	9	196	15	New York	1,158	10	211	11
Delaware	678	45	153	40	North Carolina	927	26	134	48
D.C.	1,103	14	164	32	North Dakota	1,038	18	115	51
Florida	2,084	1	217	8	Ohio	721	43	185	19
Georgia	975	23	226	6	Oklahoma	1,501	4	234	4
Hawaii	957	24	221	7	Oregon	567	50	168	30
Idaho	538	51	157	36	Pennsylvania	804	36	156	37
Illinois	881	28	171	27	Rhode Island	1,233	7	182	21
Indiana	840	33	182	21	South Carolina	1,134	13	196	15
Iowa	779	40	147	45	South Dakota	789	38	118	50
Kansas	1,213	8	174	25	Tennessee	1,008	20	212	10
Kentucky	916	27	171	27	Texas[6]	1,661	3	228	5
Louisiana	1,742	2	242	2	Utah	580	49	145	46
Maine	741	42	149	43	Vermont	782	39	154	39
Maryland	837	34	160	34	Virginia	843	32	158	35
Massachusetts	1,150	11	206	14	Washington	648	47	173	26
Michigan	802	37	207	12	West Virginia	771	41	176	24
Minnesota	1,140	12	149	43	Wisconsin	631	48	130	49
Mississippi	1,314	5	244	1	Wyoming	821	35	156	37
Missouri	1,091	16	182	21	**United States**	**$1,034**		**$187**	

[1]See previous chart for state funds and residual markets included. [2]Based on the HO-3 homeowner package policy for owner-occupied dwellings, one- to four-family units. Provides all risks coverage (except those specifically excluded in the policy) on buildings and broad named-peril coverage on personal property and is the most common package written. [3]Ranked from highest to lowest. States with the same premium receive the same rank. [4]Based on the HO-4 renters insurance policy for tenants. Includes broad named-peril coverage for the personal property of tenants. [5]Data provided by the California Department of Insurance. [6]The Texas Department of Insurance developed home insurance policy forms that are similar but not identical to the standard forms. In addition, due to the Texas Windstorm Association (which writes wind-only policies) classifying HO-1, 2 and 5 premiums as HO-3, the average premium for homeowners insurance is artificially high.

Note: Average premium=Premiums/exposure per house years. A house year is equal to 365 days of insured coverage for a single dwelling. The NAIC does not rank state average expenditures and does not endorse any conclusions drawn from this data.

Source: ©2015 National Association of Insurance Commissioners (NAIC). Reprinted with permission. Further reprint or distribution strictly prohibited without written permission of NAIC.

HOMEOWNERS INSURANCE INDUSTRY UNDERWRITING EXPENSES, 2014[1]

Expense	Percent of premiums
LOSSES AND RELATED EXPENSES[2]	
Loss and loss adjustment expense (LAE) ratio	**62.1%**
Incurred losses	53.0
Defense and cost containment expenses incurred	1.6
Adjusting and other expenses incurred	7.4
OPERATING EXPENSES[3]	
Expense ratio	**29.0%**
Net commissions and brokerage expenses incurred	12.7
Taxes, licenses and fees	2.6
Other acquisition and field supervision expenses incurred	8.5
General expenses incurred	5.2
DIVIDENDS TO POLICYHOLDERS[2]	**0.5%**
COMBINED RATIO AFTER DIVIDENDS[4]	**91.6%**

[1]After reinsurance transactions.
[2]As a percent of net premiums earned ($75.3 billion in 2014).
[3]As a percent of net premiums written ($77.9 billion in 2014).
[4]Sum of loss and LAE, expense and dividends ratios.

Source: SNL Financial LC.

Claims

- In 2013, 4.8 percent of insured homes experienced a claim.

- Homeowners insurance losses, net of reinsurance, rose to $39.9 billion in 2014 from $35.5 billion in 2013, according to SNL Financial.

HOMEOWNERS INSURANCE LOSSES, 2009-2013[1]

	Total homeowner losses			Total homeowner losses	
Year	Claim frequency[2]	Claim severity[3]	Year	Claim frequency[2]	Claim severity[3]
2009	6.09	$8,411	2012	7.56	$8,801
2010	6.66	8,618	2013	4.81	10,271
2011	9.83	8,455	**Average**[4]	**7.02**	**$8,793**

[1]For homeowners multiple peril policies. Excludes tenants and condominium policies. Excludes Alaska and Texas.
[2]Claims per 100 house years (policies).
[3]Average amount paid per claim; based on accident year incurred losses, excluding loss adjustment expenses, i.e., indemnity costs per accident year incurred claims.
[4]Weighted average, 2009-2013.

Source: ISO, a Verisk Analytics company.

Causes of Homeowners Insurance Losses

In 2013, 4.8 percent of insured homes had a claim, according to ISO. Property damage, including theft, accounted for 97.0 percent of those claims. Changes in the percentage of each type of homeowners loss from one year to another are partially influenced by large fluctuations in the number and severity of weather-related events such as hurricanes and winter storms. There are two ways of looking at losses: by the average number of claims filed per 100 policies (frequency) and by the average amount paid for each claim (severity). The loss category "water damage and freezing" includes damage caused by mold, if covered.

HOMEOWNERS INSURANCE LOSSES BY CAUSE, 2009-2013[1]
(Percent of losses incurred)

Cause of loss	2009	2010	2011	2012	2013
Property damage[2]	**95.1%**	**95.2%**	**97.0%**	**97.1%**	**97.0%**
Fire and lightning	27.0	25.2	18.5	23.6	30.5
Wind and hail	32.1	35.8	46.3	49.0	29.9
Water damage and freezing	24.4	21.2	21.6	17.0	26.4
Theft	3.3	3.1	2.3	2.9	3.4
All other property damage[3]	8.2	9.9	8.3	4.6	6.8
Liability[4]	**4.9%**	**4.8%**	**3.0%**	**2.9%**	**3.0%**
Bodily injury and property damage	4.7	4.7	2.8	2.6	2.7
Medical payments and other	0.2	0.2	0.2	0.2	0.3
Credit card and other[5]	6	6	6	6	6
Total	**100.0%**	**100.0%**	**100.0%**	**100.0%**	**100.0%**

[1]For homeowners multiple peril policies. Excludes tenants and condominium owners policies. Excludes Alaska and Texas.
[2]First party, i.e., covers damage to policyholder's own property.
[3]Includes vandalism and malicious mischief.
[4]Payments to others for which policyholder is responsible.
[5]Includes coverage for unauthorized use of various cards, forgery, counterfeit money and losses not otherwise classified.
[6]Less than 0.1 percent.

Source: ISO, a Verisk Analytics company.

AVERAGE HOMEOWNERS LOSSES, 2009-2013[1]
(Weighted average, 2009-2013)

- In the five-year period, 2009-2013, 7.0 percent of insured homes had a claim. Wind and hail accounted for the largest share of claims, with 3.2 percent of insured homes having such a loss.

Cause of loss	Claim frequency[2]	Claim severity[3]
Property damage[4]	**6.87**	**$8,668**
Fire and lightning	0.40	37,153
Wind and hail	3.20	7,741
Water damage and freezing	1.79	7,479
Theft	0.50	3,620
All other[5]	0.98	4,757
Liability[6]	**0.16**	**$14,412**
Bodily injury and property damage	0.11	19,466
Medical payments and other	0.05	2,560
Credit card and other[7]	[8]	**$592**
Average (property damage and liability), 2009-2013	**7.02**	**$8,793**

[1]For homeowners multiple peril policies. Excludes tenants and condominium owners policies. Excludes Alaska and Texas.
[2]Claims per 100 house years (policies).
[3]Accident year incurred losses, excluding loss adjustment expenses, i.e., indemnity costs per accident year incurred claims.
[4]First-party, i.e., covers damage to policyholder's own property.
[5]Includes vandalism and malicious mischief.
[6]Payments to others for which policyholder is responsible. [7]Includes coverage for unauthorized use of various cards, forgery, counterfeit money and losses not otherwise classified.
[8]Less than 0.01.

Source: Source: ISO, a Verisk Analytics company.

HOMEOWNERS INSURANCE CLAIMS FREQUENCY*

- Homeowners claims related to wind or hail are the most frequent; the costliest are related to fire and lightning.

- About one in 15 insured homes has a claim each year.

- About one in 30 insured homes has a property damage claim related to wind or hail each year.

- About one in 55 insured homes has a property damage claim caused by water damage or freezing each year.

- About one in 200 insured homes has a property damage claim due to theft each year.

- About one in 250 insured homes has a property damage claim related to fire and lightning.

- About one in 900 homeowners policies has a liability claim related to the cost of lawsuits for bodily injury or property damage that the policyholder or family members cause to others.

*Insurance Information Institute calculations, based on ISO, a Verisk Analytics company, data for homeowners insurance claims from 2009-2013 (see table above).

Lightning

In 2014 the number of direct lightning fatalities rose to 26 from a record low of 23 in 2013, but were 10 fewer than the 10-year average of 33 fatalities, according to the National Oceanic and Atmospheric Administration.

HOMEOWNERS INSURANCE CLAIMS AND PAYOUTS FOR LIGHTNING LOSSES, 2010-2014

	2010	2011	2012	2013	2014	Percent change 2013-2014	Percent change 2010-2014
Number of paid claims	213,278	186,307	151,000	114,740	99,871	-13.0%	-53.2%
Insured losses ($ millions)	$1,033.5	$952.5	$969.0	$673.5	$739.0	9.7	-28.5
Average cost per claim	$4,846	$5,112	$6,400	$5,869	$7,400	26.1	52.7

Source: Insurance Information Institute, State Farm®.

TOP 10 STATES FOR HOMEOWNERS INSURANCE LIGHTNING LOSSES BY NUMBER OF CLAIMS, 2014

Rank	State	Number of paid claims	Insured losses ($ millions)	Average cost per claim
1	Florida	10,440	$73.9	$7,075
2	Georgia	9,805	62.2	6,341
3	Texas	5,622	60.0	10,671
4	Louisiana	5,007	25.1	5,009
5	North Carolina	4,886	28.8	5,891
6	Alabama	4,853	39.2	8,079
7	Illinois	4,049	25.7	6,348
8	Pennsylvania	3,960	21.7	5,491
9	Tennessee	3,638	31.2	8,583
10	Indiana	3,262	22.3	6,832

Source: Insurance Information Institute, State Farm®.

- As of October 2015, 79 insurance companies participated in the Write Your Own program, started in 1983, in which insurers issue policies and adjust flood claims on behalf of the federal government under their own names.

- As of August 2015, 67 percent of policies covered single family homes, 21 percent covered condominiums, and 6 percent covered businesses and other non-residential properties. Two- to four-family units and other residential policies accounted for the remainder.

- Superstorm Sandy, which occurred in October 2012, resulted in $8.0 billion in NFIP payouts as of October 2015, second only to 2005's Hurricane Katrina with $16.3 billion in payouts.

National Flood Insurance Program

Flood damage is excluded under standard homeowners and renters insurance policies. However, flood coverage is available in the form of a separate policy both from the National Flood Insurance Program (NFIP) and from a few private insurers.

Congress created the NFIP in 1968 in response to the rising cost of taxpayer-funded disaster relief for flood victims and the increasing amount of damage caused by floods. The NFIP makes federally backed flood insurance available in communities that agree to adopt and enforce floodplain management ordinances to reduce future flood damage. The NFIP is self-supporting for the average historical loss year. This means that unless there is a widespread disaster, operating expenses and flood insurance claims are financed through premiums collected.

The NFIP provides coverage for up to $250,000 for the structure of the home and up to $100,000 for personal possessions. Private flood insurance is available for those who need additional insurance protection, known as excess coverage, over and above the basic policy or for people whose communities do not participate in the NFIP. Some insurers have introduced special policies for high-value properties. These policies may cover homes in noncoastal areas and/or provide enhancements to traditional flood coverage. The comprehensive portion of an auto insurance policy includes coverage for flood damage.

A 2015 poll by the Insurance Information Institute found that 14 percent of American homeowners had a flood insurance policy. This percentage has been at about the same level every year since 2009. The percentage of homeowners with flood insurance was highest in the South, at 21 percent, compared with 20 percent in 2014. Eleven percent of homeowners in the Northeast had a flood insurance policy, which is unchanged from 2014. Nine percent of homeowners in the West had a flood insurance policy, compared with 8 percent in 2014, while 10 percent of homeowners in the Midwest had flood insurance, compared with 7 percent in 2014.

Flood Insurance Losses

National Flood Insurance Program (NFIP) payouts vary widely from year to year. Flood loss payments totaled $351 million in 2014, lower than the 2013 losses of $489 million and down significantly from $9.1 billion in 2012, the year of superstorm Sandy. In 2005 loss payments totaled $17.8 billion, the highest amount on record, including losses from Hurricanes Katrina, Rita and Wilma. See page 151 for information on flood insurance losses.

The widespread flooding associated with Hurricane Katrina in 2005 set in motion a debate about how to improve the NFIP. The Biggert-Waters Flood Insurance Reform Act of 2012 sought to make the federal flood insurance program more financially self-sufficient in part by eliminating rate subsidies. In response to complaints that the law was making flood insurance unaffordable, in March 2014 Congress repealed and modified the law, rescinding many of the rate increases.

- There were 129,360 NFIP claims from superstorm Sandy as of October 2015. The average paid loss was $61,809, compared with 167,970 claims from Katrina, with an average paid loss of $97,140.

- In 2014 the average amount of flood coverage was $241,736, and the average premium was $665.

- The average flood claim in 2014 was $29,033, down from $60,488 in 2012, the year of superstorm Sandy.

- NFIP earned premiums rose slightly to $3.56 billion in 2014 from $3.51 billion in 2013.

- As of the end of October the federal government had declared 26 major flood disasters in 2015, compared with 31 in all of 2014.

NATIONAL FLOOD INSURANCE PROGRAM, 1980-2014

Year	Policies in force at year-end	Losses paid	
		Number	Amount ($000)
1980	2,103,851	41,918	$230,414
1985	2,016,785	38,676	368,239
1990	2,477,861	14,766	167,897
1995	3,476,829	62,441	1,295,578
2000	4,369,087	16,362	251,721
2005	4,962,011	213,515	17,768,904
2007	5,655,919	23,183	614,007
2008	5,684,275	74,852	3,487,554
2009	5,700,235	31,027	780,115
2010	5,645,436	29,152	774,689
2011	5,646,144	78,057	2,427,308
2012	5,620,017	149,808	9,061,580
2013	5,568,642	18,046	488,815
2014	5,350,887	12,105	351,446

Source: U.S. Department of Homeland Security, Federal Emergency Management Agency.

FLOOD INSURANCE IN THE UNITED STATES, 2014[1]

State	Direct NFIP business		WYO business		Total NFIP/WYO	
	Number of policies	Insurance in force[2] ($ millions)	Number of policies	Insurance in force[2] ($ millions)	Number of policies	Insurance in force[2] ($ millions)
Alabama	10,964	$2,185.3	45,429	$10,410.0	56,393	$12,595.3
Alaska	794	171.7	2,220	580.8	3,014	752.5
Arizona	6,650	1,505.2	29,639	7,046.0	36,289	8,551.2
Arkansas	3,730	550.6	16,251	2,652.0	19,981	3,202.6
California	39,609	10,149.8	194,699	53,352.4	234,308	63,502.3
Colorado	4,757	1,106.0	18,887	4,743.2	23,644	5,849.3
Connecticut	2,913	649.7	38,941	9,825.6	41,854	10,475.3
Delaware	5,012	1,308.6	20,023	5,394.9	25,035	6,703.6
D.C.	97	25.9	2,338	438.6	2,435	464.5
Florida	163,567	41,853.7	1,783,937	425,872.4	1,947,504	467,726.1
Georgia	18,494	4,457.0	74,251	18,913.4	92,745	23,370.4
Hawaii	2,540	563.5	58,116	12,651.4	60,656	13,214.9
Idaho	1,204	271.0	5,365	1,241.0	6,569	1,512.0
Illinois	12,859	2,204.2	34,246	6,706.7	47,105	8,910.9
Indiana	6,797	1,055.4	21,179	4,026.3	27,976	5,081.7
Iowa	3,065	465.3	12,576	2,422.6	15,641	2,887.9
Kansas	2,879	444.0	9,221	1,631.7	12,100	2,075.8
Kentucky	3,912	548.3	19,572	3,137.6	23,484	3,685.9
Louisiana	127,531	30,062.3	345,011	83,712.7	472,542	113,775.0
Maine	699	139.2	8,479	1,942.2	9,178	2,081.4
Maryland	7,583	1,803.6	64,702	14,569.0	72,285	16,372.6
Massachusetts	5,646	1,242.3	53,505	14,429.4	59,151	15,671.7
Michigan	4,897	727.1	19,726	3,638.3	24,623	4,365.4
Minnesota	2,145	452.9	9,845	2,179.8	11,990	2,632.7
Mississippi	16,514	3,764.6	54,121	12,456.4	70,635	16,220.9
Missouri	4,681	730.7	19,850	3,582.0	24,531	4,312.7
Montana	1,044	199.4	5,070	1,004.2	6,114	1,203.6
Nebraska	2,642	386.6	9,277	1,687.8	11,919	2,074.4
Nevada	2,433	546.8	10,885	2,793.4	13,318	3,340.1

(table continues)

FLOOD INSURANCE IN THE UNITED STATES, 2014[1] (Cont'd)

State	Direct NFIP business		WYO business		Total NFIP/WYO	
	Number of policies	Insurance in force[2] ($ millions)	Number of policies	Insurance in force[2] ($ millions)	Number of policies	Insurance in force[2] ($ millions)
New Hampshire	683	$139.2	8,356	$1,801.3	9,039	$1,940.5
New Jersey	22,333	4,319.5	215,025	53,344.0	237,358	57,663.5
New Mexico	2,602	464.7	12,645	2,492.2	15,247	2,957.0
New York	26,773	5,642.4	162,099	45,052.0	188,872	50,694.4
North Carolina	16,024	3,910.3	119,487	28,737.5	135,511	32,647.8
North Dakota	2,168	552.7	10,110	2,608.1	12,278	3,160.8
Ohio	8,127	1,155.8	31,911	5,732.7	40,038	6,888.4
Oklahoma	3,782	662.5	12,740	2,484.4	16,522	3,146.9
Oregon	6,966	1,587.7	25,055	5,945.1	32,021	7,532.8
Pennsylvania	10,786	1,712.2	58,476	11,797.8	69,262	13,509.9
Rhode Island	612	145.7	14,884	3,896.9	15,496	4,042.6
South Carolina	25,622	6,893.4	164,848	44,629.5	190,470	51,522.9
South Dakota	1,037	211.6	4,212	938.6	5,249	1,150.2
Tennessee	5,920	1,328.3	25,356	5,930.4	31,276	7,258.7
Texas	111,070	29,459.2	489,540	127,863.4	600,610	157,322.6
Utah	718	158.8	3,525	867.2	4,243	1,026.1
Vermont	378	65.8	3,937	854.3	4,315	920.1
Virginia	19,040	4,657.3	93,116	23,382.9	112,156	28,040.2
Washington	6,669	1,457.0	35,941	8,716.2	42,610	10,173.2
West Virginia	5,120	575.0	14,315	2,059.6	19,435	2,634.6
Wisconsin	2,276	359.2	13,107	2,461.1	15,383	2,820.4
Wyoming	464	101.0	1,839	430.6	2,303	531.7
Amer. Samoa	1	0.0	0	0.0	1	0.0
Guam	168	31.0	68	15.5	236	46.5
N Mariana Islands	5	0.4	2	1.0	7	1.4
Puerto Rico	145	16.5	13,464	1,856.2	13,609	1,872.7
Virgin Islands	295	55.1	1,417	266.1	1,712	321.2
United States	**745,442**	**$175,233.2**	**4,522,836**	**$1,097,206.2**	**5,268,278**	**$1,272,439.4**

[1]Direct and WYO business may not add to total due to rounding.
[2]Total limits of liability for all policies in force.

Source: U.S. Department of Homeland Security, Federal Emergency Management Agency.

Earthquake Insurance

Standard homeowners, renters and business insurance policies do not cover damage from earthquakes. Coverage is available either in the form of an endorsement or as a separate policy. Earthquake insurance provides protection from the shaking and cracking that can destroy buildings and personal possessions. Coverage for other kinds of damage that may result from earthquakes, such as fire and water damage due to burst gas and water pipes, is provided by standard home and business insurance policies. Earthquake coverage is available mostly from private insurance companies. In California homeowners can also get coverage from the California Earthquake Authority (CEA), a privately funded, publicly managed organization. Only about 10 percent of California residents currently have earthquake coverage, down from about 30 percent in 1996, two years after the Northridge, California, earthquake.

Ten percent of homeowners responding to a 2015 poll by the Insurance Information Institute said they have earthquake insurance. Eighteen percent of homeowners in the West were most likely to buy earthquake coverage; followed by the Northeast at 9 percent; the Midwest at 8 percent; and the South at 7 percent. See page 155 for information on earthquake insurance losses.

EARTHQUAKE INSURANCE, 2005-2014
($000)

Year	Net premiums written[1]	Annual percent change	Combined ratio[2]	Annual point change[3]
2005	$1,106,671	0.7%	50.9	2.3 pts.
2006	1,315,423	18.9	40.4	-10.5
2007	1,246,538	-5.2	30.0	-10.4
2008	1,259,872	1.1	33.5	3.5
2009	1,288,353	2.3	36.3	2.8
2010	1,443,598	12.0	41.4	5.1
2011	1,467,372	1.6	55.8	14.4
2012	1,593,451	8.6	36.3	-19.5
2013	1,586,985	-0.4	30.3	-6.0
2014	1,641,847	3.5	34.1	3.8

[1]After reinsurance transactions, excludes state funds
[2]After dividends to policyholders. A drop in the combined ratio represents an improvement; an increase represents a deterioration.
[3]Calculated from unrounded data.

Source: SNL Financial LC.

Leading Writers of Earthquake Insurance

The California Earthquake Authority (CEA), a publicly managed, largely privately funded organization that sells its policies through participating private insurance companies, was the leading writer of earthquake insurance in the United States, based on direct premiums written in 2014, according to data from SNL Financial. The CEA had $607 million in direct premiums written in 2014, all of which covered residential California properties. It accounted for 20.8 percent of the total U.S. earthquake insurance market in 2014. The nine other largest earthquake insurers in 2014 were all private insurance companies.

TOP 10 WRITERS OF EARTHQUAKE INSURANCE BY DIRECT PREMIUMS WRITTEN, 2014
($000)

Rank	Group/company	Direct premiums written[1]	Market share[2]
1	California Earthquake Authority	$606,977	20.8%
2	Zurich Insurance Group[3]	232,700	8.0
3	State Farm Mutual Automobile Insurance	228,547	7.8
4	American International Group (AIG)	148,390	5.1
5	Travelers Companies Inc.	140,077	4.8
6	GeoVera Insurance Holdings Ltd.	117,634	4.0
7	Liberty Mutual	90,195	3.1
8	ACE Ltd.	87,253	3.0
9	Swiss Re Ltd.	72,589	2.5
10	Chubb Corp.	62,542	2.1

[1]Before reinsurance transactions, includes state funds.
[2]Based on U.S. total, includes territories.
[3]Data for Farmers Group and Zurich Financial Group (which owns Farmers' management company) are reported separately by SNL Financial.

Source: SNL Financial LC.

Property/Casualty Insurance by Line

The commercial lines sector of the property/casualty insurance industry generally provides insurance products for businesses as opposed to the personal lines sector, which offers products for individuals. However, the division between commercial and personal coverages is not precise. For example, inland marine insurance, which is included in the commercial lines sector, may cover some personal property such as expensive jewelry and fine art.

Leading Companies

TOP 10 WRITERS OF COMMERCIAL LINES INSURANCE BY DIRECT PREMIUMS WRITTEN, 2014
($000)

Rank	Group/company	Direct premiums written[1]	Market share[2]
1	American International Group (AIG)	$17,116,239	6.0%
2	Travelers Companies Inc.	16,164,807	5.7
3	Liberty Mutual	14,047,958	5.0
4	Zurich Insurance Group[3]	10,961,490	3.9
5	ACE Ltd.	8,892,619	3.1
6	CNA Financial Corp.	8,633,944	3.0
7	Nationwide Mutual Group	7,978,557	2.8
8	Chubb Corp.	7,475,185	2.6
9	Hartford Financial Services	7,265,273	2.6
10	Berkshire Hathaway Inc.	5,990,165	2.1

[1]Before reinsurance transactions, includes state funds. [2]Based on U.S. total, includes territories. [3]Data for Farmers Insurance Group of Companies and Zurich Financial Group (which owns Farmers' management company) are reported separately by SNL Financial.

Source: SNL Financial LC.

TOP 10 COMMERCIAL INSURANCE BROKERS OF U.S. BUSINESS BY REVENUES, 2014[1]
($ millions)

Rank	Company	Brokerage revenues
1	Marsh & McLennan Cos. Inc.[2]	$5,835
2	Aon P.L.C.	5,811
3	Arthur J. Gallagher & Co.[2]	2,400
4	Willis Group Holdings P.L.C.[2]	1,733
5	BB&T Insurance Holdings Inc.[2]	1,714
6	Brown & Brown Inc.[2]	1,567
7	Wells Fargo Insurance Services USA Inc.	1,299
8	USI Holdings Corp.[2]	913
9	Lockton Cos. L.L.C.[3]	911
10	Hub International Ltd.[2]	907

[1]Companies that derive less than 50 percent of revenues from commercial retail brokerage or employee benefits are not ranked. [2]Reported U.S. acquisitions in 2014. [3]Fiscal year ending April 30.

Source: Business Insurance, July 20, 2015.

Workers Compensation Insurance and Excess Workers Compensation

Workers compensation insurance provides for the cost of medical care and rehabilitation for injured workers and lost wages and death benefits for the dependents of persons killed in work-related accidents. Workers compensation systems vary from state to state. Workers compensation combined ratios are expressed in two ways. Calendar year results reflect claim payments and changes in reserves for accidents that happened in that year or earlier. Accident year results only include losses from a particular year. Excess workers compensation, a coverage geared to employers that self-insure for workers compensation, comes into play when claims exceed a designated dollar amount.

WORKERS COMPENSATION INSURANCE, 2005-2014
($000)

| Year | Net premiums written[2] | Annual percent change | Combined ratio[1] | | | |
			Calendar year[3]	Annual point change[4]	Accident year[5]	Annual point change
2005	$38,981,699	6.1%	102.1	-4.8 pts.	87	-1 pts.
2006	41,820,419	7.3	95.4	-6.7	86	-1
2007	40,610,991	-2.9	101.7	6.3	99	13
2008	36,939,016	-9.0	101.5	-0.2	106	7
2009	32,247,870	-12.7	107.9	6.4	110	4
2010	31,643,087	-1.9	116.1	8.2	118	8
2011	35,664,230	12.7	117.6	1.5	113	-5
2012	38,747,594	8.6	110.4	-7.3	106	-7
2013	40,921,639	5.6	103.0	-7.4	99	-7
2014	43,546,737	6.4	102.4	-0.6	95[6]	-4

[1]After dividends to policyholders. A drop in the combined ratio represents an improvement; an increase represents a deterioration. [2]After reinsurance transactions, excludes state funds. [3]Calendar year data are from SNL Financial. [4]Calculated from unrounded data. [5]Accident year data are from the National Council on Compensation Insurance (NCCI) and exclude state funds. [6]Estimated by NCCI. Source: SNL Financial LC; ©National Council on Compensation Insurance.

EXCESS WORKERS COMPENSATION INSURANCE, 2008-2014
($000)

Year	Net premiums written[1]	Annual percent change	Combined ratio[2]	Annual point change[3]
2008	$926,487	NA	148.3	NA
2009	941,117	1.6%	34.8	-113.5 pts.
2010	799,733	-15.0	50.9	16.0
2011	816,435	2.1	134.7	83.8
2012	815,770	-0.1	153.6	18.9
2013	844,098	3.5	69.3	-84.3
2014	920,223	9.0	112.3	43.0

[1]After reinsurance transactions, excludes state funds. [2]After dividends to policyholders. A drop in the combined ratio represents an improvement; an increase represents a deterioration. [3]Calculated from unrounded data. NA=Data not available. Source: SNL Financial LC.

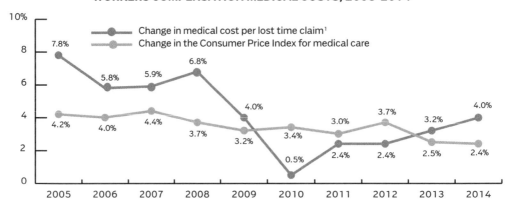

WORKERS COMPENSATION MEDICAL COSTS, 2005-2014

Legend:
- Change in medical cost per lost time claim[1]
- Change in the Consumer Price Index for medical care

Change in medical cost per lost time claim values by year: 7.8% (2005), 5.8% (2006), 5.9% (2007), 6.8% (2008), 4.0% (2009), 0.5% (2010), 2.4% (2011), 2.4% (2012), 3.2% (2013), 4.0% (2014)

Change in the Consumer Price Index for medical care values: 4.2% (2005), 4.0% (2006), 4.4% (2007), 3.7% (2008), 3.2% (2009), 3.4% (2010), 3.0% (2011), 3.7% (2012), 2.5% (2013), 2.4% (2014)

[1]Based on states where the National Council on Compensation Insurance provides ratemaking services. Represents costs for injuries that resulted in time off from work. Data for 2014 are preliminary.

Source: U.S. Bureau of Labor Statistics; ©National Council on Compensation Insurance.

WORKERS COMPENSATION BENEFITS, COVERAGE AND COSTS, 2012-2013

	2012	2013	Percent change
Covered workers (000)	127,904	129,602	1.3%
Covered wages ($ billions)	$6,309	$6,458	2.4
Workers compensation benefits paid ($ billions)	63.0	63.6	1.0
Medical benefits	31.5	31.5	[1]
Cash benefits	31.0	32.0	3.2
Employer costs for workers compensation ($ billions)	83.2	88.5	6.4

[1]Less than 0.1 percent.

Source: *Workers Compensation: Benefits, Coverage, and Costs, 2013*, National Academy of Social Insurance.

Liability Insurance

Commercial coverage known as other liability protects the policyholder from legal liability arising from negligence, carelessness or a failure to act that causes property damage or personal injury to others. It encompasses a wide variety of coverages including errors and omissions, umbrella liability and liquor liability. It excludes product liability, which is a separate line of insurance. Product liability protects the manufacturer, distributor or seller of a product from legal liability resulting from a defective condition that caused personal injury or damage associated with the use of the product.

OTHER LIABILITY INSURANCE, 2005-2014
($000)

Year	Net premiums written[1]	Annual percent change	Combined ratio[2]	Annual point change[3]	Year	Net premiums written[1]	Annual percent change	Combined ratio[2]	Annual point change[3]
2005	$39,266,103	-1.0%	110.5	-3.6 pts.	2010	$35,802,772	-1.1%	108.1	2.6 pts.
2006	42,229,148	7.5	94.8	-15.8	2011	36,511,575	2.0	96.1	-12.0
2007	40,997,132	-2.9	99.2	4.4	2012	38,307,679	4.9	103.2	7.0
2008	38,602,734	-5.8	93.8	-5.4	2013	42,053,358	9.8	96.8	-6.4
2009	36,184,065	-6.3	105.5	11.7	2014	44,181,272	5.1	94.8	-2.0

[1]After reinsurance transactions, excludes state funds. [2]After dividends to policyholders. A drop in the combined ratio represents an improvement; an increase represents a deterioration. [3]Calculated from unrounded data.

Source: SNL Financial LC.

PRODUCT LIABILITY INSURANCE, 2005-2014
($000)

Year	Net premiums written[1]	Annual percent change	Combined ratio[2]	Annual point change[3]
2005	$3,546,009	4.2%	131.1	-21.3 pts.
2006	3,621,671	2.1	77.8	-53.3
2007	3,265,035	-9.8	99.8	22.0
2008	2,777,587	-14.9	124.0	24.2
2009	2,365,681	-14.8	124.0	[4]
2010	2,050,619	-13.3	157.1	33.1
2011	2,320,540	13.2	160.0	2.9
2012	2,575,225	11.0	102.7	-57.3
2013	2,718,879	5.6	155.3	52.6
2014	2,674,183	-1.6	138.5	-16.8

[1]After reinsurance transactions, excludes state funds. [2]After dividends to policyholders. A drop in the combined ratio represents an improvement; an increase represents a deterioration. [3]Calculated from unrounded data. [4]Less than 0.1 point.

Source: SNL Financial LC.

Commercial and Farmowners Multiple Peril Insurance

Commercial multiple peril insurance is a package policy that includes property, boiler and machinery, crime and general liability coverages. Farmowners multiple peril insurance, similar to homeowners insurance, provides coverage to farmowners and ranchowners against a number of named perils and liabilities. It covers a dwelling and its contents, as well as barns, stables and other structures.

COMMERCIAL MULTIPLE PERIL INSURANCE, 2005-2014

	Total ($000)				
Year	Net premiums written[1]	Annual percent change	Year	Net premiums written[1]	Annual percent change
2005	$29,577,004	1.9%	2010	$28,913,516	[2]
2006	31,856,902	7.7	2011	29,995,201	3.7%
2007	31,261,039	-1.9	2012	31,502,689	5.0
2008	30,306,109	-3.1	2013	33,244,677	5.5
2009	28,926,363	-4.6	2014	34,375,128	3.4

	Nonliability portion ($000)								
Year	Net premiums written[1]	Annual percent change	Combined ratio[3]	Annual point change[4]	Year	Net premiums written[1]	Annual percent change	Combined ratio[3]	Annual point change[4]
2005	$17,672,953	4.3%	95.3	-2.9 pts.	2010	$18,210,612	1.6%	102.9	4.5 pts.
2006	18,250,773	3.3	83.9	-11.5	2011	18,657,799	2.5	119.1	16.2
2007	18,334,139	0.5	89.6	5.7	2012	19,513,568	4.6	113.9	-5.1
2008	18,235,095	-0.5	107.7	18.1	2013	21,058,405	7.9	93.3	-20.6
2009	17,927,074	-1.7	98.3	-9.4	2014	21,986,370	4.4	96.9	3.6

	Liability portion ($000)								
Year	Net premiums written[1]	Annual percent change	Combined ratio[3]	Annual point change[4]	Year	Net premiums written[1]	Annual percent change	Combined ratio[3]	Annual point change[4]
2005	$11,904,051	-1.4%	102.9	-2.7 pts.	2010	$10,702,904	-2.7%	96.0	1.8 pts.
2006	13,606,129	14.3	104.0	1.1	2011	11,337,402	5.9	101.8	5.8
2007	12,926,900	-5.0	95.4	-8.6	2012	11,989,121	5.7	94.1	-7.7
2008	12,071,014	-6.6	97.5	2.1	2013	12,186,272	1.6	103.8	9.7
2009	10,999,289	-8.9	94.2	-3.2	2014	12,388,758	1.7	103.6	-0.2

[1]After reinsurance transactions, excludes state funds. [2]Less than 0.1 percent. [3]After dividends to policyholders. A drop in the combined ratio represents an improvement; an increase represents a deterioration. [4]Calculated from unrounded data.

Source: SNL Financial LC.

FARMOWNERS MULTIPLE PERIL INSURANCE, 2005-2014
($000)

Year	Net premiums written[1]	Annual percent change	Combined ratio[2]	Annual point change[3]
2005	$2,258,489	6.6%	95.2	3.1 pts.
2006	2,300,728	1.9	123.2	28.0
2007	2,413,562	4.9	98.1	-25.0
2008	2,586,861	7.2	119.5	21.3
2009	2,612,262	1.0	107.9	-11.6
2010	2,754,955	5.5	108.2	0.3
2011	2,932,576	6.4	117.4	9.2
2012	3,277,423	11.8	99.5	-17.9
2013	3,511,651	7.1	93.9	-5.6
2014	3,628,084	3.3	94.7	0.7

[1]After reinsurance transactions, excludes state funds. [2]After dividends to policyholders. A drop in the combined ratio represents an improvement; an increase represents a deterioration. [3]Calculated from unrounded data.

Source: SNL Financial LC.

Medical Malpractice Insurance

Medical malpractice insurance covers facilities, doctors and other professionals in the medical field for liability claims arising from the treatment of patients.

MEDICAL MALPRACTICE INSURANCE, 2005-2014
($000)

Year	Net premiums written[1]	Annual percent change	Combined ratio[2]	Annual point change[3]
2005	$8,619,612	-5.5%	95.3	-13.7 pts.
2006	10,378,325	20.4	90.6	-4.7
2007	9,958,513	-4.0	84.7	-5.9
2008	9,521,113	-4.4	79.2	-5.5
2009	9,206,794	-3.3	85.5	6.3
2010	9,096,345	-1.2	88.9	3.4
2011	8,833,365	-2.9	88.0	-1.0
2012	8,713,595	-1.4	93.1	5.2
2013	8,530,659	-2.1	89.4	-3.7
2014	8,475,474	-0.6	106.0	16.6

[1]After reinsurance transactions, excludes state funds. [2]After dividends to policyholders. A drop in the combined ratio represents an improvement; an increase represents a deterioration. [3]Calculated from unrounded data.

Source: SNL Financial LC.

Fire and Allied Lines Insurance

Fire insurance provides coverage against losses caused by fire and lightning. It is usually sold as part of a package policy such as commercial multiple peril. Allied lines insurance includes property insurance that is usually bought in conjunction with a fire insurance policy. Allied lines includes coverage for wind and water damage and vandalism.

FIRE INSURANCE, 2005-2014
($000)

Year	Net premiums written[1]	Annual percent change	Combined ratio[2]	Annual point change[3]
2005	$7,934,584	-1.1%	83.3	10.1 pts.
2006	9,365,050	18.0	78.0	-5.3
2007	9,664,054	3.2	85.6	7.6
2008	9,906,059	2.5	92.3	6.7
2009	10,109,161	2.1	78.6	-13.7
2010	10,199,101	0.9	80.2	1.7
2011	10,317,968	1.2	94.1	13.9
2012	10,795,612	4.6	87.4	-6.7
2013	11,229,431	4.0	79.1	-8.3
2014	11,500,360	2.4	84.8	5.7

[1]After reinsurance transactions, excludes state funds. [2]After dividends to policyholders. A drop in the combined ratio represents an improvement; an increase represents a deterioration. [3]Calculated from unrounded data.

Source: SNL Financial LC.

ALLIED LINES INSURANCE, 2005-2014
($000)

Year	Net premiums written[1]	Annual percent change	Combined ratio[2]	Annual point change[3]
2005	$5,944,151	-0.6%	153.1	33.1 pts.
2006	6,593,122	10.9	94.6	-58.6
2007	6,889,750	4.5	53.5	-41.1
2008	7,691,004	11.6	128.1	74.6
2009	7,744,256	0.7	93.6	-34.5
2010	7,494,281	-3.2	98.9	5.3
2011	7,800,211	4.1	132.7	33.8
2012	8,161,346	4.6	138.0	5.3
2013	9,251,852	13.4	90.2	-47.7
2014	9,209,843	-0.5	90.0	-0.2

[1]After reinsurance transactions, excludes state funds. [2]After dividends to policyholders. A drop in the combined ratio represents an improvement; an increase represents a deterioration. [3]Calculated from unrounded data.

Source: SNL Financial LC.

Inland Marine and Ocean Marine Insurance

Inland marine insurance covers bridges and tunnels, goods in transit, movable equipment, unusual property and communications-related structures as well as expensive personal property. Ocean marine insurance provides coverage on all types of vessels, for property damage to the vessels and cargo, as well as associated liabilities.

INLAND MARINE INSURANCE, 2005-2014
($000)

Year	Net premiums written[1]	Annual percent change	Combined ratio[2]	Annual point change[3]
2005	$8,248,273	3.9%	90.4	6.1 pts.
2006	9,217,002	11.7	72.7	-17.7
2007	9,775,987	6.1	79.2	6.5
2008	9,408,463	-3.8	92.7	13.5
2009	8,686,660	-7.7	89.2	-3.5
2010	8,527,512	-1.8	86.0	-3.2
2011	8,768,829	2.8	97.6	11.6
2012	9,603,749	9.5	95.9	-1.7
2013	10,147,014	5.7	83.6	-12.4
2014	10,990,045	8.3	83.4	-0.2

[1]After reinsurance transactions, excludes state funds. [2]After dividends to policyholders. A drop in the combined ratio represents an improvement; an increase represents a deterioration. [3]Calculated from unrounded data.

Source: SNL Financial LC.

OCEAN MARINE INSURANCE, 2005-2014
($000)

Year	Net premiums written[1]	Annual percent change	Combined ratio[2]	Annual point change[3]
2005	$2,948,604	4.2%	114.5	19.0 pts.
2006	3,133,674	6.3	97.3	-17.2
2007	3,261,490	4.1	113.6	16.3
2008	3,098,438	-5.0	103.2	-10.5
2009	2,941,486	-5.1	91.8	-11.3
2010	2,740,956	-6.8	96.1	4.3
2011	2,760,853	0.7	100.9	4.8
2012	2,704,665	-2.0	109.1	8.2
2013	2,863,507	5.9	98.1	-11.0
2014	2,910,377	1.6	88.1	-10.0

[1]After reinsurance transactions, excludes state funds. [2]After dividends to policyholders. A drop in the combined ratio represents an improvement; an increase represents a deterioration. [3]Calculated from unrounded data.

Source: SNL Financial LC.

Surety and Fidelity

Surety bonds provide monetary compensation in the event that a policyholder fails to perform certain acts such as the proper fulfillment of a construction contract within a stated period. They are required for public projects in order to protect taxpayers. Fidelity bonds, which are usually purchased by an employer, protect against losses caused by employee fraud or dishonesty.

SURETY BONDS, 2005-2014
($000)

Year	Net premiums written[1]	Annual percent change	Combined ratio[2]	Annual point change[3]
2005	$3,817,496	0.4%	102.1	-18.5 pts.
2006	4,434,780	16.2	81.5	-20.6
2007	4,779,117	7.8	72.2	-9.3
2008	4,960,250	3.8	67.0	-5.2
2009	4,835,409	-2.5	79.5	12.6
2010	4,851,328	0.3	70.7	-8.8
2011	4,849,480	[4]	72.9	2.2
2012	4,695,782	-3.2	76.8	3.9
2013	4,868,847	3.7	72.7	-4.0
2014	5,000,382	2.7	70.6	-2.1

[1]After reinsurance transactions, excludes state funds. [2]After dividends to policyholders. A drop in the combined ratio represents an improvement; an increase represents a deterioration. [3]Calculated from unrounded data. [4]Less than 0.1 percent.

Source: SNL Financial LC.

FIDELITY BONDS, 2005-2014
($000)

Year	Net premiums written[1]	Annual percent change	Combined ratio[2]	Annual point change[3]
2005	$1,216,647	-7.1%	85.1	5.3 pts.
2006	1,240,822	2.0	87.2	2.1
2007	1,239,760	-0.1	76.5	-10.7
2008	1,140,617	-8.0	84.2	7.7
2009	1,098,372	-3.7	105.4	21.2
2010	1,082,534	-1.4	95.8	-9.6
2011	1,098,225	1.4	102.0	6.2
2012	1,096,406	-0.2	99.4	-2.6
2013	1,124,199	2.5	92.9	-6.5
2014	1,165,280	3.7	92.9	[4]

[1]After reinsurance transactions, excludes state funds. [2]After dividends to policyholders. A drop in the combined ratio represents an improvement; an increase represents a deterioration. [3]Calculated from unrounded data. [4]Less than 0.1 points.

Source: SNL Financial LC.

Mortgage Guaranty Insurance

Private mortgage insurance (PMI), also known as mortgage guaranty insurance, guarantees that in the event of a default, the insurer will pay the mortgage lender for any loss resulting from a property foreclosure, up to a specific amount. PMI, which is purchased by the borrower but protects the lender, is sometimes confused with mortgage life insurance, a life insurance product that pays off the mortgage if the borrower dies before the loan is repaid. Banks generally require PMI for all borrowers with down payments of less than 20 percent of the home price. The industry's combined ratio, a measure of profitability, deteriorated (i.e., rose) significantly in 2007 and 2008, reflecting the economic downturn and the subsequent rise in mortgage defaults, and remained at high levels through 2012. In 2014 the combined ratio fell to 70.2, the lowest level in the past 10 years.

MORTGAGE GUARANTY INSURANCE, 2005-2014
($000)

Year	Net premiums written[1]	Annual percent change	Combined ratio[2]	Annual point change[3]
2005	$4,454,711	3.0%	75.2	-0.4 pts.
2006	4,565,899	2.5	71.0	-4.2
2007	5,192,104	13.7	129.0	58.1
2008	5,371,878	3.5	219.8	90.8
2009	4,564,406	-15.0	201.9	-17.9
2010	4,248,798	-6.9	198.4	-3.6
2011	4,242,340	-0.2	219.0	20.7
2012	3,965,896	-6.5	189.7	-29.4
2013	4,329,947	9.2	98.0	-91.7
2014	4,180,006	-3.5	70.2	-27.7

[1]After reinsurance transactions, excludes state funds. [2]After dividends to policyholders. A drop in the combined ratio represents an improvement; an increase represents a deterioration. [3]Calculated from unrounded data.

Source: SNL Financial LC.

TOP 10 WRITERS OF MORTGAGE GUARANTY INSURANCE
BY DIRECT PREMIUMS WRITTEN, 2014
($000)

Rank	Group/company	Direct premiums written[1]	Market share[2]
1	MGIC Investment Corp.	$1,024,333	22.6%
2	Radian Group Inc.	982,062	21.6
3	American International Group (AIG)	956,821	21.1
4	Genworth Financial Inc.	638,633	14.1
5	PMI Group Inc.	286,341	6.3
6	Essent US Holdings Inc.	276,778	6.1
7	Old Republic International Corp.	226,931	5.0
8	Arch Capital Group Ltd.	111,667	2.5
9	NMI Holdings Inc.	34,029	0.8
10	ACE Ltd.	112	3

[1]Before reinsurance transactions.
[2]Based on U.S. total, includes territories.
[3]Less than 0.1 percent.

Source: SNL Financial LC.

Financial Guaranty Insurance

Financial guaranty insurance, also known as bond insurance, helps expand the financial markets by increasing borrower and lender leverage. Starting in the 1970s, surety bonds began to be used to guarantee the principal and interest payments on municipal obligations. This made the bonds more attractive to investors and at the same time benefited bond issuers because having the insurance lowered their borrowing costs. Initially, financial guaranty insurance was considered a special category of surety. It became a separate line of insurance in 1986.

Financial guaranty insurers are specialized, highly capitalized companies that traditionally had the highest rating. The insurer's high rating attaches to the bonds thus lowering the risk of the bonds to investors. With their credit rating thus enhanced, municipalities can issue bonds that pay a lower interest rate, enabling them to borrow more for the same outlay of funds. The combined ratio climbed to 421.4 in 2008 at the height of the economic downturn. In 2013 the combined ratio fell below zero as several companies reduced loss reserves by more than $2 billion combined as a result of strains created by the financial crisis. Over the years financial guaranty insurers have expanded their reach beyond municipal bonds and now insure a wide array of products, including mortgage-backed securities, pools of credit default swaps and other structured transactions.

FINANCIAL GUARANTY INSURANCE, 2005-2014[1]
($000)

Year	Net premiums written[2]	Annual percent change	Combined ratio[3]	Annual point change[4]
2005	$2,014,467	-5.6%	29.8	-14.5 pts.
2006	2,163,324	7.4	47.7	17.8
2007	3,038,889	40.5	152.4	104.8
2008	3,171,560	4.4	421.4	268.9
2009	1,793,410	-43.5	100.6	-320.7
2010	1,371,908	-23.5	228.4	127.8
2011	968,898	-29.4	219.0	-9.4
2012	692,541	-28.5	181.6	-37.4
2013	710,480	2.6	-3.4	-184.9
2014	488,482	-31.2	91.3	94.7

[1]Based on Insurance Expense Exhibit (IEE) data. Ambac did not file an IEE from 2005 to 2006; Financial Guaranty Insurance Co. did not file an IEE in 2012. Several companies in 2013 reduced loss reserves as a result of strains from the financial crisis, creating a negative combined ratio.
[2]After reinsurance transactions, excludes state funds.
[3]After dividends to policyholders. A drop in the combined ratio represents an improvement; an increase represents a deterioration.
[4]Calculated from unrounded data.

Source: SNL Financial LC.

TOP 10 WRITERS OF FINANCIAL GUARANTY INSURANCE
BY DIRECT PREMIUMS WRITTEN, 2014
($000)

Rank	Group/company	Direct premiums written[1]	Market share[2]
1	Assured Guaranty Ltd.	$269,619	50.7%
2	MBIA Inc.	116,031	21.8
3	Ambac Financial Group Inc.	69,613	13.1
4	Syncora Holdings Ltd.	27,579	5.2
5	Financial Guaranty Insurance Co.	17,330	3.3
6	Build America Mutual Assurance Co.	15,434	2.9
7	CIFG Assurance North America Inc.	10,073	1.9
8	Transamerica Casualty Insurance Co.	3,000	0.6
9	Berkshire Hathaway Inc.	2,034	0.4
10	Radian Group Inc.	915	0.2

[1]Before reinsurance transactions.
[2]Based on U.S. total, includes territories.

Source: SNL Financial LC.

Property/Casualty Insurance by Line

Burglary and Theft and Boiler and Machinery Insurance

Burglary and theft insurance covers the loss of property, money and securities due to burglary, robbery or larceny. Boiler and machinery insurance is also known as mechanical breakdown, equipment breakdown or systems breakdown coverage. Among the types of equipment covered by this insurance are heating, cooling, electrical, telephone/communications and computer equipment.

BURGLARY AND THEFT INSURANCE, 2005-2014
($000)

Year	Net premiums written[1]	Annual percent change	Combined ratio[2]	Annual point change[3]
2005	$120,170	-13.1%	63.6	-4.7 pts.
2006	143,132	19.1	64.3	0.7
2007	160,703	12.3	56.4	-7.9
2008	160,434	-0.2	48.2	-8.3
2009	152,197	-5.1	59.6	11.5
2010	167,152	9.8	69.4	9.8
2011	194,661	16.5	61.6	-7.8
2012	220,831	13.4	58.6	-3.0
2013	205,239	-7.1	42.0	-16.6
2014	226,247	10.2	60.3	18.3

[1]After reinsurance transactions, excludes state funds. [2]After dividends to policyholders. A drop in the combined ratio represents an improvement; an increase represents a deterioration. [3]Calculated from unrounded data.

Source: SNL Financial LC.

BOILER AND MACHINERY INSURANCE, 2005-2014
($000)

Year	Net premiums written[1]	Annual percent change	Combined ratio[2]	Annual point change[3]
2005	$1,582,964	0.7%	60.2	-6.9 pts.
2006	1,675,347	5.8	73.1	12.9
2007	1,741,099	3.9	73.1	[4]
2008	1,728,595	-0.7	87.7	14.6
2009	1,803,376	4.3	71.7	-16.1
2010	1,721,764	-4.5	71.5	-0.2
2011	1,810,941	5.2	75.0	3.5
2012	1,887,625	4.2	80.8	5.8
2013	1,979,514	4.9	72.2	-8.6
2014	1,998,967	1.0	76.6	4.4

[1]After reinsurance transactions, excludes state funds. [2]After dividends to policyholders. A drop in the combined ratio represents an improvement; an increase represents a deterioration. [3]Calculated from unrounded data. [4]Less than 0.1 point.

Source: SNL Financial LC.

Crop Insurance

There are two kinds of crop insurance: crop-hail, which is provided by the private market and covers just hail, fire and wind; and federally sponsored multiple peril crop insurance, which is sold and serviced by the private market but subsidized and reinsured by the federal government.

CROP-HAIL INSURANCE, 2005-2014
($000)

Year	Direct premiums written[1]	Annual percent change	Loss ratio[2]	Annual point change
2005	$434,711	1.7%	44	-14 pts.
2006	405,254	-6.8	50	6
2007	489,649	20.8	48	-2
2008	669,436	36.7	83	35
2009	621,322	-7.2	91	8
2010	682,188	9.8	67	-24
2011	843,801	23.7	116	49
2012	958,163	13.6	74	-42
2013	958,857	0.1	67	-7
2014	991,748	3.4	122	55

[1]Before reinsurance transactions, total for all policyholders of crop-hail insurance. [2]The percentage of each premium dollar spent on claims and associated costs. A drop in the loss ratio represents an improvement; an increase represents a deterioration.

Source: National Crop Insurance Services.

MULTIPLE PERIL CROP INSURANCE, 2005-2014[1]
($000)

Year	Net premiums written[2]	Annual percent change	Combined ratio[3]	Annual point change[4]
2005	$2,234,630	1.4%	91.3	15.2 pts.
2006	2,824,769	26.4	77.9	-13.3
2007	3,648,996	29.2	74.7	-3.2
2008	5,077,625	39.2	90.1	15.3
2009	3,964,690	-21.9	79.7	-10.4
2010	3,501,631	-11.7	73.9	-5.8
2011	5,456,991	55.8	90.6	16.8
2012	5,321,811	-2.5	104.0	13.3
2013	4,942,547	-7.1	103.3	-0.7
2014	4,189,765	-15.2	104.9	1.6

[1]Includes private crop-hail insurance from 2005 to 2013. Data for 2014 excludes private crop-hail insurance. [2]After reinsurance transactions, excludes state funds. [3]After dividends to policyholders. A drop in the combined ratio represents an improvement; an increase represents a deterioration. [4]Calculated from unrounded numbers.

Source: SNL Financial LC.

TOP 10 WRITERS OF MULTIPLE PERIL CROP INSURANCE BY DIRECT PREMIUMS WRITTEN, 2014
($000)

Rank	Group/company	Direct premiums written[1]	Market share[2]
1	ACE Ltd.	$1,892,346	18.8%
2	Wells Fargo & Co.	1,827,226	18.2
3	QBE Insurance Group Ltd.	1,335,762	13.3
4	American Financial Group Inc.	855,114	8.5
5	Endurance Specialty Holdings	797,283	7.9
6	Farmers Mutual Hail Insurance Co. of Iowa	776,203	7.7
7	HCC Insurance Holdings Inc.	491,245	4.9
8	CGB Insurance Co.	420,429	4.2
9	Archer-Daniels-Midland Co.	362,685	3.6
10	Fairfax Financial Holdings	276,139	2.8

[1]Before reinsurance transactions, includes some state funds.
[2]Based on U.S. total, includes territories.

Source: SNL Financial LC.

Warranty Insurance

Warranty insurance coverage compensates for the cost of repairing or replacing defective products past the normal warranty period provided by manufacturers.

WARRANTY INSURANCE, 2008-2014
($000)

Year	Net premiums written[1]	Annual percent change	Combined ratio[2]	Annual point change[3]
2008	$2,086,935	NA	94.3	NA
2009	1,757,247	-15.8%	97.9	3.6 pts.
2010	1,864,139	6.1	106.4	8.5
2011	1,695,799	-9.0	97.1	-9.3
2012	1,386,404	-18.2	99.5	2.5
2013	1,155,338	-16.7	104.2	4.7
2014	1,020,188	-11.7	93.5	-10.8

[1]After reinsurance transactions, excludes state funds.
[2]After dividends to policyholders. A drop in the combined ratio represents an improvement; an increase represents a deterioration.
[3]Calculated from unrounded data.

NA=Data not available.

Source: SNL Financial LC.

Overview

In addition to Social Security and private savings, a large number of Americans rely on investments in formal plans to prepare for retirement. Employer-sponsored retirement plans, individual retirement accounts (IRAs) and annuities play an important role in the U.S. retirement system. Such retirement assets totaled $24.6 trillion at the end of 2014, up 5.6 percent from the same period in 2013, according to the Investment Company Institute (ICI). The largest components of retirement assets were IRAs and employer-sponsored defined contribution plans, holding $7.4 trillion and $6.7 trillion, respectively, at the close of 2014. An ICI report found that 63 percent of U.S. households (77 million households) reported that they had employer-sponsored retirement plans, IRAs or both in mid-2014.

U.S. RETIREMENT ASSETS, 2010 AND 2014
(\$ trillions, year-end)

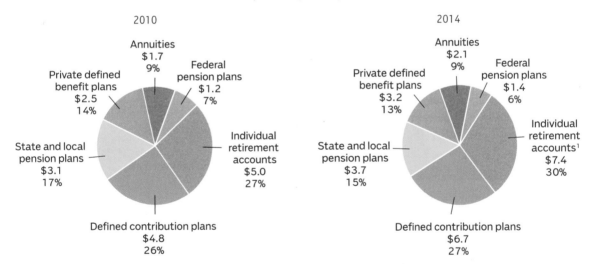

[1] Estimated.

Source: Investment Company Institute, *The U.S. Retirement Market, First Quarter 2015.*

Defined Benefit and Defined Contribution Retirement Plans

There are two basic types of workplace pension plans: defined benefit and defined contribution plans. In a defined benefit plan, the income the employee receives in retirement is guaranteed, based on predetermined benefit formulas. In a defined contribution plan, a type of savings plan in which taxes on earnings are deferred until funds are withdrawn, the amount of retirement income depends on the contributions made and the earnings generated by the securities purchased. The employer generally matches the employee contribution up to a certain level, and the employee selects investments from among the options the employer's plan offers. 401(k) plans fall into this category, as do 403(b) plans for nonprofit organizations and 457 plans for government workers.

RETIREMENT FUNDS ASSET MIX, 2014

- In defined benefit plans, equities held the largest share by type of investment in 2014, with 43 percent, followed by credit market instruments, with 27 percent and mutual funds, with 14 percent.

- In defined contribution plans, mutual funds held the largest share, with 51 percent. Equities ranked second, with 23 percent, followed by other assets (such as guaranteed investment contracts) with 17 percent.

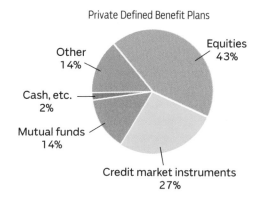

Private Defined Benefit Plans

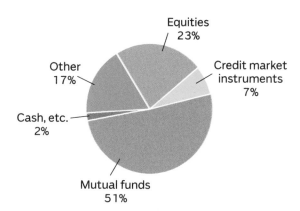

Private Defined Contribution Plans

Source: Board of Governors of the Federal Reserve System, June 11, 2015.

Individual Retirement Accounts (IRAs)

An individual retirement account (IRA) is a personal savings plan that allows individuals to set aside money for retirement, while offering tax advantages. Traditional IRAs are defined as those first allowed under the Employee Retirement Income Security Act of 1974. Amounts in a traditional IRA, including earnings, generally are not taxed until distributed to the holder. Roth IRAs were created by the Taxpayer Relief Act of 1997. Unlike traditional IRAs, Roth IRAs do not allow holders to deduct contributions. However, qualified distributions are tax-free. Other variations include Simplified Employee Pensions (SEP), which enable businesses to contribute to traditional IRAs set up for their workers, Savings Incentive Match Plans for Employees (SIMPLE) plans and a similar arrangement for small businesses and Keogh plans for the self-employed. According to the Investment Company Institute, 41.5 million households, or more than three out of 10, had at least one type of IRA as of mid-2014. Of these, 31.1 million households had traditional IRAs, 19.2 million had Roth IRAs and 7.4 million had a SEP, SIMPLE or other employer-sponsored IRA. Households may invest in one or more types of IRAs.

IRA MARKET SHARES BY HOLDER, 2010 AND 2014
(Market value, end of year)

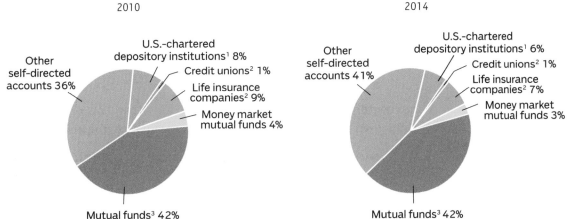

2010

Other self-directed accounts 36%

U.S.-chartered depository institutions[1] 8%

Credit unions[2] 1%

Life insurance companies[2] 9%

Money market mutual funds 4%

Mutual funds[3] 42%

2014

Other self-directed accounts 41%

U.S.-chartered depository institutions[1] 6%

Credit unions[2] 1%

Life insurance companies[2] 7%

Money market mutual funds 3%

Mutual funds[3] 42%

[1]Includes savings banks, commercial banks and Keogh accounts.
[2]Includes Keogh accounts.
[3]Excludes variable annuities.
Source: Board of Governors of the Federal Reserve System, June 11, 2015.

401(k)s

A 401(k) plan is a retirement plan offered by an employer to its workers, allowing employees to set aside tax-deferred income for retirement purposes. It is a type of defined contribution plan. (See page 132.) With $4.6 trillion in assets at year-end 2014, 401(k) plans held the largest share of employer-sponsored defined contribution plan assets, according to the Investment Company Institute (ICI). At the end of 2014, employer-sponsored defined contribution plans, including 401(k) plans and other defined contribution plans, held an estimated $6.8 trillion in assets, according to the ICI.

AVERAGE ASSET ALLOCATION FOR ALL 401(k) PLAN BALANCES, 2013[1]

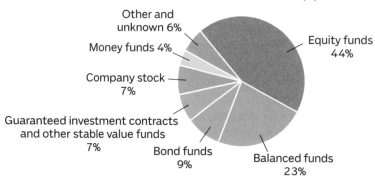

Other and unknown 6%
Money funds 4%
Company stock 7%
Guaranteed investment contracts and other stable value funds 7%
Bond funds 9%
Balanced funds 23%
Equity funds 44%

[1]Percentages are dollar-weighted averages. Source: Investment Company Institute, *ICI Research Perspective, vol. 20, no. 10.*

Mutual Funds

Mutual funds held in defined contribution plans and IRAs accounted for $7.3 trillion, or 29 percent, of the $24.7 trillion U.S. retirement market at the end of 2014, according to the Investment Company Institute.

MUTUAL FUND RETIREMENT ASSETS BY TYPE OF PLAN, 2014[1]
($ billions, end of year)

- Of the total $7.3 trillion in mutual fund assets held by retirement plans at the end of 2014, 58 percent were invested in equity funds, including 45 percent in domestic funds and 13 percent in foreign funds.

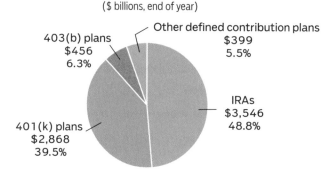

403(b) plans $456 6.3%
Other defined contribution plans $399 5.5%
IRAs $3,546 48.8%
401(k) plans $2,868 39.5%

[1]Preliminary data. Excludes defined benefit plans.
Source: Investment Company Institute, *Investment Company Fact Book 2015.*

Sales of Fixed and Variable Annuities

Annuities play an important role in retirement planning by helping individuals guard against outliving their assets. In its most general sense, an annuity is an agreement for an entity (generally a life insurance company) to pay another a stream or series of payments. While there are many types of annuities, key features can include tax savings, protection from creditors, investment options, lifetime income and benefits to heirs.

There are many types of annuities. Among the most common are fixed and variable. Fixed annuities guarantee the principal and a minimum rate of interest. Generally, interest credited and payments made from a fixed annuity are based on rates declared by the company, which can change only yearly. In contrast, variable annuity account values and payments are based on the performance of a separate investment portfolio, thus their value may fluctuate daily.

There is a variety of fixed annuities and variable annuities. One type of fixed annuity, the equity indexed annuity, contains features of fixed and variable annuities. It provides a base return, just as other fixed annuities do, but its value is also based on the performance of a specified stock index. The return can go higher if the index rises. The 2010 Dodd-Frank Act included language keeping equity indexed annuities under state insurance regulation. Variable annuities are subject to both state insurance regulation and federal securities regulation. Fixed annuities are not considered securities and are only subject to state regulation.

Annuities can be deferred or immediate. Deferred annuities generally accumulate assets over a long period of time, with withdrawals taken as a single sum or as an income payment beginning at retirement. Immediate annuities allow purchasers to convert a lump sum payment into a stream of income that begins right away. Annuities can be written on an individual or group basis. (See the Premiums by Line table, page 35.)

Annuities can be used to fund structured settlements, arrangements in which an injury victim in a lawsuit receives compensation in a number of tax-free payments over time, rather than as a lump sum.

INDIVIDUAL ANNUITY CONSIDERATIONS, 2010-2014[1]
($ billions)

- Individual variable annuity sales in the United States fell 3.6 percent in 2014, following a 1.4 percent drop the previous year. Fixed annuity sales grew 13.5 percent in 2014, after a 16.7 percent increase in 2013.

Year	Variable	Fixed	Total Amount	Total Percent change from prior year
2010	$140.5	$81.9	$222.4	-6.8%
2011	157.9	80.5	238.4	7.2
2012	147.4	72.3	219.7	-7.8
2013	145.4	84.4	229.8	4.6
2014	140.1	95.8	235.9	2.7

[1]Based on LIMRA's estimates of the total annuity sales market. Includes some considerations (i.e., premiums) that though bought in group settings involve individual buying decisions.
Source: LIMRA.

DEFFERED ANNUITY ASSETS, 2005-2014
($ billions, end of year)

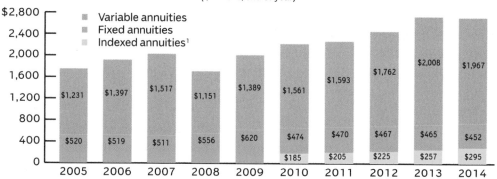

- Variable annuities
- Fixed annuities
- Indexed annuities[1]

	2005	2006	2007	2008	2009	2010	2011	2012	2013	2014
Variable annuities	$1,231	$1,397	$1,517	$1,151	$1,389	$1,561	$1,593	$1,762	$2,008	$1,967
Fixed annuities	$520	$519	$511	$556	$620	$474	$470	$467	$465	$452
Indexed annuities						$185	$205	$225	$257	$295

[1]Not reported before 2010.
Source: LIMRA.

INDIVIDUAL IMMEDIATE ANNUITY SALES, 2010-2014[1]
($ billions)

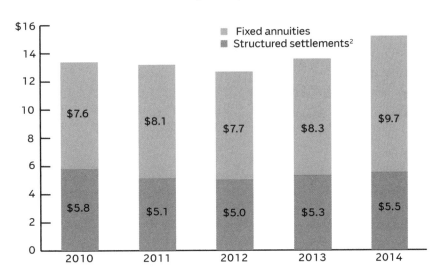

[1]Includes variable individual annuities sales which were less than $0.1 billion.
[2]Single premium contracts bought by property/casualty insurers to distribute awards in personal injury or wrongful death lawsuits over a period of time, rather than as lump sums.

Source: LIMRA.

TOP 10 WRITERS OF ANNUITIES BY DIRECT PREMIUMS WRITTEN, 2014[1]
($000)

Rank	Group/company	Direct premiums written	Market share[2]
1	Jackson National Life Group	$24,627,546	9.7%
2	American International Group (AIG)	19,020,430	7.5
3	Lincoln National Corp.	17,891,329	7.0
4	Prudential Financial Inc.	16,897,162	6.6
5	Allianz Group	14,945,846	5.9
6	Voya Financial Inc.	11,489,654	4.5
7	TIAA-CREF	11,145,986	4.4
8	New York Life Insurance Group	10,760,885	4.2
9	MetLife Inc.	10,488,535	4.1
10	AEGON	10,231,367	4.0

[1]Includes individual and group annuities.
[2]Based on U.S. total, includes territories.

Source: SNL Financial LC.

TOP 10 WRITERS OF INDIVIDUAL ANNUITIES BY DIRECT PREMIUMS WRITTEN, 2014
($000)

Rank	Group/company	Direct premiums written	Market share[1]
1	Jackson National Life Group	$21,858,690	11.1%
2	Allianz Group	14,945,846	7.6
3	Lincoln National Corp.	14,063,224	7.1
4	American International Group (AIG)	11,516,654	5.8
5	New York Life Insurance Group	10,320,255	5.2
6	AEGON	10,191,777	5.2
7	Prudential Financial Inc.	10,113,735	5.1
8	AXA	7,655,601	3.9
9	Guggenheim Capital LLC	7,652,155	3.9
10	MetLife Inc.	7,265,947	3.7

[1]Based on U.S. total, includes territories.

Source: SNL Financial LC.

TOP 10 WRITERS OF GROUP ANNUITIES BY DIRECT PREMIUMS WRITTEN, 2014
($000)

Rank	Group/company	Direct premiums written	Market share[1]
1	Voya Financial Inc.	$9,290,148	16.3%
2	American International Group (AIG)	7,503,776	13.1
3	Prudential Financial Inc.	6,783,427	11.9
4	TIAA-CREF	5,223,356	9.1
5	Great-West Insurance Group	4,311,016	7.5
6	Lincoln National Corp.	3,828,106	6.7
7	MetLife Inc.	3,222,588	5.6
8	Jackson National Life Group	2,768,856	4.8
9	OneAmerica Financial Partners	2,623,046	4.6
10	AXA	2,220,810	3.9

[1]Based on U.S. total, includes territories.

Source: SNL Financial LC.

World Insurance Losses

Natural catastrophes and man-made disasters resulted in $35 billion in insured losses in 2014, down from $44 billion in 2013, according to Swiss Re. Weather events in the United States, Europe and Japan caused the most insured losses. There were 189 worldwide natural catastrophes in 2014, the most ever recorded by *sigma*, a Swiss Re publication. The catastrophes accounted for $28 billion in insured losses. The United States experienced the largest insured loss event of 2014—a spate of severe storms with hail across five days in May struck from Colorado to Pennsylvania, causing insured losses of $2.9 billion. Harsh winters in the United States and Japan were another major cause of losses. Insured losses from all winter storms in the United States totaled $2.4 billion, more than double the average of the previous 10 years, while in Japan severe cold brought the heaviest snows in decades and caused insured losses of $2.5 billion.

TOP 15 MOST COSTLY WORLD INSURANCE LOSSES, 2014[1]
($ millions)

Rank	Date	Country	Event	Insured loss in U.S. dollars
1	May 18	U.S.	Severe thunderstorms, large hail	$2,935
2	Feb. 8	Japan	Snowstorm	2,502
3	Jun. 8	France, Germany, Belgium	Wind and hailstorm Ela	2,190
4	Sep. 14	Mexico	Hurricane Odile	1,700
5	Jan. 5	U.S.	Winter storm	1,669
6	Jun. 3	U.S.	Severe thunderstorms, large hail, tornadoes	1,269
7	Apr. 27	U.S.	Thunderstorms, large hail, 83 tornadoes, severe flash floods	1,220
8	Apr. 2	U.S.	Severe storms, large hail, tornadoes	1,084
9	Jun. 15	Russia	Major fire and explosion at oil refinery	NA
10	Sep. 27	U.S.	Thunderstorms with winds up to 67 miles per hour, hail, flash floods	905
11	Nov. 30	Australia	Hailstorm	852
12	Apr. 12	U.S.	Thunderstorms, large hail, tornadoes	678
13	Jul. 7	U.S.	Fire at petrochemical plant	NA
14	May 10	U.S.	Thunderstorms, hail, tornadoes, flash floods	635
15	Oct. 12	India	Cyclone Hudhud	632

[1]Property and business interruption losses, excluding life and liability losses. Includes flood losses in the U.S. insured via the National Flood Insurance Program. Loss data shown here may differ from figures shown elsewhere for the same event due to differences in the date of publication, the geographical area covered and other criteria used by organizations collecting the data.

NA=Data not provided.

Source: Swiss Re, *sigma*, No. 2/2015; Property Claim Services (PCS), a Verisk Analytics business, insured losses for natural catastrophes in the United States.

WORLD INSURED CATASTROPHE LOSSES, 2005-2014[1]
(2014 $ millions)

Year	Weather-related natural catastrophes	Man-made	Earthquakes	Total
2005	$123,018	$6,593	$284	$129,895
2006	14,685	5,984	95	20,764
2007	26,840	6,590	640	34,069
2008	46,909	9,094	464	56,467
2009	23,764	4,599	672	29,036
2010	32,212	5,181	14,640	52,032
2011	68,980	6,255	56,429	131,664
2012	72,235	6,030	1,894	80,159
2013	36,531	7,857	46	44,434
2014	27,437	6,958	313	34,708

[1]In order to maintain comparability of the data over the course of time, the minimum threshold for losses was adjusted annually to compensate for inflation in the United States. Adjusted to 2014 dollars by Swiss Re.

Source: Swiss Re.

TOP 10 MOST COSTLY WORLD INSURANCE LOSSES, 1970-2014[1]
(2014 $ millions)

Rank	Date	Country	Event	Insured loss
1	Aug. 25, 2005	U.S., Gulf of Mexico, Bahamas	Hurricane Katrina, storm surge, damage to oil rigs	$78,638
2	Mar. 11, 2011	Japan	Earthquake (Mw 9.0) triggers tsunami	36,828
3	Oct. 24, 2012	U.S., Caribbean	Hurricane Sandy, massive storm surge	36,079
4	Aug. 23, 1992	U.S., Bahamas	Hurricane Andrew, floods	26,990
5	Sep. 11, 2001	U.S.	Terror attacks on WTC, Pentagon and other buildings	25,104
6	Jan. 17, 1994	U.S.	Northridge earthquake (M 6.6)	22,355
7	Sep. 6, 2008	U.S., Gulf of Mexico, Caribbean, et al.	Hurricane Ike	22,258
8	Feb. 22, 2011	New Zealand	Earthquake (Mw 6.3), aftershocks	16,836
9	Sep. 2, 2004	U.S., Caribbean; Barbados, et al.	Hurricane Ivan, damage to oil rigs	16,157
10	Jul. 27, 2011	Thailand	Floods caused by heavy monsoon rains	15,783

[1]Property and business interruption losses, excluding life and liability losses. Includes flood losses in the United States insured via the National Flood Insurance Program. Adjusted to 2014 dollars by Swiss Re.

Note: Loss data shown here may differ from figures shown elsewhere for the same event due to differences in the date of publication, the geographical area covered and other criteria used by organizations collecting the data.

Source: Swiss Re, *sigma*, No. 2/2015.

TOP 10 DEADLIEST WORLD CATASTROPHES, 2014

Rank	Date	Country	Event	Victims[1]
1	Aug. 3	China	Earthquake (Mw 6.1), aftershocks and landslides	731
2	Sep. 3	India, Pakistan	Severe monsoon floods	665
3	Apr. 13	Peru	Cold wave, freezing temperatures	505
4	Apr. 16	North Pacific Ocean, South Korea	Passenger ferry sinks	304
5	May 13	Turkey	Fire at coal mine	301
6	Jul. 17	Ukraine	Malaysia Airlines Boeing 777-2H6ER (FlightMH17) crashes	298
7	May 2	Afghanistan	Heavy rains trigger massive landslide	256
8	Mar. 22	Uganda	Overcrowded boat carrying refugees capsizes on Lake Albert	251
9	Jan. 13	Sudan	Overcrowded boat capsizes on the Nile	250
10	Aug. 13	Nepal	Monsoon floods	241

[1]Dead and missing.
Source: Swiss Re, *sigma*, No. 2/2015.

TOP 10 DEADLIEST WORLD CATASTROPHES, 1970-2014

Rank	Date	Country	Event	Victims[1]
1	Nov. 11, 1970	Bangladesh	Storm and flood catastrophe	300,000
2	Jul. 28, 1976	China	Earthquake (M 7.5)	255,000
3	Jan. 12, 2010	Haiti	Earthquake (Mw 7.0), aftershocks	222,570
4	Dec. 26, 2004	Indonesia, Thailand et al.	Earthquake (Mw 9), tsunami in Indian Ocean	220,000
5	May 2, 2008	Myanmar (Burma), Bay of Bengal	Tropical cyclone Nargis	138,300
6	Apr. 29, 1991	Bangladesh	Tropical cyclone Gorky	138,000
7	May 12, 2008	China	Earthquake (Mw 7.9) in Sichuan, aftershocks	87,449
8	Oct. 8, 2005	Pakistan, India, Afghanistan	Earthquake (Mw 7.6), aftershocks, landslides	74,310
9	May 31, 1970	Peru	Earthquake (M 7.7), massive avalanche and floods	66,000
10	Jun. 15, 2010	Russia, Czech Republic	Heat wave with temperatures up to 40 Celsius	55,630

[1]Dead and missing.
Source: Swiss Re, *sigma*, No. 2/2015.

Major Catastrophes: World/United States

TOP 10 MOST COSTLY WORLD EARTHQUAKES AND TSUNAMIS BY INSURED LOSSES, 1980-2014[1]

($ millions)

Rank	Date	Location	Losses when occurred Overall	Insured[2]	Fatalities
1	Mar. 11, 2011	Japan: Aomori, Chiba, Fukushima, Ibaraki, Iwate, Miyagi, Tochigi, Tokyo, Yamagata. Includes tsunami.	$210,000	$40,000	15,880
2	Feb. 22, 2011	New Zealand: Canterbury, Christchurch, Lyttelton	24,000	16,500	185
3	Jan. 17, 1994	USA: CA: Northridge, Los Angeles, San Fernando Valley, Ventura, Orange	44,000	15,300	61
4	Feb. 27, 2010	Chile: Concepcion, Metropolitana, Rancagua, Talca, Temuco, Valparaiso. Includes tsunami.	30,000	8,000	520
5	Sep. 4, 2010	New Zealand: Canterbury, Christchurch, Avonside, Omihi, Timaru, Kaiapoi, Lyttelton	10,000	7,400	NA
6	Jan. 17, 1995	Japan: Hyogo, Kobe, Osaka, Kyoto	100,000	3,000	6,430
7	Jun. 13, 2011	New Zealand: Canterbury, Christchurch, Lyttelton	2,700	2,100	1
8	May 20 and May 29, 2012	Italy: Emilia-Romagna, San Felice del Panaro, Cavezzo, Rovereto di Novi, Carpi, Concordia. Series of earthquakes.	16,000	1,600	18
9	Dec. 26, 2004	Sri Lanka: Indonesia, Thailand, India, Bangladesh, Myanmar, Maldives, Malaysia. Includes tsunami.	10,000	1,000	220,000
10	Oct. 17, 1989	USA: CA: Loma Prieta, Santa Cruz, San Francisco, Oakland, Berkeley, Silicon Valley	10,000	960	68

[1]As of January 2015. Ranked on insured losses when occurred. [2]Based on property losses including, if applicable, agricultural, offshore, marine, aviation and National Flood Insurance Program losses in the United States and may differ from data shown elsewhere. NA=Data not available. Source: © 2015 Munich Re, Geo Risks Research, NatCatSERVICE.

Major Catastrophes: United States

Property Claim Services (PCS), a Verisk Analytics business, defines a catastrophe as an event that causes $25 million or more in insured property losses and affects a significant number of property/casualty (P/C) policyholders and insurers. PCS estimates represent anticipated insured losses from natural and man-made catastrophes on an industrywide basis, reflecting the total net insurance payment for personal and commercial property lines of insurance covering fixed property, vehicles, boats, related-property items, business interruption and additional living expenses. They exclude loss adjustment expenses. P/C insurance industry catastrophes losses in the United States rose to $15.5 billion in 2014 from $12.9 billion in 2013 according to PCS, the second consecutive below-average year of losses. The number of claims reached 2.1 million in 2014, compared with 1.8 million in 2013. The number of catastrophes rose to 31 from 28 in 2013. Munich Re estimates shown below are for natural catastrophes only.

NATURAL CATASTROPHE LOSSES IN THE UNITED STATES, 2014[1]

($ millions)

Event	Number of events	Fatalities	Estimated overall losses	Estimated insured losses[2]
Severe thunderstorm	62	98	$17,000	$12,300
Winter storm	13	115	3,700	2,300
Flood	20	5	1,800	500
Earthquake and geophysical	11	45	750	150
Tropical cyclone	2	1	95	Minor
Wildfire, heat and drought	11	2	1,700	Minor
Total	**119**	**266**	**$25,000**	**$15,300**

[1]As of December 31, 2014.
[2]Based on property losses including, if applicable, agricultural, offshore, marine, aviation and National Flood Insurance Program losses and may differ from data shown elsewhere.

Source: © 2015 Munich Re, NatCatSERVICE. As of January 2015.

CATASTROPHES BY QUARTER, 2014[1]

($ millions)

Quarter	Estimated insured losses	Number of catastrophes
1	$3,010	7
2	9,620	13
3	2,139	6
4	684	5
Full year	**$15,454**	**31**

[1]Includes catastrophes causing insured property losses of at least $25 million in 1997 dollars and affecting a significant number of policyholders and insurers. Excludes losses covered by the federally administered National Flood Insurance Program.

Source: Property Claim Services (PCS), a Verisk Analytics business.

TOP FIVE STATES BY INSURED CATASTROPHE LOSSES, 2014[1]

($ millions)

Rank	State	Estimated insured loss
1	Texas	$2,177.2
2	Colorado	1,702.1
3	Illinois	1,218.9
4	Pennsylvania	1,186.4
5	Nebraska	1,127.8

[1]Includes catastrophes causing insured property losses of at least $25 million in 1997 dollars and affecting a significant number of policyholders and insurers. Excludes losses covered by the federally administered National Flood Insurance Program.

Source: Property Claim Services (PCS), a Verisk Analytics business.

Major Catastrophes: United States

ESTIMATED INSURED PROPERTY LOSSES, U.S. CATASTROPHES, 2005-2014[1]

Year	Number of catastrophes	Number of claims (millions)	Dollars when occurred ($ billions)	In 2014 dollars[2] ($ billions)
2005	24	4.4	$62.3	$73.3
2006	31	2.3	9.2	10.5
2007	23	1.2	6.7	7.5
2008	36	4.1	27.0	29.5
2009	27	2.2	10.5	11.4
2010	33	2.4	14.3	15.3
2011	30	4.9	33.6	35.3
2012	26	4.0	35.0	36.0
2013	28	1.8	12.9	13.1
2014	31	2.1	15.5	15.5

[1]Includes catastrophes causing insured property losses of at least $25 million in 1997 dollars and affecting a significant number of policyholders and insurers. Excludes losses covered by the federally administered National Flood Insurance Program.
[2]Adjusted for inflation through 2014 by ISO using the GDP implicit price deflator.

Source: Property Claim Services (PCS), a Verisk Analytics business.

TOP 10 MOST COSTLY CATASTROPHES, UNITED STATES[1]
($ millions)

Rank	Date	Peril	Estimated Insured property losses	
			Dollars when occurred	In 2014 dollars[2]
1	Aug. 2005	Hurricane Katrina	$41,100	$48,383
2	Sep. 2001	Fire, explosion: World Trade Center, Pentagon terrorist attacks	18,779	24,279
3	Aug. 1992	Hurricane Andrew	15,500	23,785
4	Oct. 2012	Hurricane Sandy	18,750	19,307
5	Jan. 1994	Northridge, CA earthquake	12,500	18,345
6	Sep. 2008	Hurricane Ike	12,500	13,639
7	Oct. 2005	Hurricane Wilma	10,300	12,125
8	Aug. 2004	Hurricane Charley	7,475	9,083
9	Sep. 2004	Hurricane Ivan	7,110	8,639
10	Apr. 2011	Flooding, hail and wind including the tornadoes that struck Tuscaloosa and other locations	7,300	7,652

[1]Property losses only. Excludes flood damage covered by the federally administered National Flood Insurance Program.
[2]Adjusted for inflation through 2014 by ISO using the GDP implicit price deflator.

Source: Property Claim Services (PCS), a Verisk Analytics business.

INFLATION-ADJUSTED U.S. INSURED CATASTROPHE LOSSES BY CAUSE OF LOSS, 1995-2014[1]

(2014 $ billions)

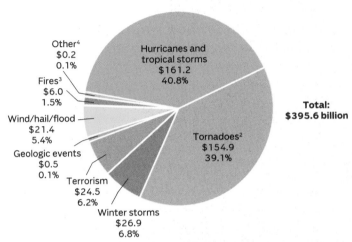

Other[4]
$0.2
0.1%

Hurricanes and
tropical storms
$161.2
40.8%

Fires[3]
$6.0
1.5%

Total:
$395.6 billion

Wind/hail/flood
$21.4
5.4%

Tornadoes[2]
$154.9
39.1%

Geologic events
$0.5
0.1%

Terrorism
$24.5
6.2%

Winter storms
$26.9
6.8%

[1]Adjusted for inflation through 2014 by ISO using the GDP implicit price deflator. Excludes catastrophes causing direct losses less than $25 million in 1997 dollars. Excludes flood damage covered by the federally administered National Flood Insurance Program. [2]Includes other wind, hail, and/or flood losses associated with catastrophes involving tornadoes. [3]Includes wildland fires. [4]Includes losses from civil disorders, water damage, utility service disruptions and any workers compensation catastrophes generating losses in excess of PCS's threshold after adjusting for inflation.

Source: Property Claim Services (PCS), a Verisk Analytics business.

TOP THREE STATES BY INFLATION-ADJUSTED INSURED CATASTROPHE LOSSES, 1985-2014[1]

(2014 $ billions)

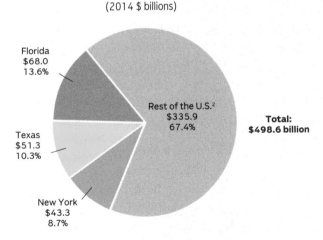

Florida
$68.0
13.6%

Rest of the U.S.[2]
$335.9
67.4%

Total:
$498.6 billion

Texas
$51.3
10.3%

New York
$43.3
8.7%

[1]Adjusted for inflation through 2014 by ISO using the GDP implicit price deflator. Excludes catastrophes causing direct losses less than $25 million in 1997 dollars. Excludes flood damage covered by the federally administered National Flood Insurance Program. [2]Includes the other 47 states plus Washington, D.C., Puerto Rico and the U.S. Virgin Islands.

Source: Property Claim Services (PCS), a Verisk Analytics business.

Losses

Major Catastrophes: Hurricanes

Hurricanes are tropical cyclones. A hurricane's winds revolve around a center of low pressure, expressed in millibars (mb) or inches of mercury. Hurricanes are categorized on the Saffir-Simpson Hurricane Wind Scale, which has a range of from 1 to 5, based on the hurricane's intensity at the time of landfall at the location experiencing the strongest winds. The scale provides examples of the type of damage and impacts in the United States associated with winds of the indicated intensity, but does not address the potential for other hurricane-related phenomena such as storm surge, rainfall-induced floods and tornadoes. The Saffir-Simpson Hurricane Wind Scale, which was introduced in 2009 and modified in 2010 and 2012, replaced the Saffir-Simpson Scale which tied specific storm surge and flooding effects to each category of hurricane. The National Oceanic and Atmospheric Administration found that storm surge values varied widely, depending on the size of the storm, among several other factors, and thus often fell significantly outside the ranges suggested in the original scale.

Insured losses from hurricanes rose in the past decade as hurricane activity intensified. When adjusted for inflation, eight of the 10 most costly hurricanes in U.S. history have struck since 2004. In addition to the increase in storm activity, building along the Gulf and East Coasts has continued to develop and property values have increased, leaving higher property values exposed to a storm.

THE SAFFIR-SIMPSON HURRICANE WIND SCALE

Category	Sustained wind speeds (mph)	Wind damage	Historical example
1	74-95	Very dangerous winds will produce some damage	Hurricane Dolly, 2008, South Padre Island, Texas
2	96-110	Extremely dangerous winds will cause extensive damage	Hurricane Frances, 2004, Port St. Lucie, Florida
3	111-129	Devastating damage will occur	Hurricane Ivan, 2004, Gulf Shores, Alabama
4	130-156	Catastrophic damage will occur	Hurricane Charley, 2004, Punta Gorda, Florida
5	More than 157	Catastrophic damage will occur	Hurricane Andrew, 1992, Cutler Ridge, Florida

Source: U.S. Department of Commerce, National Oceanic and Atmospheric Administration, National Hurricane Center.

The 2014 and 2015 Atlantic Hurricane Seasons

The 2014 Atlantic hurricane season produced eight named storms, six of which became hurricanes. Only Hurricane Arthur, the first hurricane of the 2014 Atlantic hurricane season, made landfall. Arthur was also the first hurricane to make landfall onto the U.S. mainland since Isaac in August 2012 and the first Category 2 hurricane in the United States since Ike in 2008, according to the National Weather Service. Arthur made landfall in North Carolina in July. Hurricanes Bertha and Cristobal, which developed in the Caribbean, resulted in four drowning deaths in the United States. The 2014 Pacific hurricane season was the most active since 1992, with 20 named storms, 14 of which became hurricanes, and eight of them major hurricanes, according to the National Oceanic and Atmospheric Administration. Iselle hit Hawaii in August as a tropical storm and was the first tropical cyclone to make landfall in the main Hawaiian Islands since Hurricane Iniki in 1992. Odile hit the Baja California area of Mexico as a Category 3 hurricane and caused 11 direct deaths. Odile inflicted extensive damage on two airports in Mexico in addition to causing damage in California, Texas and New Mexico.

By late November 2015, 11 tropical storms developed in the Atlantic Basin, including four hurricanes. Tropical Storm Ana made landfall near Myrtle Beach, South Carolina, on May 10 and dumped more than six inches of rain in North and South Carolina. Tropical Storm Bill made landfall on the southern coast of Louisiana on June 30 and resulted in four deaths, wind- and storm-surge damage, power outages and a tornado. Danny, the first major hurricane of the 2015 Atlantic hurricane season, formed on August 20 and became a Category 3 storm at its peak and affected the Leeward Islands. Tropical Storm Erica formed on August 24 and was responsible for at least 20 deaths on the island of Dominica. Hurricane Fred, the second hurricane of the season, briefly became a hurricane on August 31. Joaquin became a hurricane on September 30 and reached Category 4 in strength. Joaquin battered the Bahamas and Bermuda with strong winds, storm-surge flooding and torrential rainfall. Joaquin also combined with other weather systems on the southeastern coast of the United States producing record rainfall for Charleston, South Carolina, and other parts of the state. The Eastern Pacific was active again in 2015 as 17 named storms formed, with 12 becoming hurricanes. Hurricane Dolores poured on the desert Southwest, resulting in record rainfalls in Los Angeles and San Diego on July 18. On September 15 the remnants of Hurricane Linda made it the wettest day of the year in Los Angeles. Hurricane Patricia, the strongest storm on record in the Western Hemisphere, hit the west coast of Mexico on October 23 as a Category 5 storm with 165 mph winds.

CATASTROPHIC HURRICANE LOSSES IN THE UNITED STATES, 2005-2014
($ billions)

| Year | Number of catastrophic hurricanes[1] | Estimated insured loss | | Year | Number of catastrophic hurricanes[1] | Estimated insured loss | |
		Dollars when occurred	In 2014 dollars[2]			Dollars when occurred	In 2014 dollars[2]
2005	6	$58.3	$69.0	2010	0[3]	NA	NA
2006	0[3]	NA	NA	2011	1	$4.3	$4.5
2007	0[3]	NA	NA	2012	2	19.7	20.3
2008	3	15.2	16.6	2013	0[3]	NA	NA
2009	0[3]	NA	NA	2014	0[3]	NA	NA

[1]Hurricanes causing insured property losses of at least $25 million in 1997 dollars and affecting a significant number of policyholders and insurers. Excludes losses covered by the federally administered National Flood Insurance Program. [2]Adjusted for inflation through 2014 by ISO using the GDP implicit price deflator. [3]No hurricane met the PCS definition of a catastrophe.

NA=Not applicable.

Source: Property Claim Services (PCS), a Verisk Analytics business.

Major Catastrophes: Hurricanes

The following chart from PCS ranks historic hurricanes based on their insured losses, adjusted for inflation. The chart beneath it, from AIR Worldwide, estimates insured property losses from notable hurricanes from past years, if they were to hit the nation again today with the same meteorological parameters.

TOP 10 MOST COSTLY HURRICANES IN THE UNITED STATES[1]
($ millions)

Rank	Date	Location	Hurricane	Estimated insured loss[2]	
				Dollars when occurred	In 2014 dollars[3]
1	Aug. 25-30, 2005	AL, FL, GA, LA, MS, TN	Hurricane Katrina	$41,100	$48,383
2	Aug. 24-26, 1992	FL, LA	Hurricane Andrew	15,500	23,785
3	Oct. 28-31, 2012	CT, DC, DE, MA, MD, ME, NC, NH, NJ, NY, OH, PA, RI, VA, VT, WV	Hurricane Sandy	18,750	19,307
4	Sep. 12-14, 2008	AR, IL, IN, KY, LA, MO, OH, PA, TX	Hurricane Ike	12,500	13,639
5	Oct. 24, 2005	FL	Hurricane Wilma	10,300	12,125
6	Aug. 13-14, 2004	FL, NC, SC	Hurricane Charley	7,475	9,083
7	Sep. 15-21, 2004	AL, DE, FL, GA, LA, MD, MS, NC, NJ, NY, OH, PA, TN, VA, WV	Hurricane Ivan	7,110	8,639
8	Sep. 17-22, 1989	GA, NC, PR, SC, UV, VA	Hurricane Hugo	4,195	7,055
9	Sep. 20-26, 2005	AL, AR, FL, LA, MS, TN, TX	Hurricane Rita	5,627	6,624
10	Sep. 3-9, 2004	FL, GA, NC, NY, SC	Hurricane Frances	4,595	5,583

[1]Includes hurricanes occurring through 2014. [2]Property coverage only. Excludes flood damage covered by the federally administered National Flood Insurance Program. [3]Adjusted for inflation through 2014 by ISO using the GDP implicit price deflator.
Source: Property Claim Services (PCS), a Verisk Analytics business.

ESTIMATED INSURED LOSSES FOR THE TOP 10 HISTORICAL HURRICANES BASED ON CURRENT EXPOSURES[1]
($ billions)

Rank	Date	Event	Category	Insured loss (current exposures)
1	Sep. 18, 1926	Miami Hurricane	4	$125
2	Aug. 24, 1992	Hurricane Andrew	5	57
3	Sep. 17, 1947	1947 Fort Lauderdale Hurricane	4	53
4	Sep. 17, 1928	Great Okeechobee Hurricane	5	51
5	Aug. 29, 2005	Hurricane Katrina	3[2]	45
6	Sep. 9, 1965	Hurricane Betsy	3	45
7	Sep. 9, 1900	Galveston Hurricane of 1900	4	41
8	Sep. 10, 1960	Hurricane Donna	4	35
9	Sep. 21, 1938	The Great New England Hurricane	3	33
10	Sep. 15, 1950	Hurricane Easy	3	23

[1]Modeled loss to property, contents, and business interruption and additional living expenses for residential, mobile home, commercial, and auto exposures as of December 31, 2011. Losses include demand surge. [2]Refers to Katrina's second landfall in Louisiana.
Source: AIR Worldwide Corporation.

HURRICANES AND RELATED DEATHS IN THE UNITED STATES, 1995-2014

Year	Total hurricanes	Made landfall as hurricane in the U.S.	Deaths[1]	Year	Total hurricanes	Made landfall as hurricane in the U.S.	Deaths[1]	Year	Total hurricanes	Made landfall as hurricane in the U.S.	Deaths[1]
1995	3	3	29	2002	4	1	5	2009	3	1[4]	6
1996	3	2	59	2003	7	2	24	2010	12	0	11
1997	1	1	6	2004	9	6[2]	59	2011	7	1	44
1998	10	3	23	2005	15	7	1,518	2012	10	1[5]	83
1999	8	2	60	2006	5	0	0	2013	2	0	1
2000	8	0	4	2007	6	1	1	2014	6	1	2
2001	9	0	42	2008	8	4[3]	41				

[1]Includes fatalities from high winds of less than hurricane force from tropical storms.
[2]One hurricane (Alex) is considered a strike but not technically a landfall.
[3]Includes one hurricane (Hanna) which made landfall as a tropical storm.
[4]Hurricane Ida, which made landfall as a tropical storm.
[5]Excludes Hurricane Sandy which made landfall as a post-tropical storm.

Source: Insurance Information Institute from data supplied by the U.S. Department of Commerce, National Oceanic and Atmospheric Administration, National Hurricane Center.

TOP 10 DEADLIEST MAINLAND U.S. HURRICANES[1]

Rank	Year	Hurricane	Category	Deaths
1	1900	Texas (Galveston)	4	8,000[2]
2	1928	Florida (Southeast; Lake Okeechobee)	4	2,500[3]
3	2005	Hurricane Katrina (Southeast Louisiana; Mississippi)	3	1,200
4	1893	Louisiana (Cheniere Caminanda)	4	1,100-1,400[4]
5	1893	South Carolina; Georgia (Sea Islands)	3	1,000-2,000
6	1881	Georgia; South Carolina	2	700
7	1957	Hurricane Audrey (Southwest Louisiana; North Texas)	4	416
8	1935	Florida (Keys)	5	408
9	1856	Louisiana (Last Island)	4	400
10	1926	Florida (Miami, Pensacola); Mississippi; Alabama	4	372

[1]Based on a National Hurricane Center analysis of mainland U.S. tropical cyclones from 1851-2010.
[2]Could be as high as 12,000.
[3]Could be as high as 3,000.
[4]Total including offshore deaths is near 2,000.

Source: U.S. Department of Commerce, National Oceanic and Atmospheric Administration, National Hurricane Center.

Major Catastrophes: Winter Storms

TOP 15 MOST COSTLY U.S. WINTER EVENTS BY INSURED LOSSES, 1980-2014[1]
($ millions)

Rank	Date	Event	Location	Losses when occurred		Deaths
				Overall	Insured [2]	
1	Mar. 11-14, 1993	Blizzard	AL, CT, DE, FL, GA, KY, LA, MA, MD, ME, MS, NC, NH, NJ, NY, OH, PA, RI, SC, TN, TX, VA, VT, WV	$5,000	$2,000	270
2	Jan. 5-8, 2014	Winter damage, cold wave	AL, CT, GA, IL, IN, KY, MA, MD, ME, MI, MN, MO, MS, NC, NE, NJ, NY, OH, PA, SC, TN, VA, WI	2,500	1,700	NA
3	Apr. 13-17, 2007	Winter storm, tornadoes, floods	CT, DE, DC, GA, LA, MA, MD, ME, MS, NC, NH, NJ, NY, PA, RI, SC, TX, VA, VT, WV	2,000	1,600	19
4	Apr. 7-11, 2013	Winter storm	CA, IN, KS, MO, NE, SD, WI	1,500	1,200	NA
5	Dec. 10-13, 1992	Winter storm	CT, DE, NJ, NY, MA, MD, NE, PA, RI, VA	3,000	1,000	19
6	Jan. 31-Feb. 3, 2011	Winter storm, snowstorms, winter damage	CT, IA, IL, IN, KS, MA, ME, MO, NY, OH, PA, RI, TX, WI	1,300	980	36
7	Dec. 17-30, 1983	Winter damage, cold wave	FL, GA, ID, IL, IN, IA, KS, KY, LA, MD, MA, MI, MN, MS, MO, MT, NE, NJ, NY, NC, ND, OH, OK, OR, PA, RI, SC, SD, TN, TX, UT, VA, WA, WV, WI, WY	1,000	880	500
8	Jan. 17-20, 1994	Winter damage, cold wave	CT, DE, IN, IL, KY, MA, ME, MD, NC, NH, NJ, NY, OH, PA, RI, SC, TN, VA, VT, WV	1,000	800	70
9	Feb. 10-12, 1994	Winter damage	AL, AR, GA, LA, MS, NC, OK, SC, TN, TX, VA	3,000	800	9
10	Jan. 1-4, 1999	Winter storm	AL, AR, CT, DE, FL, GA, IL, IN, LA, MO, MA, MD, ME, MS, NC, NJ, NY, OH, OK, PA, RI, SC, TN, TX, VA, WV	1,000	780	25
11	Jan. 4-9, 2008	Winter storm	AR, CA, CO, IL, IN, KS, MI, MO, NV, NY, OH, OK, OR, WA, WI	1,000	745	12
12	Jan. 31-Feb. 6, 1996	Winter damage	AL, AR, CT, DE, FL, GA, IA, IL, IN, KS, KY, LA, MA, MD, MI, MO, MS, NC, NE, NJ, NY, OH, OK, PA, SC, TN, TX, VA, WV, WI	1,500	740	16
13	Feb. 24-25, 2013	Blizzard, winter damage	LA, OK, TX	1,000	690	1
14	Oct. 28-31, 2011	Winter storm, winter damage	CT, MA, NH, NJ, NY, PA	900	665	28
15	Jan. 6-9, 1996	Snowstorm	CT, DE, IN, KY, MA, MD, NC, NH, NJ, NY, OH, PA, RI, TN, VA, VT, WV	1,200	600	85

[1]Most costly U.S. blizzards and winter storms/damages based on insured losses when occurred. [2]Based on property losses including, if applicable, agricultural, offshore, marine, aviation and National Flood Insurance Program losses in the United States and may differ from data shown elsewhere.

NA=Data not available.

Source: © 2015 Munich Re, NatCatSERVICE, as of January 2015.

Major Catastrophes: Floods/Tornadoes

TOP 10 MOST SIGNIFICANT FLOOD EVENTS BY NATIONAL FLOOD INSURANCE PROGRAM PAYOUTS[1]

Rank	Date	Event	Location	Number of paid losses	Amount paid ($ millions)	Average paid loss
1	Aug. 2005	Hurricane Katrina	AL, FL, GA, LA, MS, TN	167,970	$16,317	$97,140
2	Oct. 2012	Superstorm Sandy	CT, DC, DE, MA, MD, ME, NC, NH, NJ, NY, OH, PA, RI, VA, VT, WV	129,360	7,996	61,809
3	Sep. 2008	Hurricane Ike	AR, IL, IN, KY, LA, MO, OH, PA, TX	46,593	2,690	57,730
4	Sep. 2004	Hurricane Ivan	AL, DE, FL, GA, LA, MD, MS, NJ, NY, NC, OH, PA, TN, VA, WV	28,294	1,612	56,977
5	Aug. 2011	Hurricane Irene	CT, DC, DE, MA, MD, ME, NC, NH, NJ, NY, PA, RI, VA, VT	44,244	1,338	30,242
6	Jun. 2001	Tropical Storm Allison	FL, LA, MS, NJ, PA, TX	30,786	1,107	35,958
7	May 1995	Louisiana Flood	LA	31,343	585	18,667
8	Aug. 2012	Tropical Storm Isaac	AL, FL, LA, MS	11,995	549	45,780
9	Sep. 2003	Hurricane Isabel	DE, MD, NJ, NY, NC, PA, VA, WV	19,938	500	25,091
10	Sep. 2005	Hurricane Rita	AL, AR, FL, LA, MS, TN, TX	9,528	475	49,820

[1]Includes events from 1978 to August 31, 2015, as of October 15, 2015. Defined by the National Flood Insurance Program as an event that produces at least 1,500 paid losses. Stated in dollars when occurred. Source: U.S. Department of Homeland Security, Federal Emergency Management Agency; U.S. Department of Commerce, National Oceanic and Atmospheric Administration, National Hurricane Center.

Tornadoes

A tornado is a violently rotating column of air that extends from a thunderstorm and comes into contact with the ground, according to the National Oceanic and Atmospheric Administration (NOAA). In an average year about 1,000 tornadoes are reported nationwide, according to NOAA. Tornado intensity is measured by the enhanced Fujita (EF) scale. The scale rates tornadoes on a scale of 0 through 5, based on the amount and type of wind damage. It incorporates 28 different "damage indicators," based on damage to a wide variety of structures ranging from trees to shopping malls.

THE FUJITA SCALE FOR TORNADOES

Category	Damage	Original F scale[1] Wind speed (mph)	Enhanced F scale[2] 3-second gust (mph)
F-0	Light	40-72	65-85
F-1	Moderate	73-112	86-110
F-2	Considerable	113-157	111-135
F-3	Severe	158-207	136-165
F-4	Devastating	208-260	166-200
F-5	Incredible	261-318	Over 200

[1]Original scale: wind speeds represent fastest estimated speeds over one quarter of a mile. [2]Enhanced scale: wind speeds represent maximum 3-second gusts. Source: U.S. Department of Commerce, National Oceanic and Atmospheric Administration.

Tornado Losses

Tornadoes accounted for 39.1 percent of insured catastrophe losses from 1995 to 2014, according to Property Claim Services (PCS). In 2014 insured losses from U.S. tornadoes/thunderstorms totaled $12.3 billion, up from $10.3 billion in 2013. 2014 losses were the fourth-highest annual total on record, according to Munich Re. The number of tornadoes dropped to 888 in 2014 from 907 in 2013, according to the National Oceanic and Atmospheric Administration (NOAA). There were 47 direct fatalities from tornadoes in 2014, down from 55 in 2013, according to NOAA. June was the top month for tornadoes in 2014, with 287 tornadoes. The United States experiences more tornadoes than any other country, according to a 2013 report by Lloyd's of London.

Preliminary NOAA data show that there were 1,103 tornadoes in 2015 through November 20, compared with 868 during the same period the previous year. On April 9 tornadoes developed in Illinois, Iowa, Missouri and Texas with two fatalities in Illinois. May 10 brought tornadoes to Texas and Arkansas, resulting in two fatalities in each state. Year-to-date 2015 fatalities reached 10.

TOP 10 MOST COSTLY U.S. CATASTROPHES INVOLVING TORNADOES[1]
($ millions)

- The costliest U.S. catastrophe involving tornadoes occurred in April 2011, when a spate of twisters hit Tuscaloosa, Alabama, and other areas, causing $7.7 billion in insured losses in 2014 dollars.

- The second costliest were the tornadoes that struck Joplin, Missouri, and other locations in May 2011, resulting in $7.2 billion in insured losses in 2014 dollars.

Rank	Date	Location	Estimated insured loss[2]	
			Dollars when occurred	In 2014 dollars[3]
1	Apr. 22-28, 2011	AL, AR, GA, IL, KY, LA, MO, MS, OH, OK, TN, TX, VA	$7,300	$7,652
2	May 20-27, 2011	AR, GA, IA, IL, IN, KS, KY, MI, MN, MO, NC, NE, NY, OH, OK, PA, TN, TX, VA, WI	6,900	7,232
3	May 2-11, 2003	AL, AR, CO, GA, IA, IL, IN, KS, KY, MO, MS, NC, NE, OH, OK, SC, SD, TN	3,205	4,001
4	Oct. 4-6, 2010	AZ	2,700	2,889
5	Apr. 6-12, 2001	AR, CO, IA, IL, IN, KS, KY, MI, MN, MO, NE, OH, OK, PA, TX, WI	2,200	2,844
6	Mar. 2-3, 2012	AL, GA, IN, KY, OH, TN	2,500	2,574
7	Apr. 28-29, 2012	IL, IN, KY, MO, TX	2,500	2,574
8	May 12-16, 2010	IL, MD, OK, PA, TX	2,000	2,140
9	Apr. 27-May 3, 2002	AR, GA, IL, IN, KS, KY, MD, MO, MS, NC, NY, OH, PA, TN, TX, VA, WV	1,675	2,133
10	Apr. 13-15, 2006	IA, IL, IN, WI	1,850	2,113

[1]Based on data through May 6, 2015.
[2]Property coverage only. In addition to losses due to tornadoes themselves, amounts may include losses due to hail, wind and flooding during the same event.
[3]Adjusted for inflation through 2014 by ISO using the GDP implicit price deflator.

Source: Property Claim Services (PCS), a Verisk Analytics business.

NUMBER OF TORNADOES AND RELATED DEATHS PER MONTH, 2014[1]

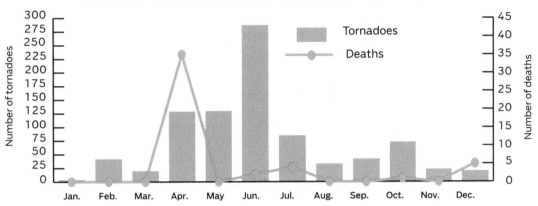

[1]Excludes Puerto Rico. A tornado that crosses state lines is counted as a single event in this chart.

Source: U.S. Department of Commerce, Storm Prediction Center, National Weather Service.

TORNADOES AND RELATED DEATHS IN THE UNITED STATES, 1995-2014[1]

Year	Tornadoes	Deaths	Year	Tornadoes	Deaths	Year	Tornadoes	Deaths
1995	1,234	30	2002	941	55	2009	1,156	21
1996	1,173	25	2003	1,376	54	2010	1,282	45
1997	1,148	67	2004	1,819	36	2011	1,691	553
1998	1,424	130	2005	1,264	38	2012	938	70
1999	1,345	94	2006	1,103	67	2013	907	55
2000	1,071	40	2007	1,098	81	2014	888	47
2001	1,216	40	2008	1,692	126			

[1]Excludes Puerto Rico. A tornado that crosses state lines is counted as one event.

Source: U.S. Department of Commerce, Storm Prediction Center, National Weather Service.

TOP 10 STATES, BY NUMBER OF TORNADOES, 2014[1]

Rank[2]	State	Number of tornadoes	Rank	State	Number of tornadoes
1	Mississippi	91	7	Colorado	54
2	Nebraska	87	8	Kansas	48
3	Alabama	65	9	South Dakota	37
4	Iowa	63	10	Georgia	35
4	Texas	63	10	Illinois	35
6	Missouri	56	10	North Carolina	35

[1]Tornadoes that cross state lines are counted in every state in which they touch down.
[2]States with the same number receive the same ranking.

Source: U.S. Department of Commerce, Storm Prediction Center, National Weather Service.

Losses

Major Catastrophes: Tornadoes

TORNADOES AND RELATED DEATHS BY STATE, 2014[1]

State	Tornadoes	Fatalities	Rank[2]	State	Tornadoes	Fatalities	Rank[2]
Alabama	65	2	3	Montana	8	0	31
Alaska	0	0	3	Nebraska	87	2	2
Arizona	2	0	38	Nevada	6	0	33
Arkansas	24	17	16	New Hampshire	0	0	3
California	11	0	28	New Jersey	0	0	3
Colorado	54	0	7	New Mexico	17	0	22
Connecticut	1	0	41	New York	10	4	29
Delaware	1	0	42	North Carolina	35	1	10
D.C.	0	0	3	North Dakota	18	0	21
Florida	29	0	14	Ohio	21	0	19
Georgia	35	0	10	Oklahoma	13	1	26
Hawaii	0	0	3	Oregon	0	0	3
Idaho	3	0	37	Pennsylvania	10	0	29
Illinois	35	0	10	Rhode Island	0	0	3
Indiana	23	0	17	South Carolina	7	0	32
Iowa	63	2	4	South Dakota	37	0	9
Kansas	48	0	8	Tennessee	23	2	17
Kentucky	33	0	13	Texas	63	0	4
Louisiana	16	0	24	Utah	0	0	3
Maine	2	0	38	Vermont	0	0	3
Maryland	2	0	38	Virginia	12	0	27
Massachusetts	5	0	35	Washington	4	0	36
Michigan	17	0	22	West Virginia	6	0	33
Minnesota	28	0	15	Wisconsin	20	0	20
Mississippi	91	16	1	Wyoming	16	0	24
Missouri	56	0	6	**United States**	**1,057**[4]	**47**	

[1]Ranked by total number of tornadoes.
[2]States with the same number receive the same ranking.
[3]No tornadoes occured in 2014.
[4]The U.S. total will not match data used in other charts because it counts tornadoes in every state in which they touch down.

Source: U.S. Department of Commerce, Storm Prediction Center, National Weather Service.

Earthquakes

The costliest U.S. earthquake, the 1994 Northridge quake, caused $15.3 billion in insured damages when it occurred (about $24 billion in 2014 dollars). It ranks as the fifth-costliest U.S. disaster, based on insured property losses (in 2014 dollars), topped only by Hurricane Katrina, the attacks on the World Trade Center, Hurricane Andrew and superstorm Sandy. Eight of the costliest U.S. quakes, based on inflation-adjusted insured losses, were in California, according to Munich Re. On August 24, 2014, a 6.0-magnitude earthquake struck South Napa, California, killing one person and causing $700 million in total damage and $150 million in insured losses, according to Munich Re.

TOP 10 MOST COSTLY U.S. EARTHQUAKES BY INFLATION-ADJUSTED INSURED LOSSES[1]

($ millions)

| Rank | Date | Location | Overall losses when occurred | Insured losses[2] | | Fatalities |
				Dollars when occurred	In 2014 dollars[3]	
1	Jan. 17, 1994	California: Northridge, Los Angeles, San Fernando Valley, Ventura, Orange	$44,000	$15,300	$24,440	61
2	Apr. 18, 1906	California: San Francisco, Santa Rosa, San Jose	524	180	4,300[4]	3,000
3	Oct. 17, 1989	California: Loma Prieta, Santa Cruz, San Francisco, Oakland, Berkeley, Silicon Valley	10,000	960	1,830	68
4	Feb. 28, 2001	Washington: Olympia, Seattle, Tacoma; Oregon	2,000	300	400	1
5	Mar. 27-28, 1964	Alaska: Anchorage, Kodiak Island, Seward, Valdez, Portage, Whittier, Cordova, Homer, Seldovia	540	45	340	131
6	Feb. 9, 1971	California: San Fernando Valley, Los Angeles	553	35	200	65
7	Oct. 1, 1987	California: Los Angeles, Whittier	360	75	160	8
8	Aug. 24, 2014	California: Napa, Vallejo, Solano, Sonoma, American Canyon	700	150	150	1
9	Apr. 4, 2010	California: San Diego, Calexico, El Centro, Los Angeles, Imperial; Arizona: Phoenix, Yuma	150	100	110	NA
10	Sep. 3, 2000	California: Napa	80	50	70	NA

[1]Costliest U.S. earthquakes occurring from 1950 to 2014, based on insured losses when occurred. Includes the 1906 San Francisco, California, earthquake, for which reliable insured losses are available.

[2]Based on property losses including, if applicable, agricultural, offshore, marine, aviation and National Flood Insurance Program losses in the United States and may differ from data shown elsewhere.

[3]Inflation-adjusted to 2014 dollars by Munich Re.

[4]Inflation-adjusted to 2014 dollars based on 1913 Bureau of Labor Statistics data (earliest year available).

NA=Data not available.

Source: © 2015 Munich Re, NatCatSERVICE.

Major Catastrophes: Earthquakes/Terrorism

The previous chart ranks historic earthquakes based on their total insured property losses, adjusted for inflation. The chart below uses a computer model to measure the estimated impact of historical quakes according to current exposures. The analysis, conducted in 2012, is based on AIR Worldwide's U.S. earthquake model. It makes use of the firm's property exposure database and takes into account the current number and value of exposed properties.

ESTIMATED INSURED LOSSES FOR THE TOP 10 HISTORICAL EARTHQUAKES BASED ON CURRENT EXPOSURES[1]

($ billions)

Rank	Date	Location	Magnitude	Insured loss (current exposures)
1	Feb. 7, 1812	New Madrid, MO	7.7	$112
2	Apr. 18, 1906	San Francisco, CA	7.8	93
3	Aug. 31, 1886	Charleston, SC	7.3	44
4	Jun. 1, 1838	San Francisco, CA	7.4	30
5	Jan. 17, 1994	Northridge, CA	6.7	23
6	Oct. 21, 1868	Hayward, CA	7.0	23
7	Jan. 9, 1857	Fort Tejon, CA	7.9	8
8	Oct. 17, 1989	Loma Prieta, CA	6.3	7
9	Mar. 10, 1933	Long Beach, CA	6.4	5
10	Jul. 1, 1911	Calaveras, CA	6.4	4

[1]Modeled loss to property, contents, business interruption and additional living expenses for residential, mobile home, commercial and auto exposures as of December 31, 2011. Losses include demand surge and fire following earthquake. Policy conditions and earthquake insurance take-up rates are based on estimates by state insurance departments and client claims data.

Source: AIR Worldwide Corporation.

Terrorism

A total of 2,976 people perished in the September 11, 2001, terrorist attacks in New York, Washington and Pennsylvania, excluding the 19 hijackers. Total insured losses from the terrorist attacks on the World Trade Center in New York City and the Pentagon are about $43.4 billion (in 2014 dollars), including property, life and liability insurance claim costs. Loss estimates may differ from estimates calculated by other organizations. It is the worst terrorist attack on record in terms of fatalities and insured property losses, which totaled about $24.3 billion (in 2014 dollars) according to Swiss Re. The April 15, 2013, Boston Marathon bombing, which killed four people and injured 264, marked the first successful terrorist attack on U.S. soil since the September 11 tragedy. As of April 2014 selected health, property/casualty and workers compensation companies have paid or are projected to pay a total of $24.9 million for medical claims and property damage claims associated with the bombings, according to the Massachusetts Division of Insurance.

TOP 20 MOST COSTLY TERRORIST ACTS BY INSURED PROPERTY LOSSES

(2014 $ millions)

Rank	Date	Country	Location	Event	Insured property loss[1]	Fatalities
1	Sep. 11, 2001	U.S.	New York, Washington, D.C., Pennsylvania	Hijacked airliners crash into World Trade Center and Pentagon	$25,122[2]	2,982
2	Apr. 24, 1993	U.K.	London	Bomb explodes near NatWest tower in the financial district	1,212	1
3	Jun. 15, 1996	U.K.	Manchester	Irish Republican Army (IRA) car bomb explodes near shopping mall	996	0
4	Apr. 10, 1992	U.K.	London	Bomb explodes in financial district	897	3
5	Feb. 26, 1993	U.S.	New York	Bomb explodes in garage of World Trade Center	835	6
6	Jul. 24, 2001	Sri Lanka	Colombo	Rebels destroy 3 airliners, 8 military aircraft and heavily damage 3 civilian aircraft	534	20
7	Feb. 9, 1996	U.K.	London	IRA bomb explodes in South Key Docklands	347	2
8	Jun. 23, 1985	North Atlantic	Irish Sea	Bomb explodes on board of an Air India Boeing 747	215	329
9	Apr. 19, 1995	U.S.	Oklahoma City, OK	Truck bomb crashes into government building	195	168
10	Sep. 12, 1970	Jordan	Zerqa, Dawson's Field (disused RAF airstrip in desert)	Hijacked Swissair DC-8, TWA Boeing 707, BOAC VC-10 dynamited on ground	170	0
11	Sep. 6, 1970	Egypt	Cairo	Hijacked PanAm B-747 dynamited on ground	147	0
12	Apr. 11, 1992	U.K.	London	Bomb explodes in financial district	129	0
13	Nov. 26, 2008	India	Mumbai	Attack on two hotels; Jewish center	113	172
14	Mar. 27, 1993	Germany	Weiterstadt	Bomb attack on a newly built, still unoccupied prison	95	0
15	Dec. 30, 2006	Spain	Madrid	Bomb explodes in car garage at Barajas Airport	77	2
16	Dec. 21, 1988	U.K.	Lockerbie	Bomb explodes on board of a PanAm Boeing 747	75	270
17	Jul. 25, 1983	Sri Lanka		Riot	63	0
18	Jul. 7, 2005	U.K.	London	Four bombs explode during rush hour in a tube and bus	63	52
19	Nov. 23, 1996	Comoros	Indian Ocean	Hijacked Ethiopian Airlines Boeing 767-260 ditched at sea	61	127
20	Mar. 17, 1992	Argentina	Buenos Aires	Bomb attack on Israel's embassy in Buenos Aires	51	24

[1]Includes bodily injury and aviation hull losses. Updated to 2014 dollars by the Insurance Information Institute using the U.S. Bureau of Labor Statistics CPI Inflation Calculator.

[2]Differs from inflation-adjusted estimates made by other organizations due to the use of different deflators.

Source: Swiss Re.

Losses

Major Catastrophes: Nuclear Incidents

The International Atomic Energy Agency (IAEA) rates the severity of nuclear incidents on the International Nuclear and Radiological Event Scale (INES) from one (indicating an anomaly) to seven (indicating a major event). The scale considers an event's impact based on three criteria: its effect on people and the environment; whether it caused unsafe levels of radiation in a facility; and if preventive measures did not function as intended. Scales six and seven designate full meltdowns, where the nuclear fuel reactor core overheats and melts. Partial meltdowns, in which the fuel is damaged, are rated four or five.

Japan's Nuclear and Industrial Safety Agency assigned a provisional rating of seven to the March 2011 accident at Japan's Fukushima Daiichi nuclear power plant. The 1986 Chernobyl accident in the former Soviet Union is the only other incident to rate a seven. The Chernobyl incident killed 56 people directly and thousands of others indirectly through cancer and other diseases. The 2011 incident released high amounts of radiation and caused widespread evacuations in affected areas but no deaths to date.

The 1979 Three Mile Island accident in Harrisburg, Pennsylvania, the worst nuclear accident in the United States, was designated a five. Insurers paid about $71 million in liability claims and litigation costs associated with the accident. In addition to the liability payments to the public under the Price-Anderson Act, $300 million was paid by a pool of insurers to the operator of the damaged nuclear power plant under its property insurance policy.

SELECTED EXAMPLES OF HISTORIC NUCLEAR EVENTS, CLASSIFIED BY THE INES[1]

Level	INES description	Example
1	Anomaly	Breach of operating limits at nuclear facilities
2	Incident	Atucha, Argentina, 2005 - Overexposure of a worker at a power reactor exceeding the annual limit
3	Serious incident	Sellafield, U.K., 2005 - Release of large quantity of radioactive material, contained within the installation
4	Accident with local consequences	Tokaimura, Japan, 1999 - Fatal exposure of workers following an event at a nuclear facility
5	Accident with wider consequences	3 Mile Island, U.S., 1979 - Severe damage to reactor core. Minimal breach of outside environment
6	Serious accident	Kyshtym, Russia, 1957 - Significant release of radioactive material from the explosion of high activity waste tank
7	Major accident	Chernobyl, Ukraine, 1986 - Widespread health and environmental effects from explosion in power plant

[1]International Nuclear and Radiological Event Scale.

Source: International Atomic Energy Agency.

Hail

Hail causes about $1 billion dollars in damage to crops and property each year, according to the National Oceanic Atmospheric Administration (NOAA). Events involving wind, hail or flood accounted for $21.4 billion in insured catastrophe losses in 2014 dollars from 1994 to 2014 (not including payouts from the National Flood Insurance Program), according to Property Claim Services. There were 5,536 major hail storms in 2014, according to the NOAA's Severe Storms database.

A report issued by Verisk Insurance Solutions in August 2014 showed that over the 14 years from 2000 to 2013 U.S. insurers paid almost 9 million claims for hail losses, totaling more than $54 billion. Most of those losses—70 percent—occurred during the past six years. In addition to the higher number of claims, the average claim severity during the past six years was 65 percent higher than the period 2000 through 2007.

HAIL FATALITIES, INJURIES AND DAMAGE, 2010-2014[1]

Year	Fatalities	Injuries	Property damage ($ millions)	Crop damage ($ millions)	Total damage ($ millions)
2010	0	42	$924.1	$99.8	$1,023.9
2011	0	31	450.5	81.9	532.4
2012	0	54	2,414.4	93.9	2,508.3
2013	0	4	1,245.5	75.0	1,320.5
2014	0	23	1,416.9	293.2	1,710.1

[1]Includes the 50 states, Puerto Rico, Guam and the Virgin Islands.

Source: U.S. Department of Commerce, Storm Prediction Center, National Weather Service.

TOP FIVE STATES FOR MAJOR HAIL EVENTS, 2014[1]

Rank	State	Number of hail events
1	Nebraska	624
2	Texas	557
3	Kansas	534
4	Iowa	290
5	Missouri	266
	United States	**5,536**

[1]One inch in diameter or larger.

Source: U.S. Department of Commerce, Storm Prediction Center, National Weather Service.

Major Catastrophes: Wildfires

Fire plays an important role in the life of a forest, clearing away dead wood and undergrowth to make way for younger trees. But for much of the last century, fire-suppression policies have sought to extinguish wildfires as quickly as possible to preserve timber and real estate. This approach has led to the accumulation of brush and other vegetation that is easily ignited and serves as fuel for wildfires. Most of the large fires with significant property damage have occurred in California, where some of the fastest developing counties are in forest areas.

WILDFIRE LOSSES IN THE UNITED STATES, 2005-2014[1]

(2014 $ millions)

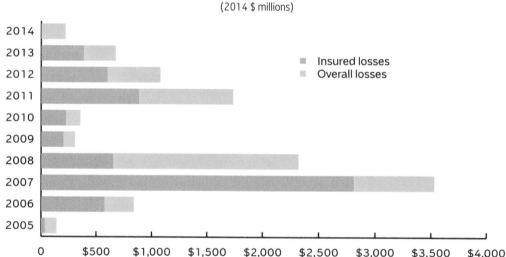

[1]Adjusted for inflation.

Source: © 2015 Munich Re, GeoRisks Research, NatCatSERVICE.

2014 and 2015 Wildfires

In 2014 there were 63,312 wildfires, which burned about 3.6 million acres. The Happy Camp Complex fire in California burned over 134,056 acres and the Carlton Complex fire in Washington state burned over 256,108 acres and was the largest fire in the state to date. Over the past 20 years the 2014 wildfire season ranks second only to 2013 for the lowest number of fires and acres burned.

Between January 1 and November 20, 2015, there were 55,636 wildfires in the United States, which burned 9.8 million acres, according to the National Interagency Fire Center. 2015 has had one of the worst wildfire seasons on record.

TOP 10 STATES FOR WILDFIRES RANKED BY NUMBER OF FIRES AND BY NUMBER OF ACRES BURNED, 2014

Rank	State	Number of fires	Rank	State	Number of acres burned
1	Texas	9,677	1	Oregon	984,629
2	California	7,865	2	California	555,044
3	North Carolina	4,625	3	Washington	386,972
4	Georgia	3,562	4	Alaska	233,561
5	Oregon	3,087	5	Arizona	205,199
6	Florida	2,436	6	Idaho	189,430
7	Alabama	2,093	7	Oklahoma	157,080
8	Montana	1,646	8	Tennessee	156,391
9	Arizona	1,543	9	Texas	131,138
10	Washington	1,480	10	Florida	101,599

Source: National Interagency Fire Center.

TOP 10 MOST COSTLY WILDLAND FIRES IN THE UNITED STATES[1]
(\$ millions)

Rank	Date	Location	Estimated insured loss	
			Dollars when occurred	In 2014 dollars[2]
1	Oct. 20-21, 1991	Oakland Fire, CA	\$1,700	\$2,668
2	Oct. 21-24, 2007	Witch Fire, CA	1,300	1,446
3	Oct. 25-Nov. 4, 2003	Cedar Fire, CA	1,060	1,323
4	Oct. 25-Nov. 3, 2003	Old Fire, CA	975	1,217
5	Nov. 2-3, 1993	Los Angeles County Fire, CA	375	562
6	Sep. 4-9, 2011	Bastrop County Complex Fire, TX	530	556
7	Oct. 27-28, 1993	Orange County Fire, CA	350	525
8	Jun. 24-28, 2012	Waldo Canyon Fire, CO	450	463
9	Jun. 27-Jul. 2, 1990	Santa Barbara Fire, CA	265	430
10	Jun. 11-16, 2013	Black Forest Fire, CO	385	391

[1]Property coverage only for catastrophic fires. Effective January 1, 1997, Property Claim Services (PCS), a Verisk Analytics business unit, defines catastrophes as events that cause more than \$25 million in insured property damage and that affect a significant number of insureds and insurers. From 1982 to 1996, PCS used a \$5 million threshold in defining catastrophes. Before 1982, PCS used a \$1 million threshold.

[2]Adjusted for inflation through 2014 by ISO using the GDP implicit price deflator.

Source: Property Claim Services (PCS), a Verisk Analytics business.

Fire Losses

Great strides have been made in constructing fire-resistant buildings and improving fire-suppression techniques, both of which have reduced the incidence of fire. However, in terms of property losses, these advances have been somewhat offset by increases in the number of and value of buildings. In 2014, on average, a fire department responded to a fire every 24 seconds in the United States, according to the National Fire Protection Association. A structure fire occurs every 64 seconds, a residential structure fire occurs every 86 seconds, and an outside property fire occurs every 52 seconds.

FIRE LOSSES IN THE UNITED STATES, BY LINE OF INSURANCE, 2014[1]

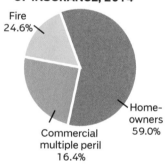

Fire 24.6%

Home-owners 59.0%

Commercial multiple peril 16.4%

[1]Estimated. Includes FAIR plan and uninsured losses.

Source: ISO, a Verisk Analytics business.

FIRE LOSSES IN THE UNITED STATES, 2005-2014[1]

Year	Property loss ($ millions)	Loss per capita[2]
2005	$20,427	$69.12
2006	20,340	68.17
2007	24,399	81.00
2008	24,734	81.34
2009	22,911	74.68
2010	20,486	66.22
2011	19,511	62.59
2012	23,977	76.33
2013	19,054	60.20
2014	21,821	68.44

[1]Including allowances for FAIR Plan and uninsured losses.
[2]Calculated by the Insurance Information Institute using ISO property loss and population estimates from the U.S. Census Bureau, Population Division.

Source: ISO, a Verisk Analytics business; U.S. Census Bureau, Population Division.

STRUCTURE FIRES, 2005-2014[1]

Year	Number of fires	Year	Number of fires
2005	511,000	2010	482,000
2006	524,000	2011	484,500
2007	530,500	2012	480,500
2008	515,000	2013	487,500
2009	480,500	2014	494,000

[1]Includes public assembly, educational, institutional and residential structures, stores and offices, industry, utility, defense, storage and special structures.

Source: Reproduced with permission from *Fire Loss in the United States During 2014* by Hylton J.G. Haynes, ©National Fire Protection Association.

- Structure fires caused $9.8 billion in damage in 2014. The majority of the damage ($7.0 billion) was to residential properties, according to the National Fire Protection Association.

CIVILIAN (NONFIREFIGHTER) FIRE DEATHS AND INJURIES BY PROPERTY USE, 2014

Property use	Civilian fire deaths	Percent change from 2013	Percent of all civilian fire deaths	Civilian fire injuries
Residential	2,795	0.4%	85.3%	12,175
One- and two-family homes[1]	2,345	-3.5	71.6	8,025
Apartments	400	23.1	12.2	3,800
Other residential[2]	50	66.7	1.5	350
Nonresidential structures[3]	65	-7.1	2.0	1,250
Highway vehicles	310	3.3	9.5	1,275
Other vehicles[4]	35	75.0	1.1	175
All other fires[5]	70	7.7	2.1	900
Total	**3,275**	**1.1%**	**100.0%**	**15,775**

[1]Includes manufactured homes. [2]Includes hotels and motels, college dormitories, boarding houses, etc. [3]Includes public assembly, educational, institutional, store and office, industry, utility, storage and special structure properties. [4]Includes trains, boats, ships, farm vehicles and construction vehicles. [5]Includes outside properties with value, as well as brush, rubbish and other outside locations.

Source: Reproduced with permission from *Fire Loss in the United States During 2014* by Hylton J.G. Haynes, ©National Fire Protection Association.

STRUCTURE FIRES BY TYPE OF USE, 2014[1]

Property use	Estimated number of fires	Percent change from 2013	Property loss[2] ($ millions)	Percent change from 2013
Public assembly	14,000	12.0%	$429	16.3%
Educational	5,000	-9.1	59	-10.6
Institutional	6,500	8.3	54	-1.7
Residential	386,500	0.1	6,992	0.3
One- and two-family homes[3]	273,500	0.7	5,844	3.9
Apartments	94,000	-4.1	982	-15.8
Other[4]	19,000	8.6	166	-6.2
Stores and offices	17,500	-2.8	708	15.9
Industry, utility, defense[5]	10,000	17.6	54	-1.7
Storage in structures	27,500	5.8	781	12.9
Special structures	27,000	12.3	211	50.7
Total	**494,000**	**1.3%**	**$9,846**	**3.4%**

[1]Estimates based on data reported by fire departments responding to the 2014 National Fire Experience Survey. May exclude reports from all fire departments.
[2]Includes overall direct property loss to contents, structures, vehicles, machinery, vegetation or any other property involved in a fire. Excludes indirect losses, such as business interruption or temporary shelter costs.
[3]Includes manufactured homes.
[4]Includes hotels and motels, college dormitories, boarding houses, etc.
[5]Excludes incidents handled only by private brigades or fixed suppression systems.

Source: Reproduced with permission from *Fire Loss in the United States During 2014* by Hylton J.G. Haynes, ©National Fire Protection Association.

TOP 10 MOST COSTLY LARGE-LOSS FIRES, 2014
($ millions)

Rank	Month	State	Type of facility	Estimated loss
1	September	California	Pier	$100.2
2	October	Kansas	Airport flight safety building	61.5
3	March	Texas	Apartment building under construction	50.0
4	March	California	Apartment building under construction	41.0
5	March	Iowa	Meatpacking plant	30.0
6	May	California	Wildland/urban complex	29.8
7	December	California	Apartment building under construction	27.1
8	June	California	Yacht	25.1
9	December	Wisconsin	Cheese storage and manufacturing	25.0
10	August	South Carolina	Gas distribution plant	25.0

Source: Reproduced with permission from *Large-Loss Fires in the United States, 2014* by Stephen G. Badger, ©National Fire Protection Association.

TOP 10 MOST COSTLY LARGE-LOSS FIRES IN U.S. HISTORY
($ millions)

Rank	Date	Location/Event	Estimated loss[1] Dollars when occurred	In 2014 dollars[2]
1	Sep. 11, 2001	World Trade Center (terrorist attacks)	$33,400[3]	$44,700[3]
2	Apr. 18, 1906	San Francisco Earthquake and Fire	350	9,150
3	Oct. 8-9, 1871	Great Chicago Fire	168	3,350
4	Oct. 20, 1991	Oakland, CA, fire storm	1,500	2,640
5	Oct. 20, 2007	San Diego County, CA, The Southern California Firestorm	1,800	2,030
6	Nov. 9, 1872	Great Boston Fire	75	1,520
7	Oct. 23, 1989	Pasadena, Texas, polyolefin plant	750	1,420
8	May 4, 2000	Los Alamos, NM, Cerro Grande wildland fire	1,000	1,420
9	Oct. 25, 2003	Julian, CA, Cedar wildland fire	1,100	1,320
10	Feb. 7, 1904	Baltimore, MD, Baltimore Conflagration	50	1,320

[1]Loss estimates are from National Fire Protection Association (NFPA) records. The list is limited to fires for which some reliable dollar loss estimates exists. [2]Adjustment to 2013 dollars made by the NFPA using the Consumer Price Index, including the U.S. Census Bureau's estimates of the index for historical times; adjusted to 2014 dollars by the Insurance Information Institute using the Bureau of Labor Statistics Inflation Calculator. [3]Differs from inflation-adjusted estimates made by other organizations due to the use of different deflators. Source: Reproduced with permission from *Large-Loss Fires in the United States, 2013* by Stephen G. Badger, ©National Fire Protection Association.

TOP 10 MOST CATASTROPHIC MULTIPLE-DEATH FIRES, 2014[1]

Rank	Month	State	Type of facility	Deaths
1	January	Kentucky	Single-family home	9
2	March	New York	Two five-story mixed-occupancy buildings	8
3	April	California	Three-vehicle (car, bus, truck tractor) interstate crash	8
4	July	Massachusetts	Three-story mixed-use building	7
5	February	Indiana	Single-family home	6
6	May	Massachusetts	Two-engine passenger jet on airport runway	6
7	June	New Jersey	Single-family home	6
8	August	North Carolina	Manufactured home	6
9	October	Pennsylvania	Single-family home	6
10	November	Maine	Three-story rooming house	6

[1]Fires that kill five or more people in home property, or three or more people in nonhome or nonstructural property.

Source: Reproduced with permission from *Catastrophic Multiple-death Fires in 2014* by Stephen G. Badger, ©National Fire Protection Association.

TOP 10 MOST CATASTROPHIC MULTIPLE-DEATH FIRES IN U.S. HISTORY[1]

Rank	Date	Location/event	Deaths
1	Sep. 11, 2001	New York, NY, World Trade Center terrorist attack	2,666[2]
2	Apr. 27, 1865	Mississippi River, SS Sultana steamship	1,547
3	Oct. 8, 1871	Peshtigo, WI, forest fire	1,152
4	Jun. 15, 1904	New York, NY, General Slocum steamship	1,030
5	Dec. 30, 1903	Chicago, IL, Iroquois Theater	602
6	Oct. 12, 1918	Cloquet, MN, forest fire	559
7	Nov. 28, 1942	Boston, MA, Cocoanut Grove night club	492
8	Apr. 16, 1947	Texas City, TX, SS Grandcamp and Monsanto Chemical Co. plant	468
9	Sep. 1, 1894	Hinckley, MN, forest fire	418
10	Dec. 6, 1907	Monongha, WV, coal mine explosion	361

[1]Fires that kill five or more people in home property, or three or more people in nonhome or nonstructural property.
[2]Revised to 2,976 by government officials.

Source: ©National Fire Protection Association.

Arson

Arson, the act of deliberately setting fire to a building, car or other property for fraudulent or malicious purposes, is a crime in all states. Church arsons, a major problem in the 1990s, have dropped significantly. Intentional fires in religious and funeral properties fell 82 percent from 1,320 in 1980 to 240 in 2002, the last year such figures were tracked. There were 1,600 structural fires in houses of worship which caused $105 million in property damage on average from 2007 to 2011, according to the NFPA. Fires in a larger category, religious and funeral properties, averaged 1,780 during the same five years. Among those fires, 16 percent, or about 285 each year, were intentional.

- In 2014 property loss from intentionally set structure fires increased 6.2 percent from 2013, according to the National Fire Protection Association, although the number of fires fell 15.6 percent.

- Intentionally set fires in vehicles fell 23.8 percent in 2014. The property loss from those fires rose 34.9 percent to $116 million in 2014.

INTENTIONALLY SET FIRES, 2005-2014

Year	Structures		Vehicles[2]	
	Number of fires	Property loss ($ millions)[1]	Number of fires	Property loss ($ millions)
2005	31,500	$664	21,000	$113
2006	31,100	755	20,500	134
2007	32,500	733	20,500	145
2008	30,500	866	17,500	139
2009	26,500	684	15,000	108
2010	27,500	585	14,000	89
2011	26,500	601	14,000	88
2012	26,000	581	12,500	480[3]
2013	22,500	577	10,500	86
2014	19,000	613	8,000	116

[1] Includes overall direct property loss to contents, structures, vehicles, machinery, vegetation or any other property involved in a fire. Excludes indirect losses, such as business interruption or temporary shelter costs.
[2] Includes highway vehicles, trains, boats, ships, aircraft and farm and construction vehicles.
[3] Includes $400 million in property loss from an intentionally set fire aboard the submarine USS Miami.

Source: 2014 data reproduced with permission from *Fire Loss in the United States During 2014* by Hylton J.G. Haynes, ©National Fire Protection Association; earlier data from prior reports.

Property Crimes

The Federal Bureau of Investigation's (FBI) Uniform Crime Reports defines property crime as larceny-theft, motor vehicle theft and burglary. These crimes involve the unlawful taking of money or property without the use of force or threat of force against the victims. Larceny theft involves the successful or attempted taking of property from another; it includes shoplifting, pocket-picking, purse-snatching and bicycle theft. While the theft of motor vehicles is a separate offense category, the thefts of motor vehicle parts and accessories are considered larceny. Burglary involves the unlawful entry into a structure such as a home or business. The burglary rate for renters was about 80 percent higher than for owners in 2011, according to a 2013 Bureau of Justice Statistics report. Home burglaries accounted for 73.2 percent of burglary offenses in 2014, according to the FBI.

NUMBER AND RATE OF PROPERTY CRIME OFFENSES IN THE UNITED STATES, 2005-2014[1]

Year	Burglary		Larceny-theft	
	Number	Rate	Number	Rate
2005	2,155,448	726.9	6,783,447	2,287.8
2006	2,194,993	733.1	6,626,363	2,213.2
2007	2,190,198	726.1	6,591,542	2,185.4
2008	2,228,887	733.0	6,586,206	2,166.1
2009	2,203,313	717.7	6,338,095	2,064.5
2010	2,168,459	701.0	6,204,601	2,005.8
2011	2,185,140	701.3	6,151,095	1,974.1
2012	2,109,932	672.2	6,168,874	1,965.4
2013	1,932,139	610.5	6,019,465	1,901.9
2014	1,729,806	542.5	5,858,496	1,837.3

Year	Motor vehicle theft		Total property crime[2]	
	Number	Rate	Number	Rate
2005	1,235,859	416.8	10,174,754	3,431.5
2006	1,198,245	400.2	10,019,601	3,346.6
2007	1,100,472	364.9	9,882,212	3,276.4
2008	959,059	315.4	9,774,152	3,214.6
2009	795,652	259.2	9,337,060	3,041.3
2010	739,565	239.1	9,112,625	2,945.9
2011	716,508	230.0	9,052,743	2,905.4
2012	723,186	230.4	9,001,992	2,868.0
2013	700,288	221.3	8,651,892	2,733.6
2014	689,527	216.2	8,277,829	2,596.1

[1]Rate is per 100,000 inhabitants. [2]Property crimes are the offenses of burglary, larceny-theft and motor vehicle theft.

Source: U.S. Department of Justice, Federal Bureau of Investigation, *Uniform Crime Reports*.

Cybersecurity

As businesses increasingly depend on electronic data and computer networks to conduct their daily operations, growing pools of personal and financial information are being transferred and stored online. This can leave individuals exposed to privacy violations and financial institutions and other businesses exposed to potentially enormous liability, if and when a breach in data security occurs.

Interest in cyber insurance and risk has grown in 2014 and 2015 as a result of high-profile data breaches, including a massive data breach at health insurer Anthem that exposed data on 78.8 million customers and employees, and another at Premera Blue Cross that compromised the records of 11 million customers. The U.S. government was targeted by hackers in two separate attacks in May 2015 that compromised personnel records on as many as 14 million current and former civilian government employees. A state-sponsored attack against Sony Pictures Entertainment, allegedly by North Korea, made headlines in late 2014.

Cyberattacks and breaches have grown in frequency, and loss costs are on the rise. In 2014 the number of U.S. data breaches hit a record 783, with 85.6 million records exposed. The majority of the 783 data breaches in 2014 affected medical/healthcare organizations (42.5 percent of total breaches) and business (33.3 percent), according to the Identity Theft Resource Center. In the first half of 2015 some 400 data breach events were publicly disclosed, with 117.6 million records exposed. These figures do not include the many attacks that go unreported. In addition, many attacks go undetected. Despite conflicting analyses, the costs associated with these losses are increasing. McAfee and the Center for Strategic and International Studies (CSIS) estimated the likely annual cost to the global economy from cybercrime is $445 billion a year, with a range of between $375 billion and $575 billion.

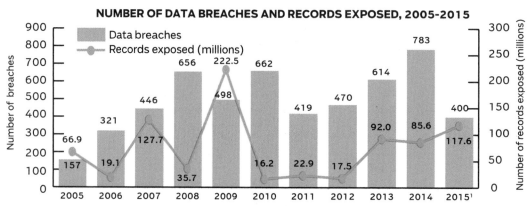

NUMBER OF DATA BREACHES AND RECORDS EXPOSED, 2005-2015

[1] As of June 30, 2015.

Source: Identity Theft Resource Center.

The Internet Crime Complaint Center (IC3), a joint project of the Federal Bureau of Investigation, the National White Collar Crime Center and the Bureau of Justice Assistance monitors Internet-related criminal complaints. In 2014 the IC3 received and processed 269,422 complaints. The IC3 reports that 123,684 of these complaints involved a dollar loss and puts total dollar losses at over $800 million. The most common complaints received in 2014 involved auto and real estate fraud, and government impersonation email scams.

CYBERCRIME COMPLAINTS, 2010-2014[1]

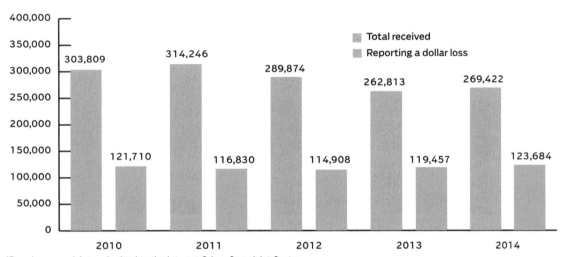

[1]Based on complaints submitted to the Internet Crime Complaint Center.

Source: Internet Crime Complaint Center.

TOP 10 STATES FOR CYBERCRIME, 2014

Rank	State	Percent[1]	Rank	State	Percent[1]
1	California	12.54%	6	Illinois	3.14%
2	Florida	7.56	7	Virginia	2.88
3	Texas	6.87	8	New Jersey	2.85
4	New York	5.85	9	Washington	2.59
5	Pennsylvania	3.30	10	Ohio	2.48

[1]Percent of complaints submitted to the Internet Crime Complaint Center via its website.

Source: Internet Crime Complaint Center.

Consumer Fraud and Identity Theft

The Consumer Sentinel Network, maintained by the Federal Trade Commission (FTC), tracks consumer fraud and identity theft complaints that have been filed with federal, state and local law enforcement agencies and private organizations. Of the 2.6 million complaints received in 2014, 60 percent were related to fraud, 13 percent were related to identity theft and 27 percent were other consumer complaints. The FTC identifies 30 types of complaints. In 2014, for the 15th year in a row, identity theft was the No. 1 type of complaint among the 30 categories, accounting for about 333,000 complaints, followed by debt collection, with about 280,000 complaints. Internet services, with about 46,000 complaints, ranked 10th.

IDENTITY THEFT AND FRAUD COMPLAINTS, 2012-2014[1]

[1]Percentages are based on the total number of Consumer Sentinel Network complaints by calendar year. These figures exclude "Do Not Call" registry complaints.

Source: Federal Trade Commission.

HOW VICTIMS' INFORMATION IS MISUSED, 2014[1]

Type of identity theft fraud	Percent
Government documents or benefits fraud	38.7%
Credit card fraud	17.4
Phone or utilities fraud	12.5
Bank fraud[2]	8.2
Attempted identity theft	4.8
Employment-related fraud	4.8
Loan fraud	4.4
Other identity theft	21.8

[1]Percentages are based on the total number of complaints in the Federal Trade Commission's Consumer Sentinel Network (332,646 in 2014). Percentages total to more than 100 because some victims reported experiencing more than one type of identity theft.
[2]Includes fraud involving checking, savings and other deposit accounts and electronic fund transfers.

Source: Federal Trade Commission.

Crime: Cybersecurity and Identity Theft

IDENTITY THEFT BY STATE, 2014

State	Complaints per 100,000 population[1]	Number of complaints	Rank[2]	State	Complaints per 100,000 population[1]	Number of complaints	Rank[2]
Alabama	77.7	3,770	22	Montana	57.2	585	40
Alaska	73.6	542	29	Nebraska	48.6	914	46
Arizona	96.0	6,460	9	Nevada	100.2	2,846	8
Arkansas	83.6	2,481	15	New Hampshire	54.7	726	41
California	100.5	38,982	7	New Jersey	79.9	7,144	19
Colorado	85.5	4,579	13	New Mexico	77.2	1,611	23
Connecticut	85.4	3,071	14	New York	80.8	15,959	17
Delaware	78.1	731	21	North Carolina	73.8	7,334	27
Florida	186.3	37,059	1	North Dakota	43.1	319	48
Georgia	112.7	11,384	5	Ohio	79.0	9,161	20
Hawaii	40.9	580	49	Oklahoma	68.5	2,656	32
Idaho	58.9	962	39	Oregon	124.6	4,946	3
Illinois	95.6	12,317	12	Pennsylvania	81.7	10,446	16
Indiana	68.2	4,498	33	Rhode Island	66.2	699	34
Iowa	48.5	1,506	47	South Carolina	73.3	3,540	30
Kansas	65.2	1,892	35	South Dakota	36.3	310	50
Kentucky	53.4	2,358	43	Tennessee	76.2	4,993	24
Louisiana	73.8	3,430	27	Texas	95.9	25,843	10
Maine	52.1	693	44	Utah	53.9	1,586	42
Maryland	95.9	5,734	10	Vermont	64.2	402	36
Massachusetts	75.8	5,116	25	Virginia	71.1	5,921	31
Michigan	104.3	10,338	6	Washington	154.8	10,930	2
Minnesota	59.2	3,229	38	West Virginia	61.4	1,136	37
Mississippi	80.5	2,409	18	Wisconsin	74.4	4,283	26
Missouri	118.7	7,195	4	Wyoming	49.1	287	45

[1]Population figures are based on the 2014 U.S. Census population estimates.
[2]Ranked per complaints per 100,000 population. The District of Columbia had 142.8 complaints per 100,000 population and 941 victims. States with the same ratio of complaints per 100,000 population receive the same rank.

Source: Federal Trade Commission.

Losses

Motor Vehicles: Crashes

The National Highway Traffic Safety Administration (NHTSA) reports that 32,719 people died in motor vehicle crashes in 2013, down 3.1 percent from 33,782 in 2012. 2012 marked the first year-to-year increase in motor vehicle crash fatalities since 2005. The fatality rate, measured as deaths per 100 million vehicle miles traveled, fell to 1.10 in 2013 from 1.14 in 2012. The 2013 fatality rate ties 2011 for the lowest fatality rate on record. NHTSA property damage figures shown below are based on accidents reported to the police and exclude fender-benders.

TRAFFIC DEATHS, 2004-2013

- The number of people injured in motor vehicle crashes fell by 2.1 percent to 2.31 million in 2013 from 2.36 million in 2012.

- The injury rate per 100 million vehicle miles traveled was 78 in 2013, down from 80 in 2012.

Year	Fatalities	Annual percent change	Fatality rate per 100 million vehicle miles traveled	Fatality rate per 100,000 registered vehicles
2004	42,836	-0.1%	1.44	18.00
2005	43,510	1.6	1.46	17.71
2006	42,708	-1.8	1.42	16.99
2007	41,259	-3.4	1.36	16.02
2008	37,423	-9.3	1.26	14.43
2009	33,883	-9.5	1.15	13.08
2010	32,999	-2.6	1.11	12.82
2011	32,479	-1.6	1.10	12.25
2012	33,782	4.0	1.14	12.72
2013	32,719	-3.1	1.10	12.26

Source: U.S. Department of Transportation, National Highway Traffic Safety Administration.

MOTOR VEHICLE CRASHES, 2004-2013

Year	Fatal	Injury	Property damage only	Total crashes
2004	38,444	1,862,000	4,281,000	6,181,000
2005	39,252	1,816,000	4,304,000	6,159,000
2006	38,648	1,746,000	4,189,000	5,973,000
2007	37,435	1,711,000	4,275,000	6,024,000
2008	34,172	1,630,000	4,146,000	5,811,000
2009	30,862	1,517,000	3,957,000	5,505,000
2010	30,296	1,542,000	3,847,000	5,419,000
2011	29,757	1,530,000	3,778,000	5,338,000
2012	31,006	1,634,000	3,950,000	5,615,000
2013	30,057	1,591,000	4,066,000	5,687,000

Source: U.S. Department of Transportation, National Highway Traffic Safety Administration.

According to the National Highway Traffic Safety Administration, vehicle occupants accounted for 68 percent of traffic deaths in 2013. Motorcycle riders accounted for 14 percent. Pedestrians accounted for another 15 percent; pedalcyclists and other nonoccupants accounted for the remainder.

MOTOR VEHICLE TRAFFIC DEATHS BY STATE, 2012-2013

State	Number of deaths		Percent change	State	Number of deaths		Percent change
	2012	2013			2012	2013	
Alabama	865	852	-1.5%	Montana	205	229	12.0%
Alaska	59	51	-14.0	Nebraska	212	211	-0.5
Arizona	821	849	3.4	Nevada	261	262	0.4
Arkansas	560	483	-14.0	New Hampshire	108	135	25.0
California	2,966	3,000	1.1	New Jersey	589	542	-8.0
Colorado	474	481	1.5	New Mexico	366	310	-15.0
Connecticut	264	276	4.5	New York	1,180	1,199	1.6
Delaware	114	99	-13.0	North Carolina	1,299	1,289	-0.8
D.C.	15	20	33.0	North Dakota	170	148	-13.0
Florida	2,431	2,407	-1.0	Ohio	1,121	989	-12.0
Georgia	1,192	1,179	-1.1	Oklahoma	709	678	-4.4
Hawaii	125	102	-18.0	Oregon	337	313	-7.1
Idaho	184	214	16.0	Pennsylvania	1,310	1,208	-7.8
Illinois	956	991	3.7	Rhode Island	64	65	1.6
Indiana	781	783	0.3	South Carolina	863	767	-11.0
Iowa	365	317	-13.0	South Dakota	133	135	1.5
Kansas	405	350	-14.0	Tennessee	1,015	995	-2.0
Kentucky	746	638	-14.0	Texas	3,408	3,382	-0.8
Louisiana	723	703	-2.8	Utah	217	220	1.4
Maine	164	145	-12.0	Vermont	77	69	-10.0
Maryland	511	465	-9.0	Virginia	776	740	-4.6
Massachusetts	383	326	-15.0	Washington	438	436	-0.5
Michigan	940	947	0.7	West Virginia	339	332	-2.1
Minnesota	395	387	-2.0	Wisconsin	615	543	-12.0
Mississippi	582	613	5.3	Wyoming	123	87	-29.0
Missouri	826	757	-8.4	**United States**	**33,782**	**32,719**	**-3.1%**

Source: U.S. Department of Transportation, National Highway Traffic Safety Administration.

VEHICLES INVOLVED IN CRASHES BY VEHICLE TYPE AND CRASH SEVERITY, 2004 AND 2013

	Fatal crashes		Injury crashes		Property damage-only crashes	
	2004	2013	2004	2013	2004	2013
Passenger cars						
Crashes	25,682	17,834	1,990,000	1,662,000	4,216,000	3,989,000
Rate per 100 million vehicle miles traveled	1.58	1.29	122	120	259	288
Rate per 100,000 registered vehicles	19.25	13.83	1,491	1,289	3,160	3,093
Light trucks[1]						
Crashes	22,486	16,857	1,246,000	1,076,000	2,886,000	2,776,000
Rate per 100 million vehicle miles traveled	2.05	1.30	114	83	263	215
Rate per 100,000 registered vehicles	25.04	13.99	1,387	893	3,213	2,305
Motorcycles						
Crashes	4,121	4,774	70,000	84,000	13,000	18,000
Rate per 100 million vehicle miles traveled	40.71	23.44	694	413	132	86
Rate per 100,000 registered vehicles	71.45	56.80	1,217	1,001	231	210

[1]Trucks with 10,000 pounds or less gross vehicle weight. Includes pickups, vans, truck-based station wagons and utility vehicles.

Source: U.S. Department of Transportation (USDOT), National Highway Traffic Safety Administration (NHTSA). Vehicle miles traveled - USDOT, Federal Highway Administration, revised by NHTSA; Registered passenger cars and light trucks - R.L. Polk & Co; Registered motorcycles - USDOT, Federal Highway Administration.

MOTOR VEHICLE DEATHS BY ACTIVITY OF PERSON KILLED, 2013

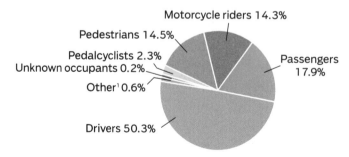

Motorcycle riders 14.3%
Pedestrians 14.5%
Pedalcyclists 2.3%
Unknown occupants 0.2%
Other[1] 0.6%
Passengers 17.9%
Drivers 50.3%

[1]Includes other non-occupants.

Source: U.S. Department of Transportation, National Highway Traffic Safety Administration.

SEX OF DRIVERS INVOLVED IN CRASHES, 2004-2013[1]

	Fatal crashes				Injury crashes			
	Male		Female		Male		Female	
Year	Number	Rate[2]	Number	Rate[2]	Number	Rate[2]	Number	Rate[2]
2004	41,876	42.06	15,272	15.38	1,911,852	1,920	1,482,315	1,493
2005	42,947	42.84	14,967	14.92	1,836,711	1,832	1,425,161	1,421
2006	41,912	41.49	14,661	14.43	1,762,552	1,745	1,387,324	1,366
2007	40,804	39.82	14,099	13.65	1,719,000	1,677	1,339,000	1,296
2008	36,881	35.59	12,568	12.00	1,609,000	1,553	1,280,000	1,223
2009	32,807	31.47	11,825	11.22	1,499,561	1,438	1,224,613	1,162
2010	31,965	30.63	11,811	11.17	1,516,000	1,453	1,265,000	1,196
2011	31,809	30.32	11,209	10.48	1,507,000	1,436	1,244,000	1,163
2012	33,124	31.55	11,509	10.77	1,634,884	1,557	1,314,534	1,230
2013	32,442	30.89	11,364	10.61	1,584,000	1,509	1,331,000	1,242

	Property damage-only crashes				Total crashes			
	Male		Female		Male		Female	
Year	Number	Rate[2]	Number	Rate[2]	Number	Rate[2]	Number	Rate[2]
2004	4,404,779	4,424	3,037,126	3,058	6,358,507	6,387	4,534,713	4,566
2005	4,357,188	4,347	3,007,038	2,998	6,236,846	6,222	4,447,166	4,435
2006	4,232,184	4,190	2,967,964	2,922	6,036,648	5,976	4,369,949	4,302
2007	4,345,000	4,241	3,066,000	2,968	6,105,000	5,968	4,418,000	4,278
2008	4,174,000	4,028	2,967,000	2,834	5,820,000	5,617	4,260,000	4,069
2009	3,913,473	3,753	2,931,260	2,782	5,445,840	5,223	4,167,698	3,956
2010	3,854,000	3,693	2,862,000	2,707	5,402,000	5,176	4,139,000	3,915
2011	3,675,000	3,503	2,921,000	2,730	5,213,000	4,970	4,176,000	3,904
2012	3,880,163	3,696	3,006,762	3,251	5,548,171	5,285	4,332,806	4,056
2013	3,990,000	3,800	3,092,000	2,886	5,607,000	5,340	4,434,000	4,138

[1]Includes motorcycle riders and restricted and graduated drivers license holders in some states.
[2]Rate per 100,000 licensed drivers.

Source: U.S. Department of Transportation, National Highway Traffic Safety Administration.

Teenage Drivers

Motor vehicle crashes are a leading cause of death among teenagers. According to the U.S. Department of Transportation (DOT), 1,651 drivers age 16 to 20 died in motor vehicle crashes in 2013, compared with 1,843 drivers in this age group in 2012. Drivers age 16 to 20 accounted for 5.8 percent of all licensed drivers, 8.7 percent of all drivers involved in fatal crashes and 12.5 percent of drivers in all crashes in 2013. Seventeen percent of drivers age 16 to 20 who were involved in fatal crashes in 2013 were alcohol-impaired, which is defined by a blood alcohol concentration of 0.08 grams per deciliter or higher. The DOT found that more teenagers are involved in motor vehicle crashes late in the day and at night than at other times of the day. Teens also have a greater chance of getting involved in an accident if other teens are present in the vehicle, according to research from the Children's Hospital of Philadelphia and State Farm.

DRIVERS IN MOTOR VEHICLE CRASHES BY AGE, 2013

Age group	Number of licensed drivers	Percent of total	Drivers in fatal crashes	Involvement rate[1]	Drivers in all crashes	Involvement rate[1]
16 to 20	12,214,248	5.8%	3,883	31.79	1,259,000	10,311
21 to 24	14,373,838	6.8	4,609	32.07	1,144,000	7,957
25 to 34	36,697,904	17.3	8,762	23.88	2,153,000	5,867
35 to 44	36,018,792	17.0	7,183	19.94	1,663,000	4,617
45 to 54	39,907,125	18.8	7,343	18.40	1,640,000	4,110
55 to 64	36,055,252	17.0	5,911	16.39	1,202,000	3,333
65 to 74	22,534,477	10.6	3,357	14.90	605,000	2,683
Over 74	14,295,739	6.7	2,567	17.96	346,000	2,420
Total	**212,159,728[2]**	**100.0%**	**44,574[2]**	**21.01**	**1,043,000[2]**	**4,733**

[1] Per 100,000 licensed drivers.
[2] Includes drivers under the age of 16 and of unknown age.

Source: U.S. Department of Transportation, National Highway Traffic Safety Administration; Federal Highway Administration.

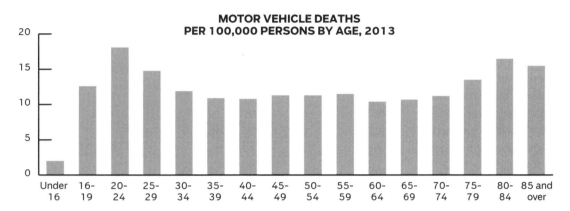

MOTOR VEHICLE DEATHS PER 100,000 PERSONS BY AGE, 2013

Source: Insurance Institute for Highway Safety.

DRIVING BEHAVIORS REPORTED FOR DRIVERS AND MOTORCYCLE OPERATORS INVOLVED IN FATAL CRASHES, 2013

Behavior	Number of drivers	Percent
Driving too fast for conditions or in excess of posted speed limit or racing	8,864	19.9%
Under the influence of alcohol, drugs or medication	6,005	13.5
Failure to keep in proper lane	3,720	8.3
Failure to yield right of way	3,149	7.1
Distracted (phone, talking, eating, etc.)	2,959	6.6
Operating vehicle in a careless manner	2,116	4.7
Overcorrecting/oversteering	1,990	4.5
Failure to obey traffic signs, signals or officer	1,780	4.0
Swerving or avoiding due to wind, slippery surface, other vehicle, object, nonmotorist in roadway, etc.	1,628	3.7
Operating vehicle in erratic, reckless, or negligent manner	1,511	3.4
Vision obscured (rain, snow, glare, lights, buildings, trees, etc.)	1,493	3.3
Drowsy, asleep, fatigued, ill, or blacked out	1,231	2.8
Driving wrong way in one-way traffic or on wrong side of road	858	1.9
Making improper turn	689	1.5
Other factors	5,165	11.6
None reported	13,692	30.7
Unknown	5,441	12.2
Total drivers[1]	**44,574**	**100.0%**

[1]The sum of percentages is greater than 100 percent because more than one factor may be present for the same driver.
Source: U.S. Department of Transportation, National Highway Traffic Safety Administration.

Losses

Motor Vehicles: Crashes

- In 2013, 10,076 people were killed in crashes where a driver had a blood alcohol concentration (BAC) of 0.08 percent or higher, down 2.5 percent from 10,336 in 2012, according to a National Highway Traffic Safety Administration report.

- The majority (68 percent) of alcohol-impaired crash fatalities in 2013 involved drivers with a BAC of 0.15 or higher—nearly double the legal limit.

ALCOHOL-IMPAIRED CRASH FATALITIES, 2004-2013[1]

Year	Alcohol impaired crash fatalities	As a percent of all crash fatalities
2004	13,099	31%
2005	13,582	31
2006	13,491	32
2007	13,041	32
2008	11,711	31
2009	10,759	32
2010	10,136	31
2011	9,865	30
2012	10,336	31
2013	10,076	31

[1]Alcohol-impaired driving crashes are crashes that involve at least one driver or a motorcycle operator with a blood alcohol concentration of 0.08 percent or above, the legal definition of drunk driving.

Source: U.S. Department of Transportation, National Highway Traffic Safety Administration.

PERCENT OF ALCOHOL-IMPAIRED DRIVERS INVOLVED IN FATAL CRASHES BY AGE, 2004 AND 2013[1]

Age	2004	2013	Point change
16 to 20	18%	17%	-1 pt.
21 to 24	33	33	0
25 to 34	27	29	2
35 to 44	23	24	1
45 to 54	19	20	1
55 to 64	12	14	2
65 to 74	8	8	0
Over 74	5	5	0

- In 2013 the percentage of drivers involved in fatal crashes who were alcohol-impaired was highest in the 21 to 24 and the 25 to 34 age groups, the same as in 2004.

[1]Alcohol-impaired driving crashes are crashes that involve at least one driver or a motorcycle operator with a blood alcohol concentration of 0.08 percent or above, the legal definition of drunk driving.

Source: U.S. Department of Transportation, National Highway Traffic Safety Administration.

PERSONS KILLED IN TOTAL AND ALCOHOL-IMPAIRED CRASHES BY PERSON TYPE, 2013

Person type	Total killed	Alcohol-impaired driving fatalities[1]	
		Number	Percent of total killed
Vehicle occupants			
Driver	16,472	5,920	36%
Passenger	5,844	1,822	31
Unknown occupant	67	2	3
Total	**22,383**	**7,744**	**35%**
Motorcyclists	**4,668**	**1,496**	**32%**
Nonoccupants			
Pedestrian	4,735	721	15
Pedalcyclist	743	92	12
Other/unknown	190	23	12
Total	**5,668**	**837**	**15%**
Total	**32,719**	**10,076**	**31%**

[1]Alcohol-impaired driving crashes are crashes that involve at least one driver or a motorcycle operator with a blood alcohol concentration of 0.08 percent or above, the legal definition of drunk driving.

Source: U.S. Department of Transportation, National Highway Traffic Safety Administration.

MOTORCYCLE HELMET USE, 1996-2014[1]

Year	Percent	Year	Percent
1996	64%	2008	63%
1998	67	2009	67
2000	71	2010	54
2002	58	2011	66
2004	58	2012	60
2005	48	2013	60
2006	51	2014	64
2007	58		

[1]Based on surveys of motorcyclists using helmets meeting Department of Transportation standards. Surveys conducted in October for 1994-2000 and in June thereafter.

Source: U.S. Department of Transportation, National Occupant Protection Use Survey, National Highway Traffic Safety Administration's (NHTSA) National Center for Statistics and Analysis.

- Motorcycle helmet usage reached 64 percent in June 2014, compared with 60 percent in 2013, a change that NHTSA indicates is not statistically significant.

- Helmet use was highest in the West, at 85 percent, down from 92 percent in 2013. In the South, helmet use rose to 78 percent from 65 percent in 2013. Helmet use was 56 percent in the Northeast, up from 52 percent in 2013, and 47 percent in the Midwest, the lowest of all the regions, up from 42 percent in 2013.

Collision Losses

The chart below shows the claim frequency and average loss payment per claim and average loss payment per insured vehicle year under collision coverage for recent model vehicles. The claim frequency is expressed as a rate per 100 insured vehicle years. A vehicle year is equal to 365 days of insurance coverage for a single vehicle.

PASSENGER VEHICLE COLLISION COVERAGE INSURANCE LOSSES, 2012-2014 MODEL YEARS

	Claim frequency[1]	Claim severity
Passenger cars and minivans	7.9	$4,633
Pickups	6.2	4,565
SUVs	6.2	4,626
All passenger vehicles	**7.2**	**$4,625**

[1]Per 100 insured vehicle years.

Source: Highway Loss Data Institute.

Aggressive Driving

Aggressive driving is a major factor in U.S. traffic accidents, playing a role not just in well-publicized incidents of road rage, but in a large number of fatal highway collisions each year. The National Highway Traffic Safety Administration (NHTSA) defines aggressive driving as occurring when "an individual commits a combination of moving traffic offenses so as to endanger other persons or property." While aggressive driving is difficult to quantify, a 2009 study by the American Automobile Association reported that, based on data tracked by NHTSA's Fatal Accident Report System, aggressive driving played a role in 56 percent of fatal crashes from 2003 through 2007, with excessive speed being the No. 1 factor. Speeding was also the leading driving behavior associated with fatal crashes in 2013 (19.9 percent), followed by driving under the influence (13.5 percent), according to NHTSA. (See chart, page 177.)

Distracted Driving

Activities that take drivers' attention off the road, including talking or texting on cellphones, eating, conversing with passengers and other distractions, are a major safety threat. The National Highway Traffic Safety Administration (NHTSA) gauges distracted driving by collecting data on "distraction-affected crashes," which focuses on distractions that are most likely to affect crash involvement such as dialing a cellphone or texting and being distracted by another person or an outside event. In 2013, 3,154 people were killed in distraction-affected crashes, and 424,000 people were injured. There were 2,910 distraction-affected fatal crashes, accounting for 10 percent of all fatal crashes in the nation, 18 percent of injury crashes and 16 percent of all motor vehicle crashes in 2013.

DRIVER HAND-HELD CELLPHONE USE BY AGE, 2004-2013[1]

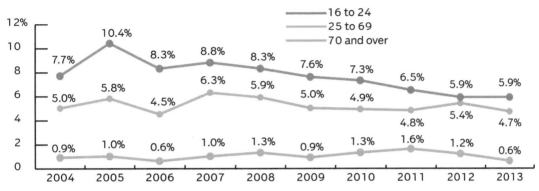

Legend:
— 16 to 24
— 25 to 69
— 70 and over

[1]Percent of drivers using hand-held cellphones.

Source: U.S. Department of Transportation, National Highway Traffic Safety Administration.

FATAL CRASHES AFFECTED BY DISTRACTED DRIVERS, 2013

	Crashes	Drivers	Fatalities
Total fatal crashes	**30,057**	**44,574**	**32,719**
Distracted-affected fatal crashes			
Number	2,910	2,959	3,154
Percent of total fatal crashes	10%	7%	10%
Cellphone in use in distracted-affected fatal crashes			
Number	411	427	445
Percent of fatal distracted-affected crashes	14%	14%	14%

- Cellphone use was a factor in 1 percent of the 30,057 fatal crashes reported in 2013.

- Distraction was a factor in 10 percent of fatal crashes reported in 2013.

Source: U.S. Department of Transportation, National Highway Traffic Safety Administration.

Motor Vehicles: Theft

The FBI includes the theft or attempted theft of automobiles, trucks, buses, motorcycles, scooters, snowmobiles and other vehicles in its definition of motor vehicle theft. A motor vehicle is stolen on average every 46 seconds in the United States.

MOTOR VEHICLE THEFT IN THE UNITED STATES, 2005-2014

- Motor vehicles were stolen at a rate of 216.2 per 100,000 people in 2014, down 2.3 percent from 2013 and down 48.1 percent from 2005.

- More than $4.5 billion was lost to motor vehicle theft in 2014. The average dollar loss per theft was $6,537.

Year	Vehicles stolen	Percent change
2005	1,235,859	-0.2%
2006	1,198,245	-3.0
2007	1,100,472	-8.2
2008	959,059	-12.9
2009	795,652	-17.0
2010	739,565	-7.0
2011	716,508	-3.1
2012	723,186	0.9
2013	700,288	-3.2
2014	689,527	-1.5

Source: U.S. Department of Justice, Federal Bureau of Investigation, *Uniform Crime Reports.*

TOP 10 U.S. METROPOLITAN STATISTICAL AREAS BY MOTOR VEHICLE THEFT RATE, 2014

- Seven of the top 10 U.S. Metropolitan Statistical Areas for motor vehicle theft were in California in 2014. Two were in Washington and one was in Texas.

Rank	Metropolitan Statistical Area[1]	Vehicles stolen	Rate[2]
1	San Francisco-Oakland-Hayward, CA	29,093	633.27
2	Bakersfield, CA	5,211	595.82
3	Stockton-Lodi, CA	4,245	593.21
4	Odessa, TX	886	575.68
5	Modesto, CA	3,047	572.75
6	Spokane-Spokane Valley, WA	3,032	560.49
7	Vallejo-Fairfield, CA	2,414	559.92
8	Seattle-Tacoma-Bellevue, WA	20,268	552.04
9	Fresno, CA	5,260	544.53
10	San Jose-Sunnyvale-Santa Clara, CA	10,531	539.26

[1]Metropolitan statistical areas are designated by the federal Office of Management and Budget and usually include areas much larger than the cities for which they are named.
[2]Rate of vehicle thefts reported per 100,000 people based on the 2014 U.S. Census Population Estimates.

Source: National Insurance Crime Bureau.

TOP 10 STATES WITH THE MOST AND THE FEWEST MOTOR VEHICLE THEFTS, 2014

	Most motor vehicle thefts			Fewest motor vehicle thefts	
Rank	State	Vehicles stolen	Rank	State	Vehicles stolen
1	California	151,852	1	Vermont	244
2	Texas	68,546	2	Wyoming	603
3	Florida	42,579	3	Maine	799
4	Washington	30,647	4	New Hampshire	857
5	Georgia	26,854	5	South Dakota	1,007
6	Michigan	21,157	6	Delaware	1,267
7	Ohio	18,015	7	North Dakota	1,514
8	Arizona	17,587	8	Idaho	1,661
9	Illinois	17,451	9	Alaska	1,739
10	Missouri	16,357	10	Rhode Island	1,833

Source: U.S. Department of Justice, Federal Bureau of Investigation, *Uniform Crime Reports*.

TOP 10 MOST FREQUENTLY STOLEN VEHICLES, 2014

Rank	Model[1]	Thefts
1	Honda Accord	51,290
2	Honda Civic	43,936
3	Ford Pickup (Full size)	28,680
4	Chevrolet Pickup (Full size)	23,196
5	Toyota Camry	14,605
6	Dodge Pickup (Full size)	11,075
7	Dodge Caravan	10,483
8	Nissan Altima	9,109
9	Acura Integra	6,902
10	Nissan Maxima	6,586

[1]Includes all model years for each vehicle.

Source: National Insurance Crime Bureau.

TOP 10 MOST FREQUENTLY STOLEN VEHICLES, 2014 MODEL YEAR

Rank	Model	Thefts
1	Ford Pickup (Full size)	964
2	Toyota Camry	869
3	Ford Fusion	819
4	Chevrolet Impala	746
5	Nissan Altima	687
6	Dodge Charger	680
7	Toyota Corolla	578
8	Chevrolet Cruze	566
9	Ford Focus	505
10	Chevrolet Malibu	410

Source: National Insurance Crime Bureau.

Recreation

Watercraft Accidents

Federal law requires owners of recreational boats and watercraft (non-commercial) to register them. In 2014 there were 11.8 million registered recreational watercraft, down from 12.0 million in 2013. A recreational boating accident must be reported to the U.S. Coast Guard if a person dies or is injured and requires medical treatment beyond first aid; if damage to the boat or other property exceeds $2,000; if the boat is lost or if a person disappears from the boat. Out of the 4,064 accidents reported in 2014, 581 occurred in Florida, accounting for 14.3 percent of all incidents. Other states with a high number of accidents were California (379), New York (175), Texas (167) and Missouri (142).

Fatalities increased by 8.9 percent to 610 in 2014 from 560 in 2013. The rate per 100,000 registered watercraft was 5.2, up from 4.7 in 2013. The number of accidents was mostly unchanged in 2014, at 4,064 compared with 4,062 in 2013. Injuries rose to 2,678 in 2014 from 2,620 in 2013, or 2.2 percent. Property damage totaled $39 million in 2014, about the same as in 2013.

The U.S. Coast Guard says that alcohol, combined with typical conditions such as motion, vibration, engine noise, sun, wind and spray can impair a person's abilities much faster than alcohol consumption on land. Operators with a blood alcohol concentration (BAC) above 0.10 percent are estimated to be more than 10 times more likely to be killed in an accident than operators with zero BAC. Alcohol was the largest primary human factor in boating deaths in 2014 (21 percent of fatalities), causing 108 deaths and 248 injuries in 277 accidents. Other primary contributing factors were operator inexperience, resulting in 44 deaths; and operator inattention, accounting for 38 deaths.

RECREATIONAL WATERCRAFT ACCIDENTS, 2010-2014[1]

Year	Accidents		Fatalities		Injuries	Property damage ($ millions)
	Total	Involving alcohol use[2]	Total	Involving alcohol use[2]		
2010	4,604	395	672	154	3,153	$36
2011	4,588	361	758	149	3,081	52
2012	4,515	368	651	140	3,000	38
2013	4,062	305	560	94	2,620	39
2014	4,064	345	610	137	2,678	39

[1]Includes accidents involving $2,000 or more in property damage.
[2]The use of alcohol by a boat's occupants was a direct or indirect cause of the accident.

Source: U.S. Department of Transportation, U.S. Coast Guard.

- 78 percent of fatal boating accident victims died by drowning in 2014, and of those, 84 percent were not wearing life jackets.

- The most common types of watercraft involved in reported accidents in 2014 were open motorboats (47 percent), personal watercraft (jet skis) (17 percent) and cabin motorboats (15 percent).

TOP 10 STATES BY RECREATIONAL WATERCRAFT ACCIDENTS, 2014[1]

Rank	State	Accidents	Deaths	People injured	Property damage ($000)
1	Florida	581	70	327	$7,387
2	California	379	38	256	2,352
3	New York	175	27	105	1,576
4	Texas	167	39	119	1,527
5	Missouri	142	14	101	1,683
6	Maryland	130	12	96	584
7	North Carolina	124	26	92	845
7	South Carolina	124	14	92	979
9	Washington	122	22	67	2,070
10	Louisiana	113	18	114	626

[1]Includes accidents involving $2,000 or more in property damage. Includes watercraft such as motorboats and sailboats and other vessels such as jet skis.

Source: U.S. Department of Transportation, U.S. Coast Guard.

Watercraft Thefts

There were 5,181 watercraft thefts in the United States in 2014, down 6 percent from 2013, according to an analysis of federal government data by the National Insurance Crime Bureau. Watercraft include motor boats, sailboats and other vessels such as jet skis. Of these thefts, 2,140, or 41 percent, were recovered by May 30, 2015. Jet skis (personal watercraft) were the most frequently stolen watercraft, with 1,121 thefts, followed by runabouts (755), utility boats (325), cruisers (186) and sailboats (49). July saw the highest number of reported thefts (667), and February had the fewest (223).

TOP 10 STATES BY WATERCRAFT THEFT, 2014[1]

Rank	State	Thefts	Rank	State	Thefts
1	Florida	1,290	6	Georgia	163
2	California	507	7	Tennessee	159
3	Texas	386	8	South Carolina	146
4	Washington	201	9	Arkansas	139
5	North Carolina	169	10	Alabama	137

[1] Includes motorboats and sailboats and other vessels such as jet skis.
Source: National Insurance Crime Bureau.

SPORTS INJURIES IN THE UNITED STATES, 2013

Sport or activity	Injuries[1]	Percent of injuries by age				
		0 to 4	5 to 14	15 to 24	25 to 64	65 and over
Basketball	533,509	0.4%	32.8%	47.8%	18.8%	0.2%
Bicycle riding[2]	521,578	4.6	33.4	18.3	39.0	4.7
Football	420,581	0.3	51.2	39.5	8.9	0.1
Exercise[3]	365,797	1.5	10.6	20.6	56.0	11.3
Soccer	229,088	0.8	44.6	37.8	16.4	0.3
Swimming[4]	184,190	9.2	41.7	17.0	27.8	4.4
Baseball	143,784	2.2	50.2	26.8	19.8	0.9
Skateboarding	120,424	1.0	35.1	51.3	12.4	0.2
Weightlifting	110,188	2.8	8.6	35.8	49.3	3.6
Softball	100,010	0.3	30.5	30.9	37.1	1.2
Fishing	70,541	3.3	16.7	16.6	50.3	13.1
Roller skating[5]	57,743	0.8	53.5	12.3	32.9	0.4
Horseback riding	54,609	1.2	16.9	23.1	53.1	5.6

(table continues)

SPORTS INJURIES IN THE UNITED STATES, 2013 (Cont'd)

Sport or activity	Injuries[1]	Percent of injuries by age				
		0 to 4	5 to 14	15 to 24	25 to 64	65 and over
Volleyball	50,845	[6]	31.9%	44.0%	23.1%	0.9%
Wrestling	42,633	[6]	42.2	53.4	4.4	[6]
Snowboarding	38,630	0.4%	23.8	51.4	24.1	0.3
Cheerleading	36,311	0.1	52.4	47.0	0.5	[6]
Gymnastics[7]	36,001	3.0	74.0	17.6	4.6	0.7
Martial arts	34,395	0.5	29.0	27.8	42.4	0.3
Golf[8]	33,101	1.7	13.7	7.6	39.2	37.8
Track and field	29,296	[6]	41.3	43.3	13.8	1.7
Ice skating[9]	20,443	0.6	47.0	21.7	28.3	2.4
Boxing	19,675	0.1	6.3	46.6	46.1	0.9
Tennis	19,292	0.5	16.2	16.3	41.3	25.7
Bowling	16,982	11.9	15.1	11.3	50.6	11.1
Ice hockey	16,871	[6]	37.3	40.4	21.2	1.0
Rugby	13,567	[6]	7.3	76.8	15.9	[6]
Mountain biking	9,763	0.8	6.5	19.7	70.9	2.1
Snowmobiling	9,270	[6]	7.2	23.3	69.1	0.4
Archery	5,153	1.6	15.7	23.4	49.8	9.4
Waterskiing	5,114	[6]	8.4	43.1	47.6	0.9
Racquetball, squash and paddleball	4,411	1.9	11.2	32.7	46.4	7.9
Mountain climbing	4,307	[6]	17.3	36.2	43.8	2.7
Hockey, field	4,241	[6]	25.3	61.6	13.1	[6]
Billiards, pool	3,698	9.4	25.2	10.8	49.5	5.1
Horseshoe pitching	1,449	5.4	6.9	12.4	64.7	10.6
Scuba diving[10]	1,437	5.0	10.3	22.6	55.2	6.9

[1]Treated in hospital emergency departments. [2]Excludes mountain biking. [3]Includes exercise equipment (60,546 injuries) and exercise activity (305,251 injuries). [4]Includes injuries associated with swimming, swimming pools, pool slides, diving or diving boards and swimming pool equipment. [5]Includes roller skating (46,023 injuries) and in-line skating (11,720 injuries). [6]Less than 0.1 percent. [7]Excludes trampolines (83,665 injuries). [8]Excludes golf carts (15,193 injuries). [9]Excludes 7,491 injuries in skating, unspecified. [10]Data for 2012.

Source: National Safety Council. (2015). Injury Facts®, 2015 Edition. Itasca, IL.

ATV Accidents

One in four people (25 percent) injured in accidents involving all-terrain vehicles (ATVs) in 2013 were children under the age of 16, according to the Consumer Product Safety Commission. ATVs are open-air vehicles with three, four or six wheels designed for off-road use. Many states require ATV insurance for vehicles operated on state-owned land.

ATV-RELATED DEATHS AND INJURIES, 2009-2013[1]

| Year | Estimated number of deaths | | | Estimated number of injuries[2] | | |
| | Total | Younger than 16 years | | Total | Younger than 16 years | |
		Number	Percent of total		Number	Percent of total
2009	721	96	13%	131,900	32,400	25%
2010	656	90	14	115,000	28,300	25
2011	620	82	13	107,500	29,000	27
2012	513	59	12	107,900	26,500	25
2013	426	62	15	99,600	25,000	25

[1]ATVs with 3, 4 or unknown number of wheels.
[2]Emergency room treated.

Source: U.S. Consumer Product Safety Commission.

Aviation

- There were 1,287 civil aviation accidents in 2014, down from 1,297 in 2013. Total fatalities rose to 439 in 2014 from 430 in 2013.

- There were no fatalities on large scheduled commercial airlines in 2014 for the fifth year running. There were no fatalities on large nonscheduled airlines (charter airlines) in 2014. There were nine fatalities in 2013.

United States

In the United States the National Transportation Safety Board compiles data on aviation flight hours, accidents and fatalities for commercial and general aviation.

Commercial airlines are divided into two categories according to the type of aircraft used: aircraft with 10 or more seats and aircraft with fewer than 10 seats. The nonscheduled commercial aircraft with more than 10 seats are also called charter airlines. Commercial airlines flying aircraft with fewer than 10 seats include commuter (scheduled) airlines, and on-demand air taxis. General aviation includes all U.S. noncommercial or privately owned aircraft.

In 2014 about 756 million people flew on commercial airlines in the United States, up 2.3 percent from 2013. The Federal Aviation Administration projects that more than 1 billion people will fly on scheduled commercial airlines in the United States annually by 2029.

AIRCRAFT ACCIDENTS IN THE UNITED STATES, 2014[1]

	Flight hours (000)	Number of accidents		Number of fatalities[2]	Accidents per 100,000 flight hours
		Total	Fatal		
Commercial airlines					
10 or more seats					
Scheduled	17,226	27	0	0	0.157
Nonscheduled	373	1	0	0	0.268
Less than 10 seats					
Commuter	349	4	0	0	1.448
On-demand	3,448	35	8	20	1.015
General aviation	18,103	1,221	253	419	6.744
Total civil aviation	**NA**	**1,287**	**261**	**439**	**NA**

[1]Preliminary data. Totals do not add because of collisions involving aircraft in different categories.
[2]Includes nonpassenger deaths.

NA=Data not available.

Source: National Transportation Safety Board.

- Small commuter airlines had four accidents in 2014 compared with seven in 2013. There were no fatalities in 2014 following five in 2013.

- The number of small on-demand airline (air taxi) accidents fell to 35 in 2014 from 44 in 2013.

- There were 1,221 general aviation (noncommercial) accidents in 2014, down from 1,224 in 2013. 2014 accidents resulted in 419 deaths, up from 391 in 2013.

LARGE AIRLINE ACCIDENTS IN THE UNITED STATES, 2005-2014[1]

Year	Flight hours	Total accidents	Fatal accidents	Total fatalities[2]	Total accidents per 100,000 flight hours
2005	19,390,029	40	3	22	0.206
2006	19,263,209	33	2	50	0.171
2007	19,637,322	28	1	1	0.143
2008	19,126,766	28	2	3	0.146
2009	17,626,832	30	2	52	0.170
2010	17,750,986	30	1	2	0.169
2011	17,962,965	31	0	0	0.173
2012	17,722,235	27	0	0	0.152
2013	17,692,748	23	2	9	0.130
2014[3]	17,599,000	28	0	0	0.159

[1]Scheduled and unscheduled planes with more than 10 seats.
[2]Includes nonpassenger deaths.
[3]Preliminary.

Source: National Transportation Safety Board.

World Aviation Losses

In 2014 more than 3.3 billion people flew safely on 38.0 million flights, according to the International Air Transport Association. The global accident rate (as measured by the rate of hull losses on Western-built jets) was 0.23 in 2014, or about one accident for every 4.4 million flights and the lowest rate in history. The 2013 accident rate was 0.41. (A hull loss is an accident in which the aircraft is destroyed or substantially damaged and is not subsequently repaired.) There were 73 accidents in 2014 (on Eastern- and Western-built aircraft), down from 81 in 2013. A Malaysia Airlines jet shot down on July 17, 2014, over Ukraine became the seventh deadliest crash in history, with 298 fatalities. This crash is not counted in the accident statistics. Malaysia Airlines Flight 370 en route to Beijing disappeared on March 8, 2014, with 239 on board.

FATAL WORLD AVIATION ACCIDENTS, 2010-2014

Year	Fatal accidents[1]	Fatalities[1]	Accident rate[2]
2010	23	786	0.79
2011	22	490	0.58
2012	15	414	0.28
2013	16	210	0.41
2014	12	641	0.23

[1]On Eastern- and Western-built jet aircraft.
[2]Measured in hull losses per million flights of Western-built jet aircraft. A hull loss is an accident in which the aircraft is destroyed or substantially damaged and is not subsequently repaired.

Source: International Air Transport Association.

TOP 10 DEADLIEST AVIATION CRASHES

Rank	Date	Location	Country	Operator	Fatalities
1	Mar. 27, 1977	Tenerife	Spain	Pan Am, KLM	583
2	Aug. 12, 1985	Yokota AFB	Japan	JAL	520
3	Nov. 12, 1996	New Delhi	India	Saudi Arabian Airlines, Kazakhstan Airlines	349
4	Mar. 3, 1974	Ermenonville	France	Turkish Airlines	346
5	Jun. 23, 1985	Atlantic Ocean		Air India	329
6	Aug. 19, 1980	Jedda	Saudi Arabia	Saudi Arabian Airlines	301
7	Jul. 17, 2014	Grabovo	Ukraine	Malaysia Airlines	298
8	Jul. 3, 1988	Persian Gulf		Iran Air	290
9	Feb. 19, 2003	Kerman	Iran	Islamic Republic of Iran Air Force	275
10	May 25, 1979	Chicago	U.S.	American Airlines	273

Source: Aircraft Crashes Record Office, Geneva.

Workplace Losses

According to the National Safety Council (NSC), the total cost of unintentional workplace deaths and injuries in 2013 was an estimated $206.1 billion. This figure includes wage and productivity losses of injured workers of $91.0 billion, medical costs of $57.9 billion and administrative expenses of $40.6 billion. Other employers' costs include their uninsured costs which add another $11.5 billion. Also included are fire losses of $2.8 billion and $2.3 billion in motor vehicle damage. Economic losses from work injuries are not comparable from year to year; as additional or more precise data become available to the NSC, they are used from that year forward. Previously estimated figures are not revised.

WORKPLACE LOSSES AND DEATHS, 2004-2013

| Year | Workers[3] (000) | Economic loss[1] ($ millions) | | Loss per worker (In 2013 dollars)[4] | Fatalities[2] | |
		Dollars when occurred	In 2013 dollars[4]		Number	Per 100,000 workers
2004	140,504	$142,200	$175,365	$1,248	4,995	3.6
2005	142,946	160,400	191,328	1,338	4,984	3.5
2006	145,607	164,700	190,318	1,307	5,088	3.5
2007	147,203	175,300	196,957	1,338	4,829	3.3
2008	146,535	183,000	198,005	1,351	4,423	3.3
2009	141,102	168,900	183,402	1,300	3,744	2.9
2010	140,298	176,900	188,989	1,347	3,896	3.0
2011	140,298	188,900	195,633	1,394	3,901	3.0
2012	143,709	198,200	201,103	1,399	3,903	3.0
2013	145,171	206,100	206,100	1,420	3,738	2.8

[1]Economic loss from unintentional injuries. These estimates are not comparable from year to year.
[2]From unintentional injuries.
[3]Age 16 and over, gainfully employed, includes owners, managers and other paid employees, the self-employed, unpaid family workers and active duty resident military personnel.
[4]Adjusted to 2013 dollars by the Insurance Information Institute using the Bureau of Labor Statistics Inflation Calculator.

Source: National Safety Council. (2015). Injury Facts®, 2015 Edition. Itasca, IL; U.S. Department of Labor, Bureau of Labor Statistics.

PRIVATE INDUSTRIES WITH THE LARGEST NUMBER OF NONFATAL OCCUPATIONAL INJURIES AND ILLNESSES, 2013[1]

Rank	Industry	Number (000)	Incidence rate[2]
1	General medical and surgical hospitals	226.6	6.4
2	Food services and drinking places	209.5	3.3
3	Nursing and residential care facilities	181.5	7.3
4	Specialty trade contractors	136.7	4.2
5	Ambulatory healthcare services	135.2	2.7
6	Administrative and support services	108.1	2.5
7	General merchandise stores	104.0	4.8
	Total, private industry	**3,007.3**	**3.3**

[1]Based on industries with 100,000 or more cases in 2013. Excludes farms with fewer than 11 employees.
[2]The incidence rates represent the number of injuries and illnesses per 100 full-time workers.

Source: U.S. Department of Labor, Bureau of Labor Statistics.

THE 10 OCCUPATIONS WITH THE LARGEST NUMBER OF INJURIES AND ILLNESSES, 2013[1]

Rank	Occupation	Number	Percent of total
1	Laborers (nonconstruction)	53,740	5.9%
2	Truck drivers, heavy and tractor trailer	49,000	5.3
3	Nursing assistants	41,450	4.5
4	Janitors and cleaners	39,040	4.3
5	General maintenance and repair workers	28,460	3.1
6	Police and sheriff's patrol officers	28,170	3.1
7	Registered nurses	27,020	2.9
8	Retail salespersons	26,830	2.9
9	Light truck and delivery service drivers	23,980	2.6
10	Stock clerks and order fillers	22,710	2.5
	Total, top 10	**340,400**	**37.1%**
	Total, all occupations	**917,090**	**100.0%**

[1]Nonfatal injuries and illnesses involving days off from work for private industries; excludes farms with fewer than 11 employees.

Source: U.S. Department of Labor, Bureau of Labor Statistics.

Causes of Workplace Deaths

According to the U.S. Department of Labor, the highest rate of workplace fatalities in 2014 was among logging workers, with 109.5 deaths per 100,000 full-time employees, followed by fishing workers, aircraft pilots and flight engineers and roofers. The all-industry average was 3.3 deaths per 100,000 workers.

WORKPLACE DEATHS BY CAUSE, 2013-2014[1]

Cause	2013 Number	2014 Number	2014 Percent of total
All transportation (includes vehicle crashes)	1,865	1,891	40%
Vehicle crashes[2]	1,099	1,075	23
Falls	724	793	17
Assaults and violence (includes homicides)	773	749	16
Homicides	404	403	9
Contact with objects and equipment	721	708	15
Exposure to harmful substances or environments	335	390	8
Fires and explosions	149	137	3
Total workplace fatalities	**4,585**	**4,679**	**100%**

[1]From intentional and unintentional sources. [2]Roadway incidents involving motorized land vehicles.

Source: U.S. Department of Labor, Bureau of Labor Statistics, Census of Fatal Occupational Injuries.

Occupational Disease

According to the U.S. Department of Labor's Bureau of Labor Statistics, an occupational disease is any new abnormal condition or disorder, other than one resulting from an occupational injury, caused by exposure to factors associated with employment. Included are acute and chronic diseases that may be caused by inhalation, absorption, ingestion or direct contact in the workplace.

The overwhelming majority of reported new illnesses are those that directly relate to workplace activity (e.g., contact dermatitis or carpal tunnel syndrome) and are easy to identify. However some conditions, such as long-term latent illnesses caused by exposure to carcinogens, often are difficult to relate to the workplace and may be understated.

Asbestos-Related Illness

Exposure to asbestos can cause lung cancer and other respiratory diseases. The first asbestos-related lawsuit was filed in 1966. A large number of workers who may have physical signs of exposure but not a debilitating disease are filing claims now out of concern that if they later develop an illness, the company responsible may be bankrupt, due to other asbestos claims. It can take as long as 40 years after exposure for someone to be diagnosed with an asbestos-related illness.

ESTIMATED ASBESTOS LOSSES, 2005-2014[1]
($ billions)

- In 2014 incurred asbestos losses fell 25 percent to $1.5 billion from $2.0 billion in 2013.

Year	Beginning reserve	Losses		Ending reserve[3]
		Incurred[2]	Paid	
2005	$24.0	$3.8	$2.4	$25.4
2006	25.2	1.7	2.6	24.1
2007	23.2	2.5	2.5	23.5
2008	23.5	1.1	3.7	20.5
2009	20.6	1.9	2.0	20.4
2010	20.5	2.4	2.3	20.6
2011	20.6	1.8	1.8	20.6
2012	20.4	1.9	2.0	20.3
2013	20.4	2.0	2.1	20.3
2014	20.3	1.5	2.4	19.4

[1]All amounts are net of reinsurance recoveries.
[2]Incurred losses are losses related to events that have occurred, regardless of whether or not the claims have been paid, net of reinsurance. Includes loss adjustment expenses.
[3]Because of changes in the population of insurers reporting data each year, the beginning reserve may not equal the ending reserve of the prior year.

Source: SNL Financial LC.

Home

In 2013, 19.9 million Americans, or one in 16 people, experienced an unintentional injury in the home that required aid from a medical professional, according to an analysis by the National Safety Council (NSC). Injuries requiring medical attention occur more often at home than in public places, the workplace and motor vehicle crashes combined, according to the NSC. There were 66,000 deaths from unintentional home injuries in 2013. Despite population growth and a corresponding rise in the number of fatal injuries, the rate of fatal home injuries has declined dramatically over the past 100 years, falling by 25 percent to 20.9 deaths per 100,000 people in 2013 from 28 deaths per 100,000 people in 1912. However, the number and rate of unintentional home injury deaths has been steadily rising since 2000, largely due to increases in unintentional poisonings and falls.

UNINTENTIONAL HOME DEATHS AND INJURIES, 2013

Deaths	66,000
Medically consulted injuries	19,900,000
Death rate per 100,000 population	20.9
Cost	$226.1 billion

Source: National Safety Council. (2015). Injury Facts®, 2015 Edition. Itasca, IL.

PRINCIPAL TYPES OF HOME UNINTENTIONAL INJURY DEATHS, 2013

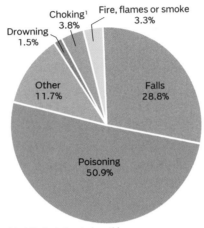

Choking[1] 3.8%
Fire, flames or smoke 3.3%
Drowning 1.5%
Other 11.7%
Falls 28.8%
Poisoning 50.9%

[1]Inhalation and ingestion of food or other object that obstructs breathing.

Source: National Safety Council. (2015). Injury Facts®, 2015 Edition. Itasca, IL.

Causes of Death

Mortality Risks

Heart disease is the leading cause of death in the United States, accounting for 611,000 fatalities in 2013, according to the Centers for Disease Control and Prevention. Influenza and pneumonia ranked eighth in 2013, accounting for some 57,000 fatalities. However, pandemic influenza viruses have the potential to be far more deadly. An estimated 675,000 Americans died during the 1918 Spanish influenza pandemic, the deadliest and most infectious known influenza strain to date.

DEATH RATES FROM MAJOR CAUSES IN THE UNITED STATES, 2012-2013

Cause of death	Number of deaths, 2013	Age-adjusted death rate[1]		
		2012	2013	Percent change
Heart disease	611,105	170.5	169.8	-0.4%
Malignant neoplasms (tumors)	584,881	166.5	163.2	-2.0
Chronic lower respiratory diseases	149,205	41.5	42.1	1.4
Accidents (unintentional injuries)	130,557	39.1	39.4	0.8
Cerebrovascular diseases (stroke)	128,978	36.9	36.2	-1.9
Alzheimer's disease	84,797	23.8	23.5	-1.3
Diabetes	75,578	21.2	21.2	[2]
Influenza and pneumonia	56,979	14.4	15.9	10.4

(table continues)

DEATH RATES FROM MAJOR CAUSES IN THE UNITED STATES, 2012-2013 (Cont'd)

Cause of death	Number of deaths, 2013	Age-adjusted death rate[1]		
		2012	2013	Percent change
Kidney disease	47,112	13.1	13.2	0.8%
Intentional self-harm (suicide)	41,149	12.6	12.6	[2]
Septicemia	38,156	10.3	10.7	3.9
Chronic liver disease and cirrhosis	36,427	9.9	10.2	3.0
Hypertension[3]	30,770	8.2	8.5	3.7
Parkinson's disease	25,196	7.0	7.3	4.3
All deaths	**2,596,993**	**732.8**	**731.9**	**-0.1%**

[1]Per 100,000 population; factors out differences based on age.
[2]Less than 0.1 percent.
[3]Essential (primary) hypertension and hypertensive renal disease.

Source: National Center for Health Statistics.

Gun Deaths and Injuries

The societal cost of U.S. injuries from firearms, including lost work time, medical care, insurance, criminal-justice expenses, pain and suffering and lost quality of life, amounted to about $174 billion in 2010, according to an analysis of Centers for Disease Control and Prevention data by the Pacific Institute for Research and Evaluation. Fatal injuries accounted for $153.3 billion, or nearly 90 percent of the costs. Suicides accounted for 53 percent of the societal cost of firearm injuries, followed by homicides and assaults, accounting for 41 percent. Unintentional acts, legal intervention and acts of undetermined intent account for the remainder.

DEATHS IN THE UNITED STATES BY FIREARM, 2012 AND 2013

Deaths caused by firearms	Number		Percent of total	
	2012	2013[1]	2012	2013[1]
Accidental discharge of firearms	548	505	1.7%	1.5%
Suicide by firearm	20,666	21,175	62.5	63.8
Assault (homicide) by firearm	11,622	11,208	35.1	33.8
Undetermined intent	256	281	0.8	0.8
Total[2]	**33,092**	**33,169**	**100.0%**	**100.0%**

[1]Preliminary.
[2]Excludes deaths resulting from legal intervention.

Source: Centers for Disease Control and Prevention, National Vital Statistics Report.

Cost of Goods and Services

The Bureau of Labor Statistics Consumer Expenditures Survey describes the buying habits of American consumers, using household expenditure records and surveys. Expenditures include goods and services purchased, whether or not payment was made at the time of purchase and all sales and excise taxes.

Income, age of family members, geographic location, taste and personal preference influence expenditures. Location often affects the cost of auto and homeowners insurance. Rural households spend less than urban households on auto insurance; regional variations in residential building costs affect spending on homeowners insurance. In addition to the number and type of cars, where they are driven and by whom, auto insurance prices are influenced by such factors as the degree of competition in the marketplace and how claimants are compensated (through the no-fault or traditional tort systems).

INSURANCE AND OTHER CONSUMER EXPENDITURES AS A PERCENT OF TOTAL HOUSEHOLD SPENDING, 1990-2014[1]

	1990	1995	2000	2005	2010	2012	2013	2014
Housing	30.0%	31.7%	31.7%	31.9%	33.7%	32.1%	32.8%	32.6%
Transportation	15.9	16.4	17.5	16.0	13.9	15.5	15.6	14.9
Food	15.0	14.0	13.6	12.8	12.7	12.8	12.9	12.6
Retirement[2]	8.8	8.0	7.8	10.4	10.5	10.2	10.2	10.1
Other	10.6	10.2	10.5	10.4	10.4	10.6	10.0	10.0
Total insurance	5.8	6.8	6.3	6.5	7.3	7.4	7.7	8.8
Health	2.0	2.7	2.6	2.9	3.8	3.9	4.4	5.4
Vehicle	2.0	2.2	2.0	2.0	2.1	2.0	2.0	2.1
Homeowners	0.5	0.7	0.7	0.7	0.8	0.8	0.7	0.7
Life	1.2	1.1	1.0	0.8	0.6	0.6	0.6	0.6
Other	0.1	0.1	0.1	0.1	[3]	[3]	[3]	0.1
Entertainment	5.0	5.0	4.9	5.1	5.2	5.1	4.9	5.1
Clothing	5.7	5.3	4.9	4.1	3.5	3.4	3.1	3.3
Healthcare	3.1	2.7	2.8	2.8	2.8	2.9	2.7	2.7

[1]Ranked by 2014 data.
[2]Mostly payroll deductions for retirement purposes such as Social Security (79% of retirement expenditures), government and private pension plans (11%) and nonpayroll deposits such as IRAs (10%) in 2014.
[3]Less than 0.1 percent.

Note: Percentages may not add up to 100 percent due to rounding.

Source: U.S. Department of Labor, Bureau of Labor Statistics.

Cost of Goods and Services

- Insurance accounted for 8.8 percent of household spending in 2014, up 1.1 percentage points from 2013. The health insurance share grew 1.0 percentage points and vehicle insurance rose 0.1 percentage points, while the shares spent on homeowners and life insurance remained the same.

INSURANCE EXPENDITURES AS A PERCENTAGE OF TOTAL HOUSEHOLD SPENDING, 2014

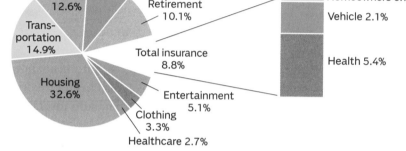

Other 10.0%
Food 12.6%
Transportation 14.9%
Retirement 10.1%
Total insurance 8.8%
Housing 32.6%
Entertainment 5.1%
Clothing 3.3%
Healthcare 2.7%

Life 0.6%
Homeowners 0.7%
Vehicle 2.1%
Health 5.4%

Source: U.S. Department of Labor, Bureau of Labor Statistics.

Consumer Prices

The Bureau of Labor Statistics consumer price index (CPI) tracks changes in the prices paid by consumers for a representative basket of goods and services. The cost of living (all items) rose 1.6 percent in 2014. The cost of hospital services and auto insurance rose more (5.0 percent and 4.2 percent, respectively). The cost of legal services rose 2.1 percent and doctors' services rose 1.4 percent.

CONSUMER PRICE INDICES FOR INSURANCE AND RELATED ITEMS AND ANNUAL RATES OF CHANGE, 2005-2014
(Base: 1982-84=100)

Year	Cost of living (all items) Index	Percent change	Motor vehicle insurance Index	Percent change	Medical care items Index	Percent change	Physicians' services Index	Percent change	Hospital services[1] Index	Percent change
2005	195.3	3.4%	329.9	2.1%	323.2	4.2%	287.5	3.3%	161.6	5.3%
2006	201.6	3.2	331.8	0.6	336.2	4.0	291.9	1.5	172.1	6.5
2007	207.3	2.8	333.1	0.4	351.1	4.4	303.2	3.9	183.6	6.7
2008	215.3	3.8	341.5	2.5	364.1	3.7	311.3	2.7	197.2	7.4
2009	214.5	-0.4	357.0	4.5	375.6	3.2	320.8	3.0	210.7	6.9
2010	218.1	1.6	375.2	5.1	388.4	3.4	331.3	3.3	227.2	7.8
2011	224.9	3.2	388.7	3.6	400.3	3.0	340.3	2.7	241.2	6.2
2012	229.6	2.1	402.5	3.6	414.9	3.7	347.3	2.1	253.6	5.1
2013	233.0	1.5	419.4	4.2	425.1	2.5	354.2	2.0	265.4	4.7
2014	236.7	1.6	437.2	4.2	435.3	2.4	359.1	1.4	278.8	5.0
Percent change 2005-2014		**21.2%**		**32.5%**		**34.7%**		**24.9%**		**72.5%**

(table continues)

**CONSUMER PRICE INDICES FOR INSURANCE AND
RELATED ITEMS AND ANNUAL RATES OF CHANGE, 2005-2014 (Cont'd)**
(Base: 1982-84=100)

Year	Motor vehicle body work		New vehicles		New cars		New trucks[2]	
	Index	Percent change	Index	Percent change	Index	Percent change	Index	Percent change
2005	215.0	3.3%	137.9	0.6%	135.2	1.0%	145.3	0.2%
2006	224.8	4.6	137.6	-0.2	136.4	0.9	142.9	-1.7
2007	232.2	3.3	136.3	-1.0	135.9	-0.4	140.7	-1.5
2008	239.7	3.2	134.2	-1.5	135.4	-0.3	137.1	-2.6
2009	248.5	3.7	135.6	1.1	136.7	0.9	138.8	1.3
2010	254.4	2.4	138.0	1.8	138.1	1.0	142.7	2.8
2011	259.9	2.2	141.9	2.8	142.2	3.0	146.5	2.7
2012	264.9	1.9	144.2	1.7	144.2	1.4	149.4	1.9
2013	271.0	2.3	145.8	1.1	144.9	0.5	151.8	1.6
2014	278.0	2.6	146.3	0.3	144.5	-0.3	153.6	1.1
Percent change 2005-2014		**29.3%**		**6.1%**		**6.9%**		**5.7%**

Year	Used cars and trucks		Tenants and household insurance[3,4]		Repair of household items[3,5]		Legal services		Existing single-family homes	
	Index	Percent change	Index	Percent change	Index	Percent change	Index	Percent change	Median price ($000)	Percent change
2005	139.4	4.6%	117.6	1.2%	147.4	5.7%	241.8	4.1%	$220	12.4%
2006	140.0	0.4	116.5	-0.9	154.7	5.0	250.0	3.4	222	1.0
2007	135.7	-3.0	117.0	0.4	161.2	4.2	260.3	4.1	219	-1.3
2008	134.0	-1.3	118.8	1.6	170.0	5.5	270.7	4.0	198	-9.5
2009	127.0	-5.2	121.5	2.2	176.0	3.5	278.1	2.7	173	-12.9
2010	143.1	12.7	125.7	3.5	181.7	3.2	288.1	3.6	173	0.3
2011	149.0	4.1	127.4	1.4	NA	NA	297.4	3.2	166	-4.0
2012	150.3	0.9	131.3	3.1	198.7	NA	303.5	2.0	177	6.6
2013	149.9	-0.3	135.4	3.1	206.7	4.0	311.8	2.8	197	11.4
2014	149.1	-0.5	141.9	4.8	212.4	2.8	318.5	2.1	209	5.8
Percent change 2005-2014		**7.0%**		**20.6%**		**44.1%**		**31.7%**		**-5.0%**

[1]December 1996=100. [2]December 1983=100. [3]December 1997=100. [4]Only includes insurance covering rental properties. [5]Includes appliances, reupholstery and inside home maintenance. NA=Data not available. Note: Percent changes after 2007 for consumer price indices and all years for the median price of existing single-family homes calculated from unrounded data.

Source: U.S. Department of Labor, Bureau of Labor Statistics; National Association of Realtors.

Insurance Fraud

Insurance fraud is a deliberate deception perpetrated against or by an insurance company or agent for the purpose of financial gain. Fraud may be committed at different points in the insurance transaction by applicants for insurance, policyholders, third-party claimants or professionals who provide services to claimants. Insurance agents and company employees may also commit insurance fraud. Common frauds include padding, or inflating actual claims, misrepresenting facts on an insurance application, submitting claims for injuries or damage that never occurred and staging accidents.

The exact amount of fraud committed is difficult to determine. The proportion of fraud varies among different lines of insurance, with healthcare, workers compensation and auto insurance believed to be the most vulnerable lines. The nature of fraud is constantly evolving.

Insurers are at the front line in combatting insurance fraud despite the increase in the number of states that have passed laws to criminalize the practice. One of the most effective means of combatting fraud is the adoption of data technologies that cut the time needed to recognize fraud.

In 2014 the Coalition Against Insurance Fraud and the SAS Institute published a report entitled *The State of Insurance Fraud Technology* to track how insurers deploy technology to combat insurance fraud. An online survey of 42 insurers compared 2014 results to a 2012 survey and found that by 2014, 95 percent of insurers reported using anti-fraud technology, up from 88 percent in 2012. These technologies focused on claims—71 percent of respondents said detecting claims fraud is the primary use of anti-fraud technology. Less than half use these tools for nonclaim issues such as underwriting and internal fraud.

Other findings of the Coalition study included:

■ More than half of the study respondents said the amount of suspected fraud against their company had increased over the past three years. Only 2 percent said it had decreased.

■ When asked what benefits the insurers who use fraud-detection systems have received, the most-cited benefits were more and better referrals, uncovering complex or organized fraud activity and improved investigator efficiency.

■ Compared to 2012 a larger share of referrals came from automated systems in 2014.

■ One of the most common technologies used today are automated red flags, which automatically highlight suspected fraudulent activity. Eighty-one percent of respondents reported using automated red flags, followed by:

  • Link analysis, a tool that enables insurers to unravel complex or organized fraud rings by recognizing the relationships between groups across multiple claims, is used by 50 percent of respondents; and

  • Anomaly detection, which warns investigators that information seems improbable, is used by 45 percent of respondents.

- Most insurers think that no single technology is sufficient to combat fraud. They believe a combination of technologies is necessary to uncover both opportunistic and organized fraud.
- Eighty-five percent of insurers predict that funds for anti-fraud detection will remain the same or increase.

KEY STATE LAWS AGAINST INSURANCE FRAUD

State	Insurance fraud classified as a crime	Immunity statutes	Fraud bureau	Mandatory insurer fraud plan	Mandatory auto photo inspection
Alabama	X	X	X		
Alaska	X	X	X		
Arizona	X	X	X		
Arkansas	X	X	X	X	
California	X	X	X	X	
Colorado	X	X	[4]	X	
Connecticut	X	X	X[1,5]		
Delaware	X	X	X		
D.C.	X	X	X[6]	X	
Florida	X	X	X	X	X
Georgia	X	X	X		
Hawaii	X[1,2]	X	X		
Idaho	X	X	X		
Illinois	X	X	X[1]		
Indiana	X	X			
Iowa	X	X	X		
Kansas	X	X	X	X	
Kentucky	X	X	X	X	
Louisiana	X	X	X	X	
Maine	X	X	X[1]	X	
Maryland	X	X	X	X	
Massachusetts	X	X	X		X
Michigan	X	X			
Minnesota	X	X	X	X	
Mississippi	X	X[3]	X[1,5]		

- Immunity statutes protect the person or insurance company that reports insurance fraud from criminal and civil prosecution.

- Fraud bureaus are state law enforcement agencies, mostly set up in insurance departments, where investigators review fraud reports and begin the prosecution process.

(table continues)

- State-mandated insurer fraud plans require insurance companies to formulate a program for fighting fraud and sometimes to establish special investigation units to identify fraud patterns.

KEY STATE LAWS AGAINST INSURANCE FRAUD (Cont'd)

State	Insurance fraud classified as a crime	Immunity statutes	Fraud bureau	Mandatory insurer fraud plan	Mandatory auto photo inspection
Missouri	X	X	X		
Montana	X	X	X		
Nebraska	X	X	X		
Nevada	X	X	X[5]		
New Hampshire	X	X	X	X	
New Jersey	X	X	X[5]	X	X
New Mexico	X	X	X	X	
New York	X	X	X[1]	X	X
North Carolina	X	X	X		
North Dakota	X	X	X[1]		
Ohio	X	X	X	X	
Oklahoma	X	X	X		
Oregon	X	X			
Pennsylvania	X	X	X[5]	X	
Rhode Island	X	X[7]	X[5,8]	X	X
South Carolina	X	X	X[5]		
South Dakota	X	X	X[5]		
Tennessee	X	X		X	
Texas	X	X	X	X	
Utah	X	X	X		
Vermont	X	X		X	
Virginia	X	X	X[8]		
Washington	X	X	X	X	
West Virginia	X	X	X		
Wisconsin	X	X			
Wyoming	X	X[3]			

[1]Workers compensation insurance only. [2]Healthcare insurance only. [3]Arson only. [4]No fraud bureau. Industry assessment payable to the Insurance Cash Fund. Attorney General's office conducts fraud prosecution. [5]Fraud bureau set up in the state Attorney General's office. [6]In the District of Columbia fraud is investigated by the Enforcement and Consumer Protection Bureau in the Department of Insurance, Securities and Banking which investigates fraud in all three financial sectors. [7]Auto insurance only. [8]Fraud bureau set up in the state police office.

Source: Property Casualty Insurers Association of America; Coalition Against Insurance Fraud.

Insurers' Legal Defense Costs

Lawsuits against businesses affect the cost of insurance and the products and services of the industries sued. Travelers Insurance 2015 Business Risk Index showed that legal liability was the fourth-highest rated worry for business leaders in the United States, down from No. 3 a year earlier. Of 1,210 business leaders surveyed, 56 percent indicated they worry about it somewhat or a great deal.

Businesses address their liability concerns through many types of risk management, of which insurance is an important component. A Swiss Re study indicated that in 2013 the United States had the largest commercial liability insurance market in the world both in premium volume ($84 billion) and as a percentage of Gross Domestic Product (0.50 percent). More than half of all global liability premiums were written in the United States.

TOP 10 LARGEST COMMERCIAL LIABILITY MARKETS, 2013
($ billions)

Rank	Country	Direct premiums written, 2013			Liability as a percentage of	
		Liability	Total nonlife	GDP[1]	Total nonlife	GDP[1]
1	U.S.	$84.0	$531.2	$16,802	15.8%	0.50%
2	U.K.	9.9	99.2	2,521	10.0	0.39
3	Germany	7.8	90.4	3,713	8.6	0.21
4	France	6.8	83.1	2,750	8.2	0.25
5	Japan	6.0	81.0	4,964	7.4	0.12
6	Canada	5.2	50.5	1,823	10.3	0.29
7	Italy	5.0	47.6	2,073	10.5	0.24
8	Australia	4.8	32.7	1,506	14.7	0.32
9	China	3.5	105.5	9,345	3.3	0.04
10	Spain	2.2	31.0	1,361	7.1	0.16
	World	**$160.0**	**$1,550.0**	**$61,709**	**10.3%**	**0.26%**

[1]Gross Domestic Product.
Source: Swiss Re, *sigma*, No. 4/2014.

Insurers are required to defend their policyholders against lawsuits. The costs of settling a claim are reported on insurers' financial statements as "defense and cost containment expenses incurred." These expenses include defense, litigation and medical cost containment. Expenditures for surveillance, litigation management and fees for appraisers, private investigators, hearing representatives and fraud investigators are included. In addition, attorney legal fees may be incurred owing to a duty to defend, even when coverage does not exist, because attorneys must be hired to issue opinions about coverage. Insurers' defense costs as a percentage of incurred losses are relatively high in some lines such as product liability and medical malpractice, reflecting the high cost of defending certain types of lawsuits, such as medical injury cases and class actions against pharmaceutical companies. For example, in addition to $1.2 billion in product liability incurred losses in 2014, insurers spent $953 million on settlement expenses, equivalent to 77.4 percent of the losses.

**DEFENSE COSTS AND COST CONTAINMENT EXPENSES
AS A PERCENT OF INCURRED LOSSES, 2012-2014[1]**
($000)

	2012		2013		2014	
	Amount	As a percent of incurred losses	Amount	As a percent of incurred losses	Amount	As a percent of incurred losses
Product liability	$873,860	114.7%	$1,166,236	75.1%	$952,997	77.4%
Medical malpractice	1,686,009	45.7	1,656,257	53.3	1,873,874	43.2
Commercial multiple peril[2]	2,022,739	46.0	2,096,543	37.7	2,083,103	39.1
Other liability	4,959,838	24.8	4,914,374	25.4	4,365,569	21.1
Workers compensation	3,071,093	12.3	3,018,372	12.3	3,357,813	12.9
Commercial auto liability	1,091,434	10.4	1,207,681	10.7	1,266,046	10.6
Private passenger auto liability	4,353,427	6.7	4,600,395	6.8	4,714,584	6.5
All liability lines	**$18,058,400**	**13.9%**	**$18,659,858**	**14.0%**	**$18,613,986**	**13.1%**

[1]Net of reinsurance, excludes state funds.
[2]Liability portion only.

Source: SNL Financial LC.

Personal Injury Awards

Most lawsuits are settled out of court. Of those that are tried and proceed to verdict, Jury Verdict Research data show that in 2013 the median (or midpoint) award in personal injury cases was $68,218, down from $75,000 the previous year. The average award dropped to $1,009,788 from $1,045,048 during the same period. Thomson Reuters notes that average awards can be skewed by a few very high awards and that medians are more representative. In cases of product liability the highest median award was in industrial/construction products cases ($2,541,000). In disputes concerning medical malpractice the highest median award was in childbirth cases ($2,160,420). In cases involving business negligence the highest median award was against transportation industries ($588,500).

Awards of $1 million or more accounted for 16 percent of all personal injury awards in 2012 and 2013, up from 14 percent in the prior two-year period. In 2012 and 2013, 71 percent of product liability awards and 53 percent of medical malpractice awards amounted to $1 million or more, the highest proportion of awards. Vehicular liability and premises liability cases had the lowest proportion of awards of $1 million or more, at 7 percent and 12 percent, respectively.

TRENDS IN PERSONAL INJURY LAWSUITS, 2009-2013[1]

Year	Award median	Probabiity range[2]	Award range	Award mean
2009	$40,000	$9,887 - $207,828	$1 - $77,418,670	$750,392
2010	39,216	10,000 - 200,000	1 - 71,000,000	653,898
2011	60,924	12,249 - 343,958	1 - 58,619,989	782,657
2012	75,000	18,975 - 350,000	1 - 155,237,000	1,045,048
2013	68,218	15,647 - 300,000	1 - 165,972,503	1,009,788
Overall	**$45,001**	**$10,170 - $250,000**	**$1 - $188,000,000**	**$825,804**

[1]Excludes punitive damages.
[2]Twenty-five percent above and below the median award. The median represents the midpoint jury award. Half of the awards are above the median and half are below. This helps establish where awards tend to cluster.
Source: Reprinted with permission of Thomson Reuters, *Current Award Trends in Personal Injury*, 54th edition.

AVERAGE PERSONAL INJURY JURY AWARDS, 2009-2013

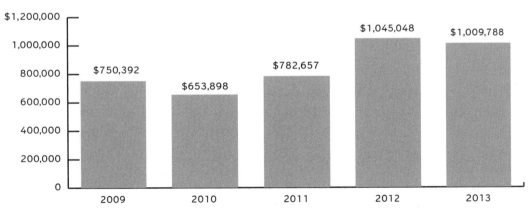

Source: Reprinted with permission of Thomson Reuters, *Current Award Trends in Personal Injury*, 54th edition.

MEDIAN AND AVERAGE PERSONAL INJURY JURY AWARDS BY TYPE OF LIABILITY, 2013

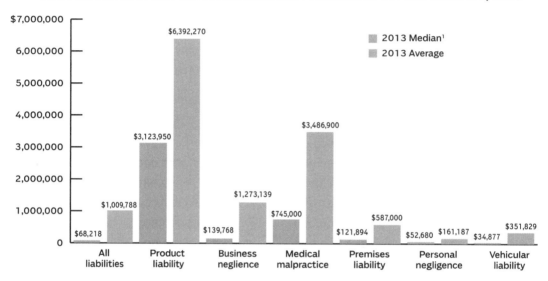

[1]Represents the midpoint jury award. Half of awards are above the median and half are below.

Source: Reprinted with permission of *Thomson Reuters, Current Award Trends in Personal Injury*, 54th edition.

PERCENT OF PERSONAL INJURY JURY AWARDS OVER $1 MILLION, 2007-2013

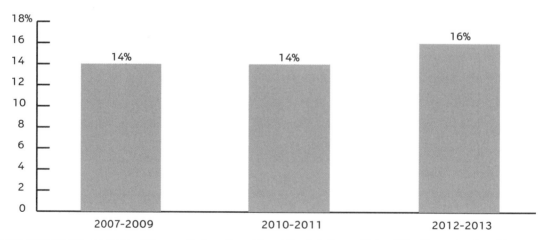

Source: Reprinted with permission of Thomson Reuters, *Current Award Trends in Personal Injury*, 54th edition and earlier editions.

Directors and Officers Liability Insurance

Directors and officers liability insurance (D&O) covers directors and officers of a company for negligent acts or omissions and for misleading statements that result in suits against the company. There are various forms of D&O coverage. Corporate reimbursement coverage indemnifies directors and officers of the organization. Side-A coverage provides D&O coverage for personal liability when directors and officers are not indemnified by the firm. Entity coverage for claims made specifically against the company is also available. D&O policies may be broadened to include coverage for employment practices liability (EPL). EPL coverage may also be purchased as a stand-alone policy.

Sixty-four percent of corporations purchased D&O coverage in 2014 according to the Cost of Risk survey from the Risk and Insurance Management Society, based on a survey of 1,457 corporations. Banks were the most likely to purchase D&O coverage, with 87 percent of industry respondents purchasing the coverage, followed by 85 percent of respondents in telecommunication services. JLT Specialty's 2015 U.S. Directors and Officers Liability Survey of 157 U.S. organizations that purchase D&O liability insurance found that the group's average D&O limits that were purchased was $131 million and the median limit purchased was $105 million. For public companies the average limit was $170 million. For private companies the average was $98 million. Twenty-four percent of public companies and 17 percent of private companies increased their D&O limits from their previous purchase. According to the 2014 survey 31 percent of respondents reported having had a claim in the past five years, with nonprofits reporting the highest proportion of claims (58 percent).

TYPES OF DIRECTORS AND OFFICERS LIABILITY CLAIMS BY OWNERSHIP, 2011-2014[1]

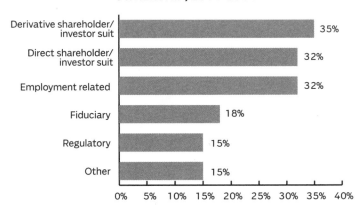

- The percentage of respondents reporting derivative shareholder/ investor lawsuits, the most widespread claim, dropped from 39 percent in 2013 to 35 percent in 2014.

[1]Based on participants in the survey that reported one or more claims over the five-year period.

Source: *2015 JLT Specialty U.S. Directors and Officers Liability Survey*, JLT Specialty Bermuda.

TOP 10 WRITERS OF DIRECTORS AND OFFICERS INSURANCE BY DIRECT PREMIUMS WRITTEN, 2014[1]

($000)

- Directors and officers liability insurance direct premiums written totaled $6.4 billion in 2014, according to SNL Financial.

Rank	Group/company	Direct premiums written	Market share
1	American International Group (AIG)	$1,049,547	16.3%
2	XL Group PLC	649,365	10.1
3	Chubb Corp.	588,587	9.2
4	CNA Financial Corp.	428,484	6.7
5	HCC Insurance Holdings Inc.	327,307	5.1
6	Travelers Companies Inc.	325,300	5.1
7	ACE Ltd.	314,891	4.9
8	Zurich Insurance Group[2]	246,665	3.8
9	Tokio Marine Group	229,555	3.6
10	American Financial Group Inc.	224,373	3.5

[1]Includes property/casualty insurers that provided monoline directors and officers policies. The coverage may also be purchased as part of a package commercial multiperil policy. Includes some state funds. [2]Data for Farmers Insurance Group of Companies and Zurich Financial Group (which owns Farmers' management company) are reported separately by SNL Financial. Source: SNL Financial LC.

DIRECTORS AND OFFICERS LIABILITY CLAIMS BY TYPE OF CLAIMANT IN THE UNITED STATES, 2011-2014[1]

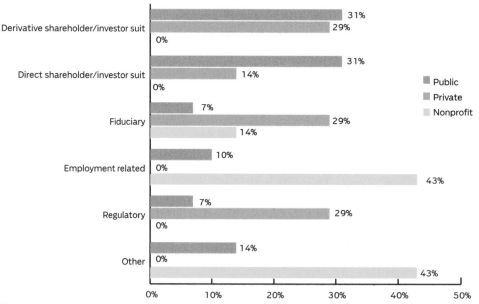

Derivative shareholder/investor suit: Public 31%, Private 29%, Nonprofit 0%
Direct shareholder/investor suit: Public 31%, Private 14%, Nonprofit 0%
Fiduciary: Public 7%, Private 29%, Nonprofit 14%
Employment related: Public 10%, Private 0%, Nonprofit 43%
Regulatory: Public 7%, Private 29%, Nonprofit 0%
Other: Public 14%, Private 0%, Nonprofit 43%

Legend: Public, Private, Nonprofit

[1]Based on participants in the survey that reported one or more claims over the four-year period.

Source: *2015 JLT Specialty U.S. Directors and Officers Liability Survey*, JLT Specialty Bermuda.

Employment Practices Liability

Employment practices are a frequent source of claims against directors, officers and their organizations. Organizations that purchase insurance for employment practices liability (EPL) claims typically either buy a stand-alone EPL insurance policy or endorse their directors and officers liability (D&O) policy to cover employment practices liability. In 2014, 9 percent of public companies responding to a JLT Specialty survey shared or blended their D&O limits with another coverage such as EPL or fiduciary liability, compared with 44 percent of private companies and 67 percent of nonprofits.

In 2014, 35 percent of the 1,457 respondents to the 2014 Cost of Risk survey from the Risk and Insurance Management Society said they bought EPL policies. Banks were the most likely to purchase EPL coverage, with 59 percent of industry respondents purchasing the coverage, followed by telecommunications services (48 percent), consumer staples (46 percent), and consumer discretionary firms (45 percent). American International Group Inc. was the leading writer, based on EPL premiums written, with a 25.9 percent market share in 2014, followed by Chubb Corp. (11.5 percent), AXIS Capital Holdings Ltd. (10.9 percent), Zurich Insurance Group Ltd. (10.3 percent) and The Travelers Companies Inc. (5.7 percent).

TRENDS IN EMPLOYMENT PRACTICES LIABILITY, 2009-2013

Year	Median (midpoint) award	Probability range[1]
2009	$207,235	$60,000 - $600,281
2010	172,000	50,000 - 385,000
2011	271,000	82,121 - 555,000
2012	65,460	11,000 - 249,081
2013	109,300	25,000 - 258,564

[1]The middle 50 percent of all awards arranged in ascending order in a sampling, 25 percent above and below the median award.

Source: Reprinted with permission of Thomson Reuters, *Employment Practice Liability: Jury Award Trends And Statistics*, 2014 edition.

EMPLOYMENT PRACTICES LIABILITY, BY DEFENDANT TYPE, 2007-2013[1]

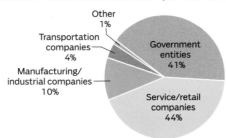

Other 1%
Transportation companies 4%
Manufacturing/industrial companies 10%
Government entities 41%
Service/retail companies 44%

[1]Based on plaintiff and defendant verdicts rendered.

Source: Reprinted with permission of Thomson Reuters, *Employment Practice Liability: Jury Award Trends And Statistics*, 2014 edition.

Shareholder Lawsuits

Cornerstone Research has conducted annual studies of securities class-action lawsuit settlements and filings each year since the passage of the 1995 Private Securities Litigation Reform Act, enacted to curb frivolous shareholder lawsuits.

Filings

The number of new federal securities class actions filed rose 2.4 percent to 170 in 2014 from 166 in 2013, according to Cornerstone's 2015 study. The 170 filings in 2014 compare with an annual average of 189 recorded between 1997 and 2013. In 2014 healthcare, biotechnology and pharmaceutical companies accounted for 37 percent of all filings, totaling 63 filings, up from 45 filings in 2013. Filings related to mergers and acquisitions have been at the same level for the past three years while Chinese reverse merger filings have continued to subside and were minimal in 2014. Reverse mergers involve the acquisition of a private company by a public "shell" company, giving it access to capital markets.

Settlements

Total settlement dollars in court-approved securities class actions in 2014 dropped to the lowest level in 16 years according to Cornerstone Research. The average settlement amount fell to the lowest level since 2000 at the same time. However the number of securities class action settlements was almost unchanged from year ago, 63 in 2014 versus 67 in 2013. Reflecting an absence of large cases, total settlement dollars fell 78 percent, to $1.1 billion in 2014 from $4.8 billion in 2013. In 2014 the percentage of settlement dollars from mega-settlements (i.e., those in excess of $100 million) was the lowest in 16 years. The median settlement amount, which represents the typical case, fell slightly, to $6.0 million in 2014 from $6.6 million in 2013. However the average settlement size fell faster, to $17 million in 2014 from $73.5 million in 2013.

POST-REFORM ACT SETTLEMENTS OF SECURITIES LAWSUITS, 1996-2014[1]
(2014 dollars)

	1996-2013	2014
Minimum	$0.1 million	$0.3 million
Median	8.3 million	6.0 million
Average	57.2 million	17.0 million
Maximum	8.5 billion	265.0 million
Total settlements	**$79.8 billion**	**$1.1 billion**

[1]Private Securities Litigation Reform Act of 1995; adjusted for inflation by Cornerstone Research.

Source: Cornerstone Research, *Securities Class Action Settlements—2014 Review and Analysis* © 2015 by Cornerstone Research, Inc. All Rights Reserved.

I.I.I. Store

The I.I.I. Store is your gateway to a wide array of books and brochures from the Insurance Information Institute.

Print, PDF and ebook formats. Quantity discounts are available for many products. Order online at www.iii.org/publications, call 212-346-5500 or email publications@iii.org.

I.I.I. Insurance Fact Book

Thousands of insurance facts, figures, tables and graphs designed for quick and easy reference.

Insurance Handbook

A guide to the insurance industry for reporters, public policymakers, students, insurance company employees, regulators and others.

Online version available at www.iii.org/insurancehandbook

Insuring Your Business: A Small Business Owners' Guide to Insurance

A comprehensive insurance guide for small business owners.

Online version available at www.iii.org/smallbusiness

A Firm Foundation Online: How Insurance Supports the Economy

Shows the myriad ways in which insurance provides economic support—from offering employment and fueling the capital markets, to providing financial security and income to individuals and businesses. Provides national and state data. Selected state versions are also available.

Available at www.iii.org/economics

International Insurance Fact Book Online

Facts and statistics on the property/casualty and life insurance industries of dozens of countries.

Available at www.iii.org/international

Commercial Insurance Online

A guide to the commercial insurance market—what it does, how it functions and its key players.

Available at www.iii.org/commerciallines

I.I.I. Insurance Daily

Keeps thousands of readers up-to-date on important events, issues and trends in the insurance industry. Transmitted early each business day via email.

Contact: daily@iii.org

Consumer Brochures

Renters Insurance

Your Home Inventory

Nine Ways to Lower Your Auto Insurance Costs

Settling Insurance Claims After a Disaster

Twelve Ways to Lower Your Homeowners Insurance Costs ...and many others

Appendices

Digital, Social and Mobile

Apps

 Know Your Plan™ is the award-winning disaster preparedness app that helps you, your family and even your pets be ready to safely get out of harm's way before trouble starts.

 Know Your Stuff® – Home Inventory ensures you'll always have an up-to-date record of your belongings. An upgraded and redesigned version will be available in February 2016. Available in the Apple App Store and Google Play, and on the Web at www.KnowYourStuff.org.

Social

Find us on:

 facebook.com/InsuranceInformationInstitute

 @iiiorg   @IIIindustryblog
@III_Research   @InsuringFlorida
@InsuringCAL

 youtube.com/user/iiivideo

 linkedin.com/company/insurance-information-institute

 pinterest.com/iiiorg

Google Plus plus.google.com/+IiiOrg/

Blogs

Terms + Conditions: An inside look at the insurance industry and current issues.

Insuring Florida: The Insuring Florida blog helps Florida residents understand insurance coverage and related issues in the Sunshine State.

Insuring California: Coming soon.

YEAR	EVENT
1601	First insurance legislation in the United Kingdom was enacted. Modern insurance has its roots in this law which concerned coverage for merchandise and ships.
1666	Great Fire of London demonstrated destructive power of fire in an urban environment, leading entrepreneur Nicholas Barbon to form a business to repair houses damaged by fire.
1684	Participants in the Friendly Society in England formed a mutual insurance company to cover fire losses.
1688	Edward Lloyd's coffee house, the precursor of Lloyd's of London, became the central meeting place for ship owners seeking insurance for a voyage.
1696	Hand in Hand Mutual Fire Company was formed in London. Aviva, the world's oldest continuously operating insurance company traces its origins to this company.
1710	Charles Povey formed the Sun in London, the oldest insurance company in existence which still conducts business in its own name. It is the forerunner of the Royal & Sun Alliance Group.
1735	The Friendly Society, the first insurance company in the United States, was established in Charleston, South Carolina. This mutual insurance company went out of business in 1740.
1752	The Philadelphia Contributionship for the Insurance of Houses from Loss by Fire, the oldest insurance carrier in continuous operation in the United States, was established in Philadelphia.
1759	Presbyterian Ministers Fund, the first life insurance company in the United States was founded in Philadelphia.
1762	Equitable Life Assurance Society, the world's oldest mutual life insurer, was formed in England.
1776	Charleston Insurance Company and the South Carolina Insurance Company, the first two United States marine insurance companies, were formed in South Carolina.
1779	Lloyd's of London introduced the first uniform ocean marine policy.
1792	Insurance Company of North America, the first stock insurance company in the United States, was established in Philadelphia.
1813	Eagle Fire Insurance Company of New York assumed all outstanding risks of the Union Insurance Company, in the first recorded fire reinsurance agreement in the United States.
1849	New York passed the first general insurance law in the United States.
1850	Franklin Health Assurance Company of Massachusetts offered the first accident and health insurance.
1851	New Hampshire created the first formal agency to regulate insurance in the United States.
1861	First war-risk insurance policies were issued, written by life insurance companies during the Civil War.
1866	National Board of Fire Underwriters was formed in New York City, marking the beginning of insurance rate standardization.
	Hartford Steam Boiler Inspection and Insurance Company, the first boiler insurance company, was established in Hartford, Connecticut.
1873	The Massachusetts Legislature adopted the first standard fire insurance policy.
1878	Fidelity and Casualty Company of New York began providing fidelity and surety bonds.
1885	Liability protection was first offered with the introduction of employers liability policies.

Appendices

Brief History

YEAR	EVENT
1890	First policies providing benefits for disabilities from specific diseases were offered.
1894	National Board of Fire Underwriters established Underwriters' Laboratories to investigate and test electrical materials to ensure they meet fire safety standards.
1898	Travelers Insurance Company issued the first automobile insurance policy in the United States.
1899	First pedestrian killed by an automobile, in New York City.
1910	New York passed the first United States workers compensation law. It was later found to be unconstitutional.
1911	Wisconsin enacted the first permanent workers compensation law in the United States.
1912	Lloyd's of London introduced aviation insurance coverage.
1925	Massachusetts passed the first compulsory automobile insurance legislation.
	Connecticut passed the first financial responsibility law for motorists.
1938	Federal Crop Insurance Act created the first federal crop insurance program.
1945	McCarran-Ferguson Act (Public Law 15) was enacted. It provided the insurance industry with a limited exemption to federal antitrust law, assuring the pre-eminence of state regulation of the industry.
1947	New York established the Motor Vehicle Liability Security Fund to cover auto insurance company insolvencies. This organization was a precursor of the state guaranty funds established by insurers in all states to absorb the claims of insolvent insurers.
1950	First package insurance policies for homeowners coverage were introduced.
1960	Boston Plan was established to address insurance availability problems in urban areas in Boston.
1968	First state-run Fair Access to Insurance Requirements (FAIR) Plans were set up to ensure property insurance availability in high-risk areas.
	The federal flood insurance program was established with the passage of the National Flood Insurance Act. It enabled property owners in communities that participate in flood reduction programs to purchase insurance against flood losses.
1971	Massachusetts became the first state to establish a true no-fault automobile insurance plan.
1974	Hawaii became first U.S. state to enact a law creating a near universal healthcare coverage system.
1981	Federal Risk Retention Act of 1981 was enacted. The law fostered the growth of risk retention groups and other nontraditional insurance mechanisms.
	The Illinois Legislature created the Illinois Insurance Exchange, a cooperative effort of individual brokers and risk bearers operating as a single market, similar to Lloyd's of London.
1985	Mission Insurance Group failed. The insolvency incurred the largest payout by state guaranty funds for a single property/casualty insurance company failure at that time. This and other insolvencies in the 1980s led to stricter state regulation of insurer solvency.
	Montana became the first state to forbid discrimination by sex in the setting of insurance rates.
1992	European Union's Third Nonlife Insurance Directive became effective, establishing a single European market for insurance.

YEAR	EVENT
1996	Florida enacted rules requiring insurers to offer separate deductibles for hurricane losses, marking a shift to hurricane deductibles based on a percentage of insured property value rather than a set dollar figure.
	Catastrophe bonds, vehicles for covering disaster risk in the capital markets, were introduced.
1997	World Trade Organization agreement to dismantle barriers to trade in financial services, including insurance, banking and securities, was signed by the United States and some 100 other countries.
1998	Travelers became first insurer to sell auto insurance on the Internet.
1999	Financial Services Modernization Act (Gramm-Leach-Bliley) enacted, allowing insurers, banks and securities firms to affiliate under a financial holding company structure.
2001	Terrorist attacks upon the World Trade Center in New York City and the Pentagon in Washington, D.C. caused about $40 billion in insured losses.
	New York became the first state to ban the use of hand-held cellphones while driving.
2002	Terrorism Risk Insurance Act enacted to provide a temporary federal backstop for terrorism insurance losses.
2003	In a landmark ruling, upheld in 2004, the U.S. Supreme Court placed limits on punitive damages, holding in State Farm v. Campbell that punitive damages awards should generally not exceed nine times compensatory awards.
2004	New York Attorney General Eliot Spitzer and a number of state regulators launched investigations into insurance industry sales and accounting practices.
2005	Citigroup sold off its Travelers life insurance unit, following the spin off of its property/casualty business in 2002. This dissolved the arrangement that led to the passage of Gramm-Leach-Bliley in 1999.
	The federal Class Action Fairness Act moved most class-action lawsuits to federal courts, offering the prospect of lower defense costs and fewer and less costly verdicts.
	A string of hurricanes, including Hurricane Katrina, hit the Gulf Coast, making 2005 the most active hurricane season.
2006	Massachusetts passed a mandatory universal health insurance law that established a statewide health insurance exchange.
	Congress passed legislation extending the Terrorism Risk Insurance Act to December 2007. The act, originally passed in 2002, had been set to expire at the end of 2005. Extended again in 2007.
2007	Washington became the first state to ban the practice of texting with a cellphone while driving.
	Congress passes legislation extending the Terrorism Risk Insurance Act through the end of 2014.
2008	The federal government acquired a 79.9 percent share in AIG in exchange for rescue program that eventually cost $182 billion. The funds were fully repaid by the end of 2012, ending the government stake.
	Troubled Asset Relief Program established to stabilize the financial sector. Insurers that own a federally regulated bank or thrift were eligible to participate.
2010	President Obama signed the Patient Protection and Affordable Care Act, requiring most U.S. citizens to have health insurance.

YEAR	EVENT
2010	The Dodd-Frank Wall Street Reform and Consumer Protection Act, a landmark regulatory overhaul of the financial services industry, was signed into law. While retaining state regulation of insurance, the act established the Federal Insurance Office, an entity that reports to Congress and the President on the insurance industry.
2011	Former Illinois Insurance Department Commissioner Michael McRaith appointed by the Secretary of the Treasury as the first director of the Federal Insurance Office, established under the Dodd-Frank Act. Serves in a nonvoting, advisory capacity to the Financial Stability Oversight Council.
2012	On June 28, 2012 the Supreme Court ruled that the 2010 Patient Protection and Affordable Care Act, requiring most U.S. citizens to have health insurance, is constitutional.
	Biggert-Waters Flood Reform Act, landmark legislation requiring flood insurance rates to better reflect risks, was passed. Many of its key provisions were revoked in 2014.
	Nevada became the first state to approve a license to test driverless cars on public roads.
2013	Health insurance exchanges, established under the 2010 Patient Protection and Affordable Care Act to expand access to insurance, began operations.
	Target discovered a computer breach affecting up to 70 million customers that would cost the retailer $235 million, of which $90 million was insured. The breach and 2014 events at Home Depot and JPMorgan Chase increased interest in and sales of cyberrisk insurance.
2014	Via Medicaid and insurance exchanges, millions of Americans gained health insurance mandated by the Patient Protection and Affordable Care Act. The percentage of uninsured Americans fell to 13.4 percent, from 18.0 percent a year earlier, according to Gallup.
	California and Colorado became the first states to pass laws clarifying the insurance responsibilities of drivers using their own cars to earn money by ferrying passengers using ride-sharing services such as UberX and Lyft.
2015	The Terrorism Risk Insurance Act (TRIA) was signed into law for a six-year reauthorization on January 12, 2015.
	In February 2015 health insurer Anthem Inc. announced a data breach that affected about 78.8 million people. Premera Blue Cross, another health insurer, said that the cyberattacks had compromised the records of 11 million people.
	On August 12, 2015 two massive explosions hit China's Port of Tianjin. The explosions likely will ultimately result in billions of dollars of losses and may be one of the largest insured man-made losses to date in Asia.
	2015 was one of the worst wildfire seasons on record. Between January 1 and October 30, 2015 there were 53,798 wildfires in the United States, which burned 9,407,571 acres, according to the National Interagency Fire Center.
	On November 13 a series of coordinated terrorist attacks in Paris killed more than 125 people, only two weeks after a terrorist bombing of a Russian airliner on October 31 killed 224 people in Egypt. Both events produced insured losses amid an increase in terrorist attacks worldwide.
	According to Conning Research, insurance merger and acquisition activity through the end of the third quarter in 2015 amounted to $220 billion in announced global transaction value, several times the average annual transaction value of $60 billion. Most of the activity occurred in the third quarter, accounting for $165 billion in aggregate announced value in 185 transactions worldwide, a record.

The majority of state commissioners are appointed by state governors and serve at their pleasure. The states designated with an asterisk (*) presently elect insurance commissioners to four-year terms.

Alabama • Jim L. Ridling, Commissioner of Insurance, 201 Monroe St., Suite 502, Montgomery, AL 36104. Tel. 334-269-3550. Fax. 334-241-4192. www.aldoi.gov

Alaska • Lori K. Wing-Heier, Director of Insurance, 550 W. Seventh Ave., Suite 1560, Anchorage, AK 99501-3567. Tel. 907-269-7900. Fax. 907-269-7910. www.commerce.state.ak.us/insurance

American Samoa • Tau Tanuvasa, Commissioner of Insurance, A P Lutali Executive Office Building, Pago Pago, American Samoa 85018-7269. Tel. 684-633-4116. www.americansamoa.gov

Arizona • Darren Ellingson, Acting Director of Insurance, 2910 N. 44th St., Suite 210, Phoenix, AZ 85018-7269. Tel. 602-364-3100. Fax. 602-364-3470. www.id.state.az.us

Arkansas • Allen W. Kerr, Insurance Commissioner, 1200 W. Third St., Little Rock, AR 72201-1904. Tel. 501-371-2600. Fax. 501-371-2618. www.insurance.arkansas.gov

*California • Dave Jones, Commissioner of Insurance, 300 Spring St., South Tower, Los Angeles, CA 90013. Tel. 213-897-8921. Fax. 213-897-9051. www.insurance.ca.gov

Colorado • Marguerite Salazar, Commissioner of Insurance, 1560 Broadway, Suite 850, Denver, CO 80202. Tel. 303-894-7499. Fax. 303-894-7455. www.dora.state.co.us/insurance

Connecticut • Katharine L. Wade, Insurance Commissioner, PO Box 816, Hartford, CT 06142-0816. Tel. 860-297-3900. Fax. 860-566-7410. www.ct.gov/cid

*Delaware • Karen Stewart, Insurance Commissioner, The Rodney Bldg., 841 Silver Lake Blvd., Dover, DE 19904. Tel. 302-674-7300. Fax. 302-739-5280. www.delawareinsurance.gov

District of Columbia • Stephen C. Taylor, Acting Commissioner, 810 First St. NE, Suite 701, Washington, DC 20002. Tel. 202-727-8000. Fax. 202-535-1196. www.disb.dc.gov

Florida • Kevin McCarty, Commissioner Office of Insurance Regulation, The Larsen Building, 200 E. Gaines St., Room 101A, Tallahassee, FL 32399-0301. Tel. 850-413-3140. Fax. 850-488-3334. www.floir.com

*Georgia • Ralph Hudgens, Insurance Commissioner, 2 Martin L. King Jr. Dr., 704 West Tower, Atlanta, GA 30334. Tel. 404-656-2070. Fax. 404-657-8542. www.gainsurance.org

Guam • Artemio B. Llagan, Banking & Insurance Commissioner, 1240 Route 16 Army Drive, Barrigada, Guam 96913. Tel. 671-635-1817. Fax. 671-633-2643. www.guamtax.com

Hawaii • Gordon Ito, Insurance Commissioner, PO Box 3614, Honolulu, HI 96811. Tel. 808-586-2790. Fax. 808-586-2806. www.state.hi.us/dcca/ins

Idaho • Dean L. Cameron, Director, Department of Insurance, 700 W. State St., PO Box 83720, Boise, ID 83720-0043. Tel. 208-334-4250. Fax. 208-334-4398. www.doi.idaho.gov

Illinois • Anne Melissa Dowling, Acting Director, Department of Insurance, 320 W. Washington St., Springfield, IL 62767-0001. Tel. 217-782-4515. Fax. 217-782-5020. www.insurance.illinois.gov

Indiana • Stephen W. Robertson, Commissioner of Insurance, 311 W. Washington St., Suite 300, Indianapolis, IN 46204-2787. Tel. 317-232-2385. Fax. 317-232-5251. www.in.gov/idoi

Iowa • Nick Gerhart, Commissioner of Insurance, 601 Locust St., Fourth Floor, Des Moines, IA 50309-3438. Tel. 515-281-5705. Fax 515-281-3059. www.iid.state.ia.us

Appendices

*Kansas • Ken Selzer, Commissioner of Insurance, 420 S. West Ninth St., Topeka, KS 66612-1678. Tel. 785-296-3071. Fax. 785-296-7805. www.ksinsurance.org

Kentucky • Sharon P. Clark, Insurance Commissioner, PO Box 517, Frankfort, KY 40602-0517. Tel. 502-564-3630. Fax. 502-564-1453. http://insurance.ky.gov

*Louisiana- • James J. Donelon, Commissioner of Insurance, 1702 N. Third St., Baton Rouge, LA 70802. Tel. 225-342-5423. Fax. 225-342-8622. www.ldi.la.gov

Maine • Eric A. Cioppa, Superintendent of Insurance, 34 State House Station, Augusta, ME 04333-0034. Tel. 207-624-8475. Fax. 207-624-8599. www.maine.gov/pfr/insurance

Maryland • Al Redmer Jr., Insurance Commissioner, 200 St. Paul Place, Suite 2700, Baltimore, MD 21202. Tel. 410-468-2090. Fax. 410-468-2020. www.mdinsurance.state.md.us

Massachusetts • Daniel R. Judson, Commissioner of Insurance, 1000 Washington St., Eighth Floor, Boston, MA 02118-6200. Tel. 617-521-7794. Fax. 617-753-6830. www.state.ma.us/doi

Michigan • Patrick M. McPharlin, Director of the Department of Insurance and Financial Services, Mason Building, 8th Floor, 530 W. Allegon Street, Lansing, MI 48933, Telephone 517-284-8800 www.michigan.gov/difs

Minnesota • Mike Rothman, Commissioner of Commerce, 85 Seventh Place E., Suite 500, St. Paul, MN 55101. Tel. 651-539-1500. Fax. 651-539-1547. www.insurance.mn.gov

*Mississippi • Mike Chaney, Commissioner of Insurance, 1001 Woolfolk State Office Building, 501 N. West St., Jackson, MS 39201. Tel. 601-359-3569. Fax. 601-359-2474. www.mid.state.ms.us

Missouri • John M. Huff, Director of Insurance, 301 W. High St., PO Box 690, Jefferson City, MO 65102-0690. Tel. 573-751-4126. Fax. 573-751-1165. www.insurance.mo.gov

*Montana • Monica Lindeen, Commissioner of Insurance, 840 Helena Ave., Room 270, Helena, MT 59601. Tel. 406-444-2040. Fax. 406-444-3497. www.csi.mt.gov

Nebraska • Bruce R. Ramge, Director of Insurance, Terminal Bldg., 941 O St., Suite 400, Lincoln, NE 68508-3639. Tel. 402-471-2201. Fax. 402-471-4610. www.doi.ne.gov

Nevada • Amy L. Parks, Acting Insurance Commissioner, 1818 E. College Parkway, Suite 103, Carson City, NV 89706. Tel. 775-687-0700. Fax. 775-687-0787. www.doi.state.nv.us

New Hampshire • Roger Sevigny, Insurance Commissioner, 21 S. Fruit St., Suite 14, Concord, NH 03301-7317. Tel. 603-271-2261. Fax. 603-271-1406. www.nh.gov/insurance

New Jersey • Richard J. Badolato, Acting Commissioner of the Department of Banking and Insurance, 20 W. State St., PO Box 325, Trenton, NJ 08625. Tel. 609-292-5360. Fax. 609-984-5273. www.dobi.nj.gov

New Mexico • John G. Franchini, Superintendent of Insurance, PERA Building, 1120 Paseo De Peralta, Santa Fe, NM 87501. Tel. 505-827-4601. Fax. 505-476-0326. www.nmprc.state.nm.us/id.htm

New York • Anthony Albanese, Anthony J. Albanese, Acting Superintendent of Financial Services, 1 State St., New York, NY 10004-1511. Tel. 212-480-6400. Fax. 212-480-2310. www.dfs.ny.gov

*North Carolina • Wayne Goodwin, Commissioner of Insurance, 1201 Mail Service Center, Raleigh, NC 27699-1201. Tel. 919-807-6750. Fax. 919-733-6495. www.ncdoi.com

*North Dakota • Adam Hamm, Commissioner of Insurance, State Capitol, Fifth Floor, 600 East Boulevard Ave., Bismarck, ND 58505-0320. Tel. 701-328-2440. Fax. 701-328-4880. www.nd.gov/ndins

Ohio • Mary Taylor, Lieutenant Governor/Director of Insurance, 50 W. Town St., Third Floor, Suite 300, Columbus, OH 43215 Tel. 614-644-2658. Fax. 614-644-3743. www.insurance.ohio.gov

*Oklahoma • John Doak, Commissioner of Insurance, Five Corporate Plaza, 3625 NW 56th, Suite 100, Oklahoma City, OK 73112. Tel. 405-521-2828. Fax. 405-521-6635. www.oid.state.ok.us

Oregon • Laura N. Cali, Insurance Commissioner, PO Box 14480, Salem, OR 97309-0405. Tel. 503-947-7980. Fax. 503-378-4351. www.cbs.state.or.us/external/ins

Pennsylvania • Teresa D. Miller, Insurance Commissioner, 1326 Strawberry Square, Harrisburg, PA 17120. Tel. 717-787-2317. Fax. 717-787-8585. www.ins.state.pa.us

Puerto Rico • Angela Weyne, Commissioner of Insurance, B5 Calle Tabonuco, Suite 216, PMB 356, Guaynabo, PR 00968-3029. Tel. 787-304-8686. Fax. 787-273-6365. www.ocs.gobierno.pr

Rhode Island • Joseph Torti III, Superintendent of Insurance, 1511 Pontiac Ave., Cranston, RI 02920. Tel. 401-462-9500. Fax. 401-462-9532. www.dbr.state.ri.us

South Carolina • Raymond Farmer, Director of Insurance, PO Box 100105, Columbia, SC 29202-3105. Tel. 803-737-6160. Fax. 803-737-6205. www.doi.sc.gov

South Dakota • Larry Deiter, Director of Insurance, 124 South Euclid Ave., Pierre, SD 57501, Telephone 605-773-3563, 445 E. Capitol Ave., Pierre, SD 57501-3185. Tel. 605-773-4104. Fax. 605-773-5369. www.sd.gov/insurance

Tennessee • Julie Mix McPeak, Commissioner of Commerce & Insurance, 500 James Robertson Parkway, Nashville, TN 37243-0565. Tel. 615-741-2241. Fax. 615-532-6934. www.state.tn.us/commerce

Texas • David Mattax, Commissioner of Insurance, 333 Guadalupe St., Austin, TX 78701. Tel. 512-463-6464. Fax. 512-475-2005. www.tdi.state.tx.us

Utah • Todd E. Kiser, Commissioner of Insurance, 3110 State Office Building, Salt Lake City, UT 84114-6901. Tel. 801-538-3800. Fax. 801-538-3829. www.insurance.utah.gov

Vermont • Susan L. Donegan, Commissioner of the Department of Financial Regulation, 89 Main St., Drawer 20, Montpelier, VT 05620-3101. Tel. 802-828-3301. Fax. 802-828-3306. www.bishca.state.vt.us

Virgin Islands • Osbert Potter, Lieutenant Governor/Commissioner of Insurance, 1131 King St., Third Floor, Suite 101, Christiansted, St. Croix, VI 00820. Tel. 340-773-6459. Fax. 340-774-9458. ltg.gov.vi

Virginia • Jacqueline K. Cunningham, Commissioner of Insurance, PO Box 1157, Richmond, VA 23218. Tel. 804-371-9694. Fax. 804-371-9349. www.scc.virginia.gov/boi

*Washington • Mike Kreidler, Insurance Commissioner, PO Box 40256, Olympia, WA 98504-0256. Tel. 360-725-7100. Fax. 360-586-2018. www.insurance.wa.gov

West Virginia • Michael D. Riley, Insurance Commissioner, 1124 Smith St., Charleston, WV 25301. Tel. 304-558-3354. Fax. 304-558-4965. www.wvinsurance.gov

Wisconsin • Ted Nickel, Commissioner of Insurance, 125 S. Webster St., Madison, WI 53703-3474. Tel. 608-266-3585. Fax. 608-266-9935. www.oci.wi.gov

Wyoming • Tom Glause, Insurance Commissioner, Herschler Bldg., 106 E. Sixth Ave., Cheyenne, WY 82002. Tel. 307-777-7401. Fax. 307-777-2446. insurance.state.wy.us

Appendices

Insurance and Related Service Organizations

The following organizations are supported by insurance companies or have activities closely related to insurance. National and state organizations which subscribe to the services of the Insurance Information Institute are identified by an asterisk (*).

A.M. BEST COMPANY INC. • Ambest Road, Oldwick, NJ 08858. Tel. 908-439-2200. www.ambest.com — Rating organization and publisher of reference books and periodicals relating to the insurance industry.

ACORD • One Blue Hill Plaza, 15th Floor, P.O. Box 1529, Pearl River, NY 10965-8529. Tel. 845-620-1700. www.acord.com — An industry-sponsored institute serving as the focal point for improving the computer processing of insurance transactions through the insurance agency system.

THE ACTUARIAL FOUNDATION • 475 North Martingale Road, Suite 600, Schaumburg, IL 60173-2226. Tel. 847-706-3535. www.actuarialfoundation.org — Develops, funds and executes education and research programs that serve the public by harnessing the talents of actuaries.

ADVOCATES FOR HIGHWAY AND AUTO SAFETY • 750 First Street NE, Suite 1130, Washington, DC 20002. Tel. 202-408-1711. www.saferoads.org — An alliance of consumer, safety and insurance organizations dedicated to highway and auto safety.

AIR WORLDWIDE CORPORATION • 131 Dartmouth Street, Boston, MA 02116. Tel. 617-267-6645. www.air-worldwide.com — Risk modeling and technology firm that develops models of global natural hazards, enabling companies to identify, quantify and plan for the financial consequences of catastrophic events.

AMERICA'S HEALTH INSURANCE PLANS (AHIP) • 601 Pennsylvania Avenue, NW, South Building, Suite 500, Washington, DC 20004. Tel. 202-778-3200. www.ahip.org — National trade association representing the health insurance industry.

AMERICAN ACADEMY OF ACTUARIES • 1850 M Street NW, Suite 300, Washington, DC 20036. Tel. 202-223-8196. www.actuary.org — Professional association for actuaries. Issues standards of conduct and provides government liaison and advisory opinions.

AMERICAN ASSOCIATION FOR LONG-TERM CARE INSURANCE • 3835 E. Thousand Oaks Blvd., Suite 336, Westlake Village, CA 91362. Tel. 818-597-3227. www.aaltci.org — A national professional organization exclusively dedicated to promoting the importance of planning for long-term care needs.

AMERICAN ASSOCIATION OF CROP INSURERS • 1 Massachusetts Avenue NW, Suite 800, Washington, DC 20001-1401. Tel. 202-789-4100. www.cropinsurers.com — Trade association of insurance companies to promote crop insurance.

AMERICAN ASSOCIATION OF INSURANCE SERVICES • 701 Warrenville Road, Lisle, IL 60532. Tel. 800-564-AAIS. www.aaisonline.com — Rating, statistical and advisory organization, made up principally of small and medium-sized property/casualty companies.

AMERICAN ASSOCIATION OF MANAGING GENERAL AGENTS • 610 Freedom Business Center, Suite 110, King of Prussia, PA 19406. Tel. 610-992-0022. www.aamga.org — Membership association of managing general agents of insurers.

AMERICAN BANKERS INSURANCE ASSOCIATION • 1120 Connecticut Avenue, NW, Washington, DC 20036. Tel. 202-663-5172. www.aba.com — A separately chartered affiliate of the American Bankers Association. A full service association for bank insurance interests dedicated to furthering the policy and business objectives of banks in insurance.

THE AMERICAN COLLEGE • 270 South Bryn Mawr Avenue, Bryn Mawr, PA 19010. Tel. 610-526-1000. www.theamericancollege.edu — An independent, accredited nonprofit institution, originally The American College of Life Underwriters. Provides graduate and professional education in insurance and other financial services.

AMERICAN COUNCIL OF LIFE INSURERS (ACLI) • 101 Constitution Avenue NW, Suite 700, Washington, DC 20001-2133. Tel. 202-624-2000. www.acli.com — Trade association responsible for the public affairs, government, legislative and research aspects of the life insurance business.

*AMERICAN INSTITUTE OF MARINE UNDERWRITERS • 14 Wall Street, New York, NY 10005. Tel. 212-233-0550. www.aimu.org — Provides information of concern to marine underwriters and promotes their interests.

AMERICAN INSURANCE ASSOCIATION (AIA) - NATIONAL OFFICE • 2101 L Street, NW, Suite 400, Washington, DC 20037. Tel. 202-828-7139. www.aiadc.org — Trade and service organization for property/casualty insurance companies. Provides a forum for the discussion of problems as well as safety, promotional and legislative services.

AMERICAN LAND TITLE ASSOCIATION • 1800 M Street, NW, Suite 300S, Washington, DC 20036-5828. Tel. 202-296-3671. www.alta.org — Trade organization for title insurers, abstractors and agents. Performs statistical research and lobbying services.

AMERICAN NUCLEAR INSURERS • 95 Glastonbury Boulevard, Suite 300, Glastonbury, CT 06033. Tel. 860-682-1301. www.amnucins.com — A nonprofit unincorporated association through which liability insurance protection is provided against hazards arising out of nuclear reactor installations and their operations.

AMERICAN PREPAID LEGAL SERVICES INSTITUTE • 321 North Clark Street, Chicago, IL 60654. Tel. 312-988-5751. www.aplsi.org — National membership organization providing information and technical assistance to lawyers, insurance companies, administrators, marketers and consumers regarding group and prepaid legal service plans.

AMERICAN RISK AND INSURANCE ASSOCIATION • 716 Providence Road, Malvern, PA 19355-3402. Tel. 610-640-1997. www.aria.org — Association of scholars in the field of risk management and insurance, dedicated to advancing knowledge in the field and enhancing the career development of its members.

AMERICAN TORT REFORM ASSOCIATION • 1101 Connecticut Avenue NW, Suite 400, Washington, DC 20036. Tel. 202-682-1163. www.atra.org — A broad based, bipartisan coalition of more than 300 businesses, corporations, municipalities, associations and professional firms that support civil justice reform.

Appendices

APIW: A PROFESSIONAL ASSOCIATION OF WOMEN IN INSURANCE • 990 Cedar Bridge Ave, Suite B&PMB 210, Brick, NJ 08723-4157. Tel. 973-941-6024. www.apiw.org — A professional association of women in the insurance and reinsurance industry and related fields. Provides professional education, networking and support services to encourage the development of professional leadership among its members.

ARBITRATION FORUMS, INC. • 3820 Northdale Boulevard, Suite 200A, Tampa, FL 33624. Tel. 866-977-3434. www.arbfile.org — Nonprofit provider of interinsurance dispute resolution services for self-insureds, insurers and claim service organizations.

ASSOCIATION OF FINANCIAL GUARANTY INSURERS • Mackin & Company, 139 Lancaster Street, Albany, NY 12210. Tel. 518-449-4698. www.afgi.org — Trade association of the insurers and reinsurers of municipal bonds and asset-backed securities.

ASSOCIATION OF GOVERNMENTAL RISK POOLS • 9 Cornell Rd., Latham, NY 12110. Tel. 518-389-2782. www.agrip.org — Organization for public entity risk and benefits pools in North America.

AUTOMOBILE INSURANCE PLANS SERVICE OFFICE • 302 Central Avenue, Johnston, RI 02919. Tel. 401-946-2310. www.aipso.com — Develops and files rates and provides other services for state-mandated automobile insurance plans.

BANK INSURANCE & SECURITIES ASSOCIATION • 2025 M Street, NW, Suite 800, Washington, DC 20036. Tel. 202-367-1111. www.bisanet.org — Fosters the full integration of securities and insurance businesses with depository institutions' traditional banking businesses. Participants include executives from the securities, insurance, investment advisory, trust, private banking, retail, capital markets and commercial divisions of depository institutions.

BISRA - BANK INSURANCE & SECURITIES RESEARCH ASSOCIATES • 300 Day Hill Road, Windsor, CT 06095-4761. Tel. 860-298-3935. www.bisra.com — Consultant focusing on the financial services marketplace. Conducts studies of sales penetration, profitability, compensation and compliance. (formerly Kehrer-LIMRA).

CAPTIVE INSURANCE COMPANIES ASSOCIATION • 4248 Park Glen Rd., Minneapolis, MN 55416. Tel. 952-928-4655. www.cicaworld.com — Organization that disseminates information useful to firms that utilize the captive insurance company concept to solve corporate insurance problems.

*CASUALTY ACTUARIAL SOCIETY • 4350 North Fairfax Drive, Suite 250, Arlington, VA 22203. Tel. 703-276-3100. www.casact.org — Promotes actuarial and statistical science in property/casualty insurance fields.

CERTIFIED AUTOMOTIVE PARTS ASSOCIATION • 1000 Vermont Ave., NW Suite 1010, Washington, DC 20005. Tel. 202-737-2212. www.capacertified.org — Nonprofit organization formed to develop and oversee a test program guaranteeing the suitability and quality of automotive parts.

COALITION AGAINST INSURANCE FRAUD • 1012 14th Street NW, Suite 200, Washington, DC 20005. Tel. 202-393-7330. www.insurancefraud.org — An alliance of consumer, law enforcement, and insurance industry groups dedicated to reducing all forms of insurance fraud through public advocacy and education.

THE COMMITTEE OF ANNUITY INSURERS • c/o Davis & Harman LLP, 1455 Pennsylvania Avenue, NW, Suite 1200, Washington, DC 20004. Tel. 202-347-2230. www.annuity-insurers.org — Group whose goal is to address federal legislative and regulatory issues relevant to the annuity industry and to participate in the development of federal tax and securities policies regarding annuities.

CONNING RESEARCH AND CONSULTING, INC. • One Financial Plaza, Hartford, CT 06103-2627. Tel. 860-299-2000. www.conningresearch.com — Research and consulting firm that offers an array of specialty information products, insights and analyses of key issues confronting the insurance industry.

CORELOGIC • 40 Pacifica, Suite 900, Irvine, CA 92618. Tel. 800-426-1466. www.corelogic.com — Provides comprehensive data, analytics and services to financial services and real estate professionals.

COUNCIL OF INSURANCE AGENTS AND BROKERS • 701 Pennsylvania Avenue NW, Suite 750, Washington, DC 20004-2608. Tel. 202-783-4400. www.ciab.com — A trade organization representing leading commercial insurance agencies and brokerage firms.

CROP INSURANCE AND REINSURANCE BUREAU • 440 First St NW, Suite 500, Washington, DC 20001. Tel. 202-544-0067. www.cropinsurance.org — Crop insurance trade organization.

DEFENSE RESEARCH INSTITUTE • 55 W. Monroe St., Suite 2000, Chicago, IL 60603. Tel. 312-795-1101. www.dri.org — A national and international membership association of lawyers and others concerned with the defense of civil actions.

EASTBRIDGE CONSULTING GROUP, INC. • 50 Avon Meadow Lane #101, Avon, CT 06001. Tel. 860-676-9633. www.eastbridge.com — Provides consulting, marketing, training and research services to financial services firms, including those involved in worksite marketing and the distribution of individual and employee benefits products.

EMPLOYEE BENEFIT RESEARCH INSTITUTE • 1100 13th Street NW, Suite 878, Washington, DC 20005-4051. Tel. 202-659-0670. www.ebri.org — The Institute's mission is to advance the public's, the media's and policymakers' knowledge and understanding of employee benefits and their importance to the U.S. economy.

EQECAT • 475 14th Street, Suite 550, Oakland, CA 94612-1938. Tel. 510-817-3100. www.eqecat.com — Provider of products and services for managing natural and man-made risks. Provides innovative catastrophe management solutions for property and casualty insurance underwriting, accumulation management and transfer of natural hazard and terrorism risk.

THE FINANCIAL SERVICES ROUNDTABLE • 600 13th Street NW, Suite 400, Washington, DC 20005. Tel. 202-289-4322. www.fsround.org — A forum for U.S. financial industry leaders working together to determine and influence the most critical public policy concerns related to the integration of the financial services.

FITCH CREDIT RATING COMPANY • 33 Whitehall Street, New York, NY 10004. Tel. 212-908-0500. www.fitchratings.com — Assigns claims-paying ability ratings to insurance companies.

GLOBAL AEROSPACE, INC. • One Sylvan Way, Parsippany, NJ 07054. Tel. 973-490-8500. www.global-aero.co.uk — A pool of property/casualty companies engaged in writing all classes of aviation insurance.

GLOBAL ASSOCIATION OF RISK PROFESSIONALS • 111 Town Square Place, 14th Floor, Jersey City, NJ 07310. Tel. 201-719-7210. www.garp.com — International group whose aim is to encourage and enhance communications between risk professionals, practitioners and regulators worldwide.

GRIFFITH INSURANCE EDUCATION FOUNDATION • 720 Providence Rd, Suite 100, Malvern, PA 19355. Tel. 855-288-7743. www.griffithfoundation.org — The foundation promotes the teaching and study of risk management and insurance at colleges and universities nationwide and provides education programs for public policymakers on the basic principles of risk management and insurance.

HIGHWAY LOSS DATA INSTITUTE • 1005 North Glebe Road, Suite 700, Arlington, VA 22201. Tel. 703-247-1600. www.hldi.org — Nonprofit organization to gather, process and provide the public with insurance data concerned with human and economic losses resulting from highway accidents.

INDEPENDENT INSURANCE AGENTS & BROKERS OF AMERICA, INC. • 127 South Peyton Street, Alexandria, VA 22314. Tel. 800-221-7917. www.independentagent.com — Trade association of independent insurance agents.

INLAND MARINE UNDERWRITERS ASSOCIATION • 14 Wall Street, 8th Floor, New York, NY 10005. Tel. 212-233-0550. www.imua.org — Forum for discussion of problems of common concern to inland marine insurers.

INSURANCE ACCOUNTING AND SYSTEMS ASSOCIATION, INC. • PO Box 51340, Durham, NC 27717. Tel. 919-489-0991. www.iasa.org — Promotes the study, research and development of modern techniques in insurance accounting and systems.

INSURANCE COMMITTEE FOR ARSON CONTROL • 3601 Vincennes Road, Indianapolis, IN 46268. Tel. 317-876-6226. www.arsoncontrol.org — All-industry coalition that serves as a catalyst for insurers' anti-arson efforts and a liaison with government agencies and other groups devoted to arson control.

INSURANCE DATA MANAGEMENT ASSOCIATION, INC. • 545 Washington Boulevard, Jersey City, NJ 07310-1686. Tel. 201-469-3069. www.idma.org — An independent, nonprofit, professional, learned association dedicated to increasing the level of professionalism, knowledge and visibility of insurance data management.

INSURANCE INDUSTRY CHARITABLE FOUNDATION • 1999 Avenue of the Stars, Suite 1100, Los Angeles, CA 90067. Tel. 424-253-1107. www.iicf.org — Seeks to help communities and enrich lives by combining the collective strengths of the industry to provide grants, volunteer service and leadership.

INSURANCE INFORMATION INSTITUTE (I.I.I.) • 110 William Street, 18th Floor, New York, NY 10038. Tel. 212-346-5500. www.iii.org — A primary source for information, analysis and reference on insurance subjects.

INSURANCE INSTITUTE FOR BUSINESS & HOME SAFETY • 4775 East Fowler Avenue, Tampa, FL 33617. Tel. 813-286-3400. www.DisasterSafety.org — An insurance industry-sponsored nonprofit organization dedicated to reducing losses, deaths, injuries and property damage resulting from natural hazards.

INSURANCE INSTITUTE FOR HIGHWAY SAFETY • 1005 North Glebe Road, Suite 800, Arlington, VA 22201. Tel. 703-247-1500. www.iihs.org — Research and education organization dedicated to reducing loss, death, injury and property damage on the highways. Fully funded by property/casualty insurers.

INSURANCE LIBRARY ASSOCIATION OF BOSTON • 156 State Street, Second Floor, Boston, MA 02109. Tel. 617-227-2087. www.insurancelibrary.org — The Insurance Library Association of Boston founded in 1887, is a nonprofit insurance association that has an extensive insurance library on all lines of insurance.

INSURANCE REGULATORY EXAMINERS SOCIETY • 1821 University Ave W, Ste S256, St. Paul, MN 55104. Tel. 651-917-6250. www.go-ires.org — Nonprofit professional and educational association for examiners and other professionals working in insurance industry.

INSURANCE RESEARCH COUNCIL (A DIVISION OF THE INSTITUTES) • 718 Providence Road, Malvern, PA 19355-0725. Tel. 610-644-2212. www.insurance-research.org — Provides research relevant to public policy issues affecting risk and insurance.

INSURED RETIREMENT INSTITUTE • 1100 Vermont Avenue, NW, 10th Floor, Washington, DC 20005. Tel. 202-469-3000. www.irionline.org — Source of knowledge pertaining to annuities, insured retirement products and retirement planning; provides educational and informational resources. Formerly the National Association for Variable Annuities (NAVA).

INTEGRATED BENEFITS INSTITUTE • 595 Market Street, Suite 810, San Francisco, CA 94105. Tel. 415-222-7280. www.ibiweb.org — A private, nonprofit organization that provides research, discussion and analysis, data services and legislative review to measure and improve integrated benefits programs, enhance efficiency in delivery of all employee-based benefits and promote effective return-to-work.

INTERMEDIARIES AND REINSURANCE UNDERWRITERS ASSOCIATION, INC. • c/o The Beaumont Group, Inc., 3626 East Tremont Avenue, Suite 203, Throggs Neck, NY 10465. Tel. 718-892 0228. www.irua.com — Educational association to encourage the exchange of ideas among reinsurers worldwide writing principally treaty reinsurance.

INTERNATIONAL ASSOCIATION OF INSURANCE FRAUD AGENCIES, INC. • P.O. Box 10018, Kansas City, MO 64171. Tel. 816-756-5285. www.iaifa.org — An international association opening the doors of communication, cooperation and exchange of information in the fight against sophisticated global insurance and related financial insurance fraud.

INTERNATIONAL ASSOCIATION OF INSURANCE PROFESSIONALS • 3525 Piedmont Road, Building 5, Suite 300, Atlanta, GA 30305. Tel. 800-766-6249. www.internationalinsuranceprofessionals.org — Provides insurance education, skills enhancement and leadership development to its members.

INTERNATIONAL ASSOCIATION OF SPECIAL INVESTIGATION UNITS • N83 W13410 Leon Road, Menomonee Falls, WI 53051. Tel. 414-375-2992. www.iasiu.org — Group whose goals are to promote a coordinated effort within the industry to combat insurance fraud and to provide education and training for insurance investigators.

Insurance and Related Service Organizations

INTERNATIONAL INSURANCE SOCIETY, INC. • 101 Astor Place, Suite 202, New York, NY 10003. Tel. 212-277-5171. www.iisonline.org — A nonprofit membership organization whose mission is to facilitate international understandings, the transfer of ideas and innovations, and the development of personal networks across insurance markets through a joint effort of leading executives and academics throughout the world.

IVANS (INSURANCE VALUE ADDED NETWORK SERVICES) • 5405 Cypress Center Drive, Suite 150, Tampa,, FL 33609. Tel. 855-233-9128. www.ivans.com — An industry-sponsored organization offering a data communications network linking agencies, companies and providers of data to the insurance industry.

KAREN CLARK & COMPANY • 2 Copley Place, Tower 2, 1st Floor, Boston, MA 02116. Tel. 617-423-2800. www.karenclarkandco.com — Catastrophe risk assessment and modeling firm.

KINETIC ANALYSIS CORPORATION • 8070 Georgia Avenue, Suite 413, Silver Spring, MD 20910. Tel. 240-821-1202. www.kinanco.com — Specializes in estimating the impact of natural and man-made hazards on the structures and the economy for clients in engineering, land development, and risk management.

LATIN AMERICAN AGENTS ASSOCIATION • 8880 Rio San Diego Drive, Suite 800, San Diego, CA 90640. Tel. 800-985-1966. www.latinagents.com — An independent group of Hispanic agents and brokers, whose goal is to educate, influence and inform the insurance community about the specific needs of the Latino community in the United States.

LATIN AMERICAN ASSOCIATION OF INSURANCE AGENCIES • P.O. Box 520844, Miami, FL 33152-2844. Tel. 305-477-1442. www.laaia.com — An association of insurance professionals whose purpose is to protect the rights of its members, benefit the consumer through education, provide information and networking services, and promote active participation in the political environment and community service.

THE LIFE AND HEALTH INSURANCE FOUNDATION FOR EDUCATION • 1655 North Fort Myer Drive, Suite 610, Arlington, VA 22209. Tel. 888-LIFE-777. lifehappens.org — Nonprofit organization dedicated to addressing the public's growing need for information and education about life, health, disability and long-term care insurance.

LIFE INSURANCE SETTLEMENT ASSOCIATION • 225 South Eola Drive, Orlando, FL 32801. Tel. 407-894-3797. www.thevoiceoftheindustry.com — Promotes the development, integrity and reputation of the life settlement industry.

*LIGHTNING PROTECTION INSTITUTE • PO Box 99, Maryville, MO 64468. Tel. 800-488-6864. www.lightning.org — Nonprofit organization dedicated to ensuring that its members' lightning protection systems are the best possible quality in design, materials and installation.

LIMRA INTERNATIONAL • 300 Day Hill Road, Windsor, CT 06095. Tel. 800-235-4672. www.limra.com — Worldwide association providing research, consulting and other services to insurance and financial services companies in more than 60 countries. LIMRA helps its member companies maximize their marketing effectiveness.

LOMA (LIFE OFFICE MANAGEMENT ASSOCIATION) • 6190 Powers Ferry Road, Suite 600, Atlanta, GA 30339. Tel. 770-951-1770. www.loma.org — Worldwide association of insurance companies specializing in research and education, with a primary focus on home office management.

LOSS EXECUTIVES ASSOCIATION • P.O. Box 37, Tenafly, NJ 07670. Tel. 201-569-3346. www.lossexecutives.com — A professional association of property loss executives providing education to the industry.

MARSHALL & SWIFT • 777 South Figueroa St., 12th floor, Los Angeles, CA 90017. Tel. 800-421-8042. www.msbinfo.com — Building cost research company providing data and estimating technologies to the property insurance industry.

MIB, INC. • 50 Braintree Hill Park, Suite 400, Braintree, MA 02184-8734. Tel. 781-751-6000. www.mibsolutions.com/lost-life-insurance — Database of individual life insurance applications processed since 1995.

MICHAEL WHITE ASSOCIATES • 823 King of Prussia Road, Radnor, PA 19087. Tel. 610-254-0440. www.bankinsurance.com — Consulting firm that helps clients plan, develop and implement bank insurance sales programs. Conducts research on and benchmarks performance of bank insurance and

MOODY'S INVESTORS SERVICE • 7 World Trade Center at 250 Greenwich Street, New York, NY 10007. Tel. 212-553-1653. www.moodys.com — Global credit analysis and financial information firm.

MORTGAGE INSURANCE COMPANIES OF AMERICA (MICA) • 1101 17th Street NW, Suite 700, Washington, DC 20036. Tel. 202-280-1820. www.usmi.org — Represents the private mortgage insurance industry. MICA provides information on related legislative and regulatory issues, and strives to enhance understanding of the role private mortgage insurance plays in housing Americans.

NATIONAL AFRICAN-AMERICAN INSURANCE ASSOCIATION • 1718 M Street NW, P.O. Box 1110, Washington, DC 20036. Tel. 866-56-NAAIA. www.naaia.org — NAAIA fosters the nationwide presence, participation and long-term financial success of African-American insurance professionals within the greater insurance community and provides its members and the insurance industry a forum for sharing information and ideas that enhance business and professional development.

NATIONAL ARBITRATION FORUM • P.O. Box 50191, Minneapolis, MN 55405-0191. Tel. 800-474-2371. www.adrforum.com — A leading neutral administrator of arbitration, mediation and other forms of alternative dispute resolution worldwide.

NATIONAL ASSOCIATION OF HEALTH UNDERWRITERS • 1212 New York Avenue NW, Suite 1100, Washington, DC 20005. Tel. 202-552-5060. www.nahu.org — Professional association of people who sell and service disability income, and hospitalization and major medical health insurance companies.

NATIONAL ASSOCIATION OF INDEPENDENT INSURANCE ADJUSTERS • 1880 Radcliff Ct., Tracy, CA 95376. Tel. 209-832-6962. www.naiia.com — Association of claims adjusters and firms operating independently on a fee basis for all insurance companies.

NATIONAL ASSOCIATION OF INSURANCE AND FINANCIAL ADVISORS • 2901 Telestar Court, Falls Church, VA 22042-1205. Tel. 877-866-2432; 703-770-8100. www.naifa.org — Professional association representing health and life insurance agents.

NATIONAL ASSOCIATION OF INSURANCE COMMISSIONERS • 1100 Walnut Street, Suite 1500, Kansas City, MO 64106-2197. Tel. 816-842-3600. www.naic.org — Organization of state insurance commissioners to promote uniformity in state supervision of insurance matters and to recommend legislation in state legislatures.

NATIONAL ASSOCIATION OF MUTUAL INSURANCE COMPANIES (NAMIC) • 3601 Vincennes Road, Indianapolis, IN 46268. Tel. 317-875-5250. www.namic.org — National property/casualty insurance trade and political advocacy association.

NATIONAL ASSOCIATION OF PROFESSIONAL INSURANCE AGENTS • 400 North Washington Street, Alexandria, VA 22314-2353. Tel. 703-836-9340. www.pianet.com — Trade association of independent insurance agents. Operations: Lobbying, Education, Communications, Business Building Tools and Insurance Products

NATIONAL ASSOCIATION OF PROFESSIONAL SURPLUS LINES OFFICES, LTD. • 4131 North Mulberry Drive, Ste. 200, Kansas City, MO 64116. Tel. 816-741-3910. www.napslo.org — Professional association of wholesale brokers, excess and surplus lines companies, affiliates and supporting members.

NATIONAL ASSOCIATION OF SURETY BOND PRODUCERS (NASBP) • 1140 19th Street, Suite 800, Washington, DC 20036-5104. Tel. 202-686-3700. www.nasbp.org — NASBP members are professionals who specialize in providing surety bonds for construction and other commercial purposes to companies and individuals needing the assurance offered by surety bonds. Its members have broad knowledge of the surety marketplace and the business strategies and underwriting differences among surety companies.

*NATIONAL CONFERENCE OF INSURANCE GUARANTY FUNDS • 300 North Meridian Street, Suite 1020, Indianapolis, IN 46204. Tel. 317-464-8199. www.ncigf.org — Advisory organization to the state guaranty fund boards; gathers and disseminates information regarding insurer insolvencies.

NATIONAL CONFERENCE OF INSURANCE LEGISLATORS • 385 Jordan Road, Troy, NY 12180. Tel. 518-687-0178. www.ncoil.org — Organization of state legislators whose main area of public policy concern is insurance and insurance regulation.

NATIONAL CROP INSURANCE SERVICES, INC. • 8900 Indian Creek Parkway, Suite 600, Overland Park, KS 66210-1567. Tel. 913-685-2767. www.ag-risk.org — National trade association of insurance companies writing hail insurance, fire insurance and insurance against other weather perils to growing crops, with rating and research services for crop-hail and rain insurers.

NATIONAL FIRE PROTECTION ASSOCIATION • One Batterymarch Park, Quincy, MA 02169-7471. Tel. 617-770-3000. www.nfpa.org — Independent, nonprofit source of information on fire protection, prevention and suppression. Develops and publishes consensus fire safety standards; sponsors national Learn Not to Burn campaign.

NATIONAL FLOOD INSURANCE PROGRAM (NFIP) • 500 C Street SW, Washington, DC 20472. Tel. 800-621-FEMA. www.floodsmart.gov/floodsmart — The NFIP offers flood insurance to homeowners, renters and business owners if their community participates in the program. Participating communities agree to adopt and enforce ordinances that meet or exceed FEMA requirements to reduce the risk of flooding.

NATIONAL HIGHWAY TRAFFIC SAFETY ADMINISTRATION (NHTSA) • 1200 New Jersey Avenue SE, West Building, Washington, DC 20590. Tel. 888-327-4236. www.nhtsa.dot.gov — Carries out programs and studies aimed at reducing economic losses in motor vehicle crashes and repairs.

NATIONAL INDEPENDENT STATISTICAL SERVICE • 3601 Vincennes Road, P.O. Box 68950, Indianapolis, IN 46268. Tel. 317-876-6200. www.niss-stat.org — National statistical agent and advisory organization for all lines of insurance, except workers compensation.

*NATIONAL INSURANCE CRIME BUREAU • 1111 East Touhy Avenue, Suite 400, Des Plaines, IL 60018. Tel. 800-447-6282; 847-544-7000. www.nicb.org — A nonprofit organization dedicated to preventing, detecting and defeating insurance fraud.

NATIONAL OCEANIC AND ATMOSPHERIC ADMINISTRATION (NOAA) • 1401 Constitution Avenue, NW, Room 5128, Washington, DC 20230. Tel. 301-427-9000 (weather division). www.noaa.gov/index.html — Dr. Kathryn Sullivan, Under Secretary of Commerce for Oceans and Atmosphere and NOAA Administrator

NATIONAL ORGANIZATION OF LIFE AND HEALTH INSURANCE GUARANTY ASSOCIATIONS (NOLHGA) • 13873 Park Center Road, Suite 329, Herndon, VA 20171. Tel. 703-481-5206. www.nolhga.com — A voluntary association composed of the life and health insurance guaranty associations of all 50 states, the District of Columbia and Puerto Rico.

NATIONAL RISK RETENTION ASSOCIATION • 16133 Ventura Blvd., Suite 1055, Encino, CA 91436. Tel. 800-928-5809 x102. www.nrra-usa.org — The voice of risk retention group and purchasing group liability insurance programs, organized pursuant to the Federal Liability Risk Retention Act.

NATIONAL SAFETY COUNCIL • 1121 Spring Lake Drive, Itasca, IL 60143-3201. Tel. 630-285-1121. www.nsc.org — Provides national support and leadership in the field of safety, publishes safety material and conducts public information and publicity programs.

NATIONAL STRUCTURED SETTLEMENTS TRADE ASSOCIATION • 1100 New York Avenue, NW, Suite 750W, Washington, DC 20005. Tel. 202 289 4004. www.nssta.com — Trade association representing consultants, insurers and others who are interested in the resolution and financing of tort claims through periodic payments.

*NCCI HOLDINGS, INC. • 901 Peninsula Corporate Circle, Boca Raton, FL 33487. Tel. 561-893-1000. www.ncci.com — Develops and administers rating plans and systems for workers compensation insurance.

NEIGHBORWORKS AMERICA • 999 North Capitol Street NE, Suite 900, Washington, DC 20002. Tel. 202-760-4000. www.nw.org — The goal of this group is to develop partnerships between the insurance industry and NeighborWorks organizations to better market the products and services of both, for the benefit of the customers and communities they serve.

NEW YORK ALLIANCE AGAINST INSURANCE FRAUD • 1450 Western Ave., Suite 101, Albany, NY 12203. Tel. 518-432-3576. www.fraudny.com — A cooperative effort of insurance companies in New York State to educate the industry about the costs of insurance fraud, the many forms is can take and what can be done to fight it.

NEW YORK INSURANCE ASSOCIATION, INC. • 130 Washington Ave., Albany, NY 12210. Tel. 518-432-4227. www.nyia.org — Domestic & Non-Domestic Property/Casualty Companies Operations: Lobbying

NEW YORK PROPERTY INSURANCE UNDERWRITING ASSOCIATION • 100 William St., 4th Fl., New York, NY 10038. Tel. 212-208-9700. www.nypiua.com — Provides basic property insurance for New York State residents not able to obtain the coverage through the voluntary market. Administers the C-MAP and FAIR Plan.

NONPROFIT RISK MANAGEMENT CENTER • 204 South King Street, Leesburg, VA 20175. Tel. 703-777-3504 or 202-785-3891. www.nonprofitrisk.org — Conducts research and education on risk management and insurance issues of special concern to nonprofit organizations.

NORTH AMERICAN PET HEALTH INSURANCE ASSOCIATION • P.O. Box 37940, Raleigh, NC 27627. Tel. 877-962-7442. www.naphia.org — Group whose members work collaboratively towards establishing and maintaining universal and professional standards for terminology, best practices, quality and ethics in the pet health industry.

OPIC • 1100 New York Avenue, NW, Washington, DC 20527. Tel. 202-336-8400. www.opic.gov — Self-sustaining U.S. government agency providing political risk insurance and finance services for U.S. investment in developing countries.

PHYSICIAN INSURERS ASSOCIATION OF AMERICA • 2275 Research Boulevard, Suite 250, Rockville, MD 20850. Tel. 301-947-9000. www.thepiaa.org — Trade association representing physician-owned mutual insurance companies that provide medical malpractice insurance.

PROFESSIONAL LIABILITY UNDERWRITING SOCIETY (PLUS) • 5353 Wayzata Boulevard, Suite 600, Minneapolis, MN 55416. Tel. 952-746-2580; 800-845-0778. www.plusweb.org — An international, nonprofit association that provides educational opportunities and programs to enhance the professionalism of its members.

PROPERTY CASUALTY INSURERS ASSOCIATION OF AMERICA (PCI) • 8700 West Bryn Mawr, Suite 1200S, Chicago, IL 60031-3512. Tel. 847-297-7800. www.pciaa.net — Serves as a voice on public policy issues and advocates positions that foster a competitive market place for property/casualty insurers and insurance consumers.

PROPERTY INSURANCE PLANS SERVICE OFFICE • 27 School Street, Suite 302, Boston, MA 02108. Tel. 617-371-4175. www.pipso.com — Provides technical and administrative services to state property insurance plans.

PROPERTY LOSS RESEARCH BUREAU • 3025 Highland Parkway, Suite 800, Downers Grove, IL 60515. Tel. 630-724-2200. www.plrb.org — This property/casualty trade organization promotes productivity and efficiency in the property and liability loss and claim adjustment processes, disseminates information on property and liability issues and fosters education and new and beneficial developments within the industry.

PUBLIC RISK MANAGEMENT ASSOCIATION • 700 S. Washington St., Suite 218, Alexandria, VA 22314. Tel. 703-528-7701. www.primacentral.org — Membership organization representing risk managers in state and local public entities.

RAND INSTITUTE FOR CIVIL JUSTICE • 1776 Main Street, P.O. Box 2138, Santa Monica, CA 90407-2138. Tel. 310-393-0411. www.rand.org — Organization formed within The Rand Corporation to perform independent, objective research and analysis concerning the civil justice system.

REINSURANCE ASSOCIATION OF AMERICA • 1445 New York Ave, NW, 7th Fl., Washington, DC 20005. Tel. 202-638-0936. www.reinsurance.org — Trade association of property/casualty reinsurers; provides legislative services for members.

RISK AND INSURANCE MANAGEMENT SOCIETY, INC. • 5 Bryant Park, 13th floor, New York, NY 10018. Tel. 212-286-9292. www.rims.org — Organization of corporate buyers of insurance, which makes known to insurers the insurance needs of business and industry, supports loss prevention and provides a forum for the discussion of common objectives and problems.

RISK MANAGEMENT SOLUTIONS, INC. • 7575 Gateway Boulevard, Newark, CA 94560. Tel. 510-505-2500. www.rms.com — Provides products and services for the quantification and management of catastrophe risk associated with natural perils as well as products for weather derivatives and enterprise risk management for the property/casualty insurance industry.

RUNZHEIMER INTERNATIONAL • 1 Runzheimer Parkway, Waterford, WI 53185. Tel. 800-558-1702. www.runzheimer.com — Management consulting firm that provides workforce mobility solutions relating to business vehicles, relocation, travel management, corporate aircraft and mobile device management programs.

SCHOOL OF RISK MANAGEMENT, INSURANCE AND ACTUARIAL SCIENCE OF THE TOBIN COLLEGE OF BUSINESS AT ST. JOHN'S UNIVERSITY (FORMERLY THE COLLEGE OF INSURANCE) • 101 Astor Place, New York, NY 10003. Tel. 212-277-5198. www.stjohns.edu/academics/graduate/tobin/srm — Insurance industry-supported college providing a curriculum leading to bachelor's and master's degrees in business administration, financial management of risk, insurance finance and actuarial science. The Kathryn and Shelby Cullom Davis Library (212-277-5135) provides services, products and resources to its members.

SELF-INSURANCE INSTITUTE OF AMERICA • P.O. Box 1237, Simpsonville, SC 29681. Tel. 800-851-7789. www.siia.org — Organization that fosters and promotes alternative methods of risk protection.

SNL FINANCIAL LC • One SNL Plaza, 212 7th St. NE, Charlottesville, VA 22902. Tel. 434-977-1600. www.snl.com — Research firm that collects, standardizes and disseminates all relevant corporate, financial, market and M&A data as well as news and analytics for the industries it covers: banking, specialized financial services, insurance, real estate and energy.

SOCIETY OF ACTUARIES • 475 North Martingale Road, Suite 600, Schaumburg, aIL 60173. Tel. 847-706-3500. www.soa.org — An educational, research and professional organization dedicated to serving the public and its members. The Society's vision is for actuaries to be recognized as the leading professionals in the modeling and management of financial risk and contingent events.

SOCIETY OF CERTIFIED INSURANCE COUNSELORS • P.O. Box 27027, Austin, TX 78755-2027. Tel. 800-633-2165. www.scic.com — National education program in property, liability and life insurance, with a continuing education requirement upon designation.

SOCIETY OF FINANCIAL EXAMINERS • 12100 Sunset Hills Rd., Suite 130, Reston, VA 20190-3221. Tel. 703-234-4140. www.sofe.org — Professional society for examiners of insurance companies, banks, savings and loans, and credit unions.

SOCIETY OF INSURANCE RESEARCH • 631 Eastpointe Drive, Shelbyville, IN 46176. Tel. 317-398-3684. www.sirnet.org — Stimulates insurance research and fosters exchanges among society members on research methodology.

SOCIETY OF INSURANCE TRAINERS AND EDUCATORS • 1821 University Ave. W, Ste. S256, St. Paul, MN 55104. Tel. 651-999-5354. www.insurancetrainers.org — Professional organization of trainers and educators in insurance.

STANDARD & POOR'S RATING GROUP • 55 Water Street, New York, NY 10041. Tel. 212-438-2000. www.standardandpoors.com — Monitors the credit quality of bonds and other financial instruments of corporations, governments and supranational entities.

SURETY & FIDELITY ASSOCIATION OF AMERICA (SFAA) • 1101 Connecticut Avenue NW, Suite 800, Washington, DC 20036. Tel. 202-463-0600. www.surety.org — Statistical, rating, development and advisory organization for surety companies.

UNDERWRITERS' LABORATORIES, INC. • 2600 N.W. Lake Rd., Camas, WA 98607-8542. Tel. 360-817-5500. www.ul.com — Investigates and tests electrical materials and other products to determine that fire prevention and protection standards are being met.

*VERISK/ISO • 545 Washington Boulevard, Jersey City, NJ 07310-1686. Tel. 201-469-3000. www.verisk.com— A leading source of information about property/casualty insurance risk. Provides statistical, actuarial, underwriting and claims information; policy language; information about specific locations; fraud identification tools; and technical services. Products help customers protect people, property and financial assets.

WEATHER RISK MANAGEMENT ASSOCIATION (WRMA) • 529 14th Street, NW, Suite 750, Washington, DC 20045. Tel. 202-289-3800. www.wrma.org — Serves the weather risk management industry by providing forums for discussion and interaction with others associated with financial weather products.

*WISCONSIN INSURANCE ALLIANCE • 44 E. Mifflin St., Suite 901, Madison, WI 53703-2888. Tel. 608-255-1749. www.wial.com — A state trade association of property/casualty insurance companies conducting legislative affairs and public relations on behalf of the industry.

*WORKERS COMPENSATION RESEARCH INSTITUTE • 955 Massachusetts Avenue, Cambridge, MA 02139. Tel. 617-661-9274. www.wcrinet.org — A nonpartisan, nonprofit membership organization conducting public policy research on workers' compensation, healthcare and disability issues. Members include employers, insurers, insurance regulators and state regulatory agencies, as well as several state labor organizations.

2016 I.I.I. Member Companies

ACE USA

ACUITY

AEGIS Insurance Services Inc.

AIG

Allianz of America, Inc.

Allied World Assurance Company

Allstate Insurance Group

ALPS Corporation

American Agricultural Insurance Company

American Family Insurance

American Integrity Insurance Company

American Reliable Insurance

Amerisafe

Amerisure Insurance Companies

Arch Insurance Group

Argo Group US

Arthur J. Gallagher

Beacon Mutual Insurance Company

BITCO Insurance Companies

Canal Insurance

Catholic Mutual Insurance

Chesapeake Employers' Insurance Company

Chubb Group of Insurance Companies

Church Mutual Insurance Company

The Concord Group

COUNTRY Financial

Country-Wide Insurance Company

CNA

CSAA Insurance Group, a AAA Insurer

CUMIS Insurance Society, Inc.

Dryden Mutual Insurance Company

EMC Insurance Companies

Enumclaw Insurance Group

Erie & Niagara Insurance Association

Erie Insurance Group

Farm Bureau Town and Country Insurance Company of Missouri

Farmers Group, Inc.

GEICO

Gen Re

Germania Insurance

Grange Insurance Association

Grange Insurance Companies

GuideOne Insurance

The Hanover Insurance Group Inc.

The Harford Mutual Insurance Companies

The Hartford Financial Services Group

The Horace Mann Companies

Ironshore Insurance Ltd.

Island Insurance Companies

Kemper Corporation

Liberty Mutual Group

Lloyd's

Lockton Companies

Magna Carta Companies

MAPFRE USA

Marsh Inc.

MEMIC

MetLife Auto & Home

Michigan Millers Mutual Insurance Company

Millville Mutual Insurance Company

Missouri Employers Mutual Insurance

MMG Insurance Company

Motorists Insurance Group

Munich Re

Nationwide

New York Central Mutual Fire Insurance Company

The Norfolk & Dedham Group

Northern Neck Insurance Company

Ohio Mutual Insurance Group

OneBeacon Insurance Group

PartnerRe

Pennsylvania Lumbermens Mutual Insurance Company

Providence Mutual Fire Insurance Company

Scor U.S. Corporation

SECURA Insurance Companies

Selective Insurance Group

State Auto Insurance Companies

State Compensation Insurance Fund of California

State Farm Mutual Automobile Insurance Company

The Sullivan Group

Swiss Reinsurance America Corporation

Travelers

USAA

Utica National Insurance Group

Westfield Group

Willis

W. R. Berkley Corporation

XL Catlin

The Zenith

Zurich North America

Associate Members

ANE, Agency Network Exchange, LLC

Crawford and Company

Deloitte

Farmers Mutual Fire Insurance of Tennessee

Mutual Assurance Society of Virginia

Sompo Japan Research Institute, Inc.

Transunion Insurance Solutions

Academic and Governmental Members

Cornell University

Drake University

East Carolina University

Florida State University

Fudan University

The Glasgow Caledonian University

Illinois State University

LaSalle University

New Mexico University

Old Dominion University

Olivet College

Pennsylvania State University

St. John's University

St. Joseph's University

Temple University

TesTeachers

U.S. Department of Commerce – Bureau of Economic Analysis

University of Alabama

University of Central Arkansas

University of Cyprus

University of Georgia

University of Guelph

University of Hawaii – West Oahu

University of Illinois at Urbana-Champaign

University of Minnesota

University of Mississippi

University of Missouri Law School

University of North Texas

University of Southern Maine

University of Texas at Dallas

University of Westminster

University of Wisconsin-Madison

Insurance Information Institute
110 William Street
New York, NY 10038

Tel. 212-346-5500. Fax. 212-732-1916. www.iii.org

President – Robert P. Hartwig, Ph.D., CPCU – bobh@iii.org

Executive Vice President – Andréa C. Basora – andreab@iii.org

Senior Vice President and Chief Communications Officer – Jeanne Salvatore – jeannes@iii.org

Senior Vice President and Chief Economist – Steven N. Weisbart, Ph.D., CLU – stevenw@iii.org

Research and Information Services

Chief Actuary and Director of Research and Information Services – James Lynch, FCAS, MAAA – jamesl@iii.org

Research Manager – Mary-Anne Firneno – mary-annef@iii.org

Information Specialist – Maria Sassian – marias@iii.org

Special Consultant – Ruth Gastel, CPCU – ruthg@iii.org

Publications

Managing Editor – Jennifer Ha – jenniferh@iii.org

Manager – Publications and Web Production, Publications Orders – Katja Charlene Lewis – charlenel@iii.org

Marketing and Content Strategy

Director – Marketing and Content Strategy – James P. Ballot – jamesb@iii.org

Director – Technology and Web Production – Shorna Lewis – shornal@iii.org

Media Relations

Vice President – Media Relations – Michael Barry – michaelb@iii.org

Vice President – Communications – Loretta Worters – lorettaw@iii.org

Terms + Conditions blog – Claire Wilkinson – clairew@iii.org

Impact Magazine – Diane Portantiere – dianep@iii.org

Administrative Assistant – Rita El-Hakim – ritae@iii.org

Administrative Assistant – Lilia Giordano – liliag@iii.org

Representatives

Davis Communications – William J. Davis, Atlanta – billjoe@bellsouth.net
Tel. 770-321-5150. Fax. 770-321-5150.

Hispanic Press Officer – Elianne González, Miami – elianneg@iii.org
Tel. 954-389-9517.

Florida Representative – Lynne McChristian, Tampa – lynnem@iii.org
Tel. 813-480-6446. Fax. 813-915-3463.

California Representative – Janet Ruiz, San Francisco – janetr@iii.org
Tel. 707-490-9365

Index

residual market property plans, 100
residual/shared market property plans, 100
top coastal counties most frequently hit by
  hurricanes, 97
top 10 states, by population change in coastal
  counties, 96
mold, 107
premiums, 60, 62, 95–96, 104
top 10 writers by direct premiums written, 96
hurricanes, 146–149
Atlantic and Pacific hurricane seasons 2014-2015,
  146–147
coastal exposure, 98, 99
costliest, 148
deadliest, 149
frequency by counties, 97
losses, 147
Saffir-Simpson Hurricane Wind Scale, 146

I

identity theft, 170–171
immunity statutes, 201
Individual Retirement Accounts (IRAs), 133
injuries. *See* accidents
inland marine insurance, 61, 64, 123
insolvency funds. *See* guaranty funds
insurance companies
  domestic, by state, 23
  global top ten, 4–5
  top companies, 15, 37, 41, 42, 53, 68, 69, 115, 116,
    126, 127, 130
insurance cost factors. *See* cost factors
insurance fraud, 200–202
  automated red flags, 200
  fraud bureaus, 201
  key state laws against, 201–202
international sales, 6
Internet crime. *See* cybercrime
Internet Crime Complaint Center (IC3), 169
investments, property/casualty insurance, 50–51

K

Keogh plans, 133

L

larceny-theft, 167, 182–184
laws
  affecting drivers, 80–94 (*see also* automobile
    insurance)
  insurance fraud, 201–202
lawsuits and legal costs, 203–210
  commercial liability markets, top 10 largest, 203
  directors and officers liability insurance (D&O),
    207–208
  employment practices liability (EPL) coverage, 207,
    209
  insurers' legal defense costs, 203–204
  personal injury awards, 204–206
  shareholder lawsuits, 210

liability coverage
  automobile insurance, 83–84
  employment practices liability (EPL) coverage, 207,
    209
  general, 119
license renewal laws, 90–91
life insurance. *See also* life/health insurance
  annuities, 15, 35, 39– 40, 131, 135–138
  distribution channels, 27
  ownership statistics, 31
  top 10 writers, 15
life/health insurance, 27, 31–42
  benefits and claims, 34
  companies, number of, 23
  employment, 17
  income analysis, 32
  investments, 33
  ownership, 31
  payout data, 34
  premiums by line, 35–40
    by state, 39–40
    disability insurance, 37–38
    long-term care insurance, 38
    private health insurance, 36–37
  top 10 writers, group/individual 2014, 42
  top 20 writers 2013, 41
lightning, 107, 108, 109
link analysis, 200
liquor liability, 89, 119
litigation costs, 203–204
long-term care (LTC) insurance, 38
loss ratio, 49
losses, 139–196
  asbestos-related illness, 194
  automobile/motor vehicle crashes, 172–181
  aviation, 188–190
  catastrophes (*see also* catastrophes)
    United States, 142–156
    world, 139–142, 157
  causes of death, 195–196
  crime
    arson, 166
    cyberattacks and identity theft, 168–171
    property crimes, 167
  fire, 162–165
  home injuries/deaths, 194–195
  property/casualty insurance, 43, 56
  recreation, 184–188
  underwriting, 43, 47
  workplace, 191–194

M

malpractice insurance, 121
mandatory insurance. *See* compulsory automobile
  insurance
marine insurance (inland and ocean), commercial, 123
mechanical breakdown insurance, 128
medical insurance. *See* healthcare insurance